Web Site Usability Handbook

WEB SITE USABILITY HANDBOOK

Mark Pearrow

CHARLES RIVER MEDIA

CHARLES RIVER MEDIA, INC.
Rockland, Massachusetts

Publisher: Jenifer Niles
Interior Design/Comp: Publishers' Design and Production Services, Inc.
Cover Design: The Printed Image

CHARLES RIVER MEDIA, Inc.
20 Downer Ave, Suite 3
Hingham, MA 02043
781-740-0400
781-740-8816(FAX)
chrivmedia@aol.com
http://www.charlesriver.com

This book is printed on acid-free paper

Web Site Usability Handbook
Mark Pearrow
ISBN: 1-58450-026-3
Printed in the United States of America

00 01 02 7 6 5 4 3

CHARLES RIVER MEDIA titles are available for site license or bulk purchase by institutions, user groups, corporations, etc. For additional information, please contact the Special Sales Department at 781-871-4184.

Dedication

This book is dedicated with love to the memory of Jerry A. Davis.

Contents

Acknowledgments

The author wishes to thank a vast array of people, some of whom have contributed directly to this work, others who have indirectly contributed to this work, and other who have simply been a major influence in my life.

- My friend Melanie DeCarolis for introducing me to the good people at Charles River Media.
- The good people at Charles River Media for being easy to work with and supportive.
- Jakob Nielsen, for his inspiring work, including his Alertbox column and numerous pioneering writings in the field of Usability.
- Keith Instone, for having the most r0kk1n set of usability links on the planet, and for getting the word out about usability.
- Freddy Gonzales, for giving me the opportunity to forge ahead into untested waters.
- My students at Northeastern University for being a constant source of eye-opening questions as well as the inspiration for some of the anecdotes in this book.
- My friend Eric Ellis, for years of patience in teaching me things that I never believed I could do. I owe you a lot, Eric.
- My friend Bob Boyd for believing in me and giving me the wings go beyond what I ever dreamed possible.
- The Squid that nearly ate Parliament, for bringing me unawares to the shore of a New World.

- Devin Parker and Sherri White, for giving me inspiration from their endless courage in the face of adversity.
- Bobby Lincoln, who taught me the ways of elecronic communication long before the average individual knew what the "Internet" was.
- My cat Godzilla for helping me with much of the material (most of which I needed to translate from her otherwise humanly indecipherable cat language).
- And most of all, my wife Melissa, who has been patient with me for all the months that we haven't had lives or gotten to see each other in order to meet deadlines.

Special thanks to Ruth Villesis, Diana Hendricks, and Martha Porter, who generated the data set for the sample test plan. They can be reached at ruth.villesis@mind-hive.com, diana.hendricks@mind-hive.com, and martha.porter@mind-hive.com.

ABOUT THE ILLUSTRATOR

A friend and fellow musician, Phillip R. Ouellette, did the illustrations in this text. Phillip currently resides in Jamaica Plain, Massachusetts, where he devotes his time to art and to music. Phillip may be contacted via email at phillip@mind-hive.com.

About This Book

In the area of web site usability instruction, there are two main goals: to educate people to create more usable sites, and to train people to perform usability evaluations of web sites. One skill is proactive, the other reactive. Although both skills are crucial to the success of the usability specialist, I have chosen to focus primarily on the latter skill. Several books have been published that give the reader a topical overview of "tips and techniques" to make sites more usable.

I felt that there was a real lack of published material that focused on the web as a subject of usability evaluation and iterative redesign. Perhaps the most compelling reason for me to write this book was the fact that I had grown weary of waiting for experts in the field to publish a book that I could use as a textbook in my Northeastern University course TMG 5306: Web Site Usability.

If you have picked up this book hoping to find brand new "quick fixes" to make your web site better, there aren't too many here. Most of the design tips I have in this book are available on the web in various columns and other formats. I have included some popular ones here mainly out of convenience and as a starting point for readers who are totally unfamiliar with the topic.

My hope is that this text will provide a starting point for people interested in getting involved with making their web sites better for the users. In no way do I intend this text to be an exhaustive compendium. No such document can exist since the web is a moving target; tips that make sense today will fade into ancient history in a year. Instead, I hope to show you one methodology that is extensible and relatively future-proof.

DISCLAIMER

In this text, I use many examples of web sites. I also provide screen shots of many of the sites, occasionally to illustrate the right way to do something, but more often to demonstrate bad design. This is in no way meant to slander or unjustly accuse any organization of doing any harm to the public. If you see your web site in this book, you can either choose to ignore it or try to effect a positive change.

My inclusion or omission of particular sites in no way should be translated as an endorsement of, or attack upon, any entity, on the account of the author, the publisher, or any other parties involved in the publication of this text.

Preface

Welcome! If you are reading this book, then in all likelihood you are eager to get started in the field of Web Site Usability Specialization. This book is designed for you, the aspiring Web Site Usability Specialist. You may be interested in the topic because you have purposefully decided to pursue the field as a career change; or perhaps you have found yourself "elected" to the task by your employer.

Whatever the case, this book is designed to provide a clear and concise framework for people in the field of Web Site Usability. Up until now, people who were interested in the subject had to cobble together whatever articles and relevant bits out of software usability testing manuals they could find. The goal of this book is to provide structure and a methodology for applying principles of Usability to web site design.

I hope that you find the field of Web Site Usability to be challenging and fulfilling! I am also glad to hear your thoughts, experiences, and feelings about the content of this book. Should you find that you disagree with something I have said herein, great!

All the better, because in any field growth can only happen through iterative redesign and many hands working toward a common goal. I strongly encourage you to publish your findings and contribute to the communal pool of knowledge.

Let's get started!

CHAPTER

1

Introduction to Usability

ACHTUNG!!!

Das machine is nicht fur gefingerpoken und mittengrabben. Ist easy schnappen der springenwerk, blowenfusen, und corkenpoppen mit spitzensparken. Ist nicht fur gewerken by das dummkopfen. Das rubbernecken sightseeren keepen hands in das pockets. Relaxen und vatch das blinkenlights!!!

What Is Usability?

According to Greek legend, near Eleusis, in Attica, there lived an unusual fellow named Damastes, who eventually acquired the nickname Procrustes, or "The Stretcher." His claim to fame—or infamy—was that he had an iron bed on which he forced travelers who came through his neck of the woods to spend the night.

His modus operandi was to stretch his unwitting guests that were to small to fill the bed until they "fit." If the guest was too large to fit the bed, well, Procrustes simply cut off any part that hung over the sides. Of course, there was never a guest who came into the unfortunate inn with just the "right" proportions, and no guest ever left the inn alive.

Since that time, any action that requires the doer to "stretch" unnaturally to accommodate an action or a thing—often as a result of bad design—is referred to as "Procrustean." Therefore, design that requires the user to adapt, to accommodate, to memorize, and to suffer—the bane of this book—is called *Procrustean design.*

The Gold Rush of the 1990s

In a mad rush to race Web documents to "go live," many Web sites have been poorly designed and lack the essential features necessary to make them do what they were originally designed to do: work. The fact of the matter is, Web sites are very much a type of user interface, and increasingly, more people rely on the Web to do business, correspond, collaborate, do research, and much more. The Web site that is poorly designed is both frustrating to the end user and a blemish on the company that produced it or for which it provides a "storefront."

Our duty as usability specialists is to seek out the problems in Web sites that cause them to be frustrating, confusing, and generally useless. To accomplish this goal, we use a series of tools, techniques, and tips throughout this text. The thing that sets usability specialists apart from general nitpickers is that we attain our goal through a scientific method; furthermore, we seek to turn our findings into recommendations for change.

The First Continuum: Form vs. Function

In the grand scheme of things, usability specialists find themselves on one end of the continuum of Web site goals: form versus function. We often find ourselves playing devil's advocate to the aspiring designer in ourselves, or, most often, other members of our Web design team. In reality, the need for beauty and the need for usability can be balanced, much like the yin and the yang of Zen. The truly great Web sites combine both aspects to make a Web site that is both aesthetically pleasing and truly usable.

Although usability principles, taken to the extreme, can result in unsightly and aesthetically unpleasant Web sites, such extremes are rarely needed. The purpose of this book is not to turn you into a militant usability guerrilla. Rather, the hope is that you will walk away from this book with a sense of moderation, because anything in extreme quantities is bad.

The First Continuum discussed in this book is that of form versus Function—that is to say, how pleasing the site looks (and, perhaps, sounds) as opposed to how serviceable it is for the purpose for which it was designed. Somewhere between the two extremes lies the happy medium: the place where it all comes together. Arriving at this place can be done only through compromise and cooperation on the behalf of the designers and the usability specialists. It may be that both of these parties are you, struggling within yourself!

The area of Web site usability is currently considered a specialty area, much like that of a Web server administrator, a content developer, or a Web programmer. Unlike these other well-established Web technology roles, the role of the usability specialist is one with which, unfortunately, far too few company decision makers are familiar.

Misinformed Decisions = Unhappy Users

As of the writing of this edition of the book, most decision makers have not caught on to the fact that the state of usability of their Web sites plays a far greater role in the success of that component of the business than any flashy, last-minute display of state-of-the-art technology ever can.

In the current generation of Web site design, people who are not experts in usable systems are making lots of decisions. They are management types and marketing types who hear buzzwords and insist blindly that the company Web site needs "more Java and more flash!" They don't take into consideration that adding features does not automatically make the end user's world better; in fact, it often makes the user's world much worse![1] Such ventures are usually doomed from the start because a Web site that is not usable is useless.

The purpose of this book is to familiarize you with the principles of user-centered design (UCD) and usability concepts to enable you to educate your organization about the need for usability. A great part of your job in this new era is to educate people about usability to the point that it is ubiquitous as the word processor, the fax, and the coffee machine.

Start with a Purpose

In our journey to attain Web site usability, we must start at the beginning: we must determine the purpose of our Web site. In your career, you have probably experienced executive decision making along the lines of, "We need a Web site and we need it now." Such decisions are often devoid of calculated thought, which leaves Web site usability in the trash can. The fact of the matter is, without a carefully laid plan for what your Web site will provide, it simply cannot do anything well—except annoy your users.

---

[1] Take, for example, the major change that Microsoft made to the Macintosh version of Word during the upgrade from version 5.1 to 6.0. Many who bought the upgrade ended up reinstalling the old version and were outraged at the way the program had been changed.

The subject of determining the purpose of your Web site is outside the scope of this text. However, it is a critical concept that you must understand before you can proceed. In a nutshell, the first step toward Web site usability is to figure out the main goals of your Web site. For labeling purposes, we will call these *goals of the purpose.*

For example, if your company sells a particular product—let's say the Wonder Widget 2000—your CEO may decide that the corporate Web site should feature an online store. This online store would feature the Wonder Widget 2000 as well as all its additional accessories, in a convenient format that makes it easy to purchase products. Additionally, your company may decide to offer technical support for these products on its Web site in an effort to reduce technical support expenses.

You can summarize these two main points in two sentences:

- Provide a sales channel for the Wonder Widget series of products.
- Provide a technical support forum for existing Wonder Widget customers.

Although these points may seem like common sense, you will quickly find out that there is no such thing as common sense; common sense is quite uncommon. Focusing so clearly on the purpose of your Web site allows you to construct the remainder of your Web site usability plan.

Although this book is mainly concerned with Web site usability, a term we'll define in a moment, it is important to understand that the general concept of usability engineering, usability testing, and UCD are by no means new.

The material in this book explains the philosophy and process of applying usability principles to Web site design as opposed to avionics, platform-dependent software graphical user interfaces (GUIs), or automobile control consoles. The techniques presented are deeply rooted in the general science of human factors and usability testing. However, we approach the task of designing—or redesigning—a Web site, taking into account the toolbox of usability that we have at our disposal to make sure that the resulting site is truly usable.

For example, if we are designing a commercial Web site for a software company, we may know that one of our principal design goals is to make it easy for clients to order software over the Web via this site. In the process of accomplishing this goal, we go through many steps to ensure that when we are done, each and every end user has the easiest and most problem-free time achieving his or her goal: to order the latest software package.

As usability specialists, we have an array of tools at our disposal to ensure our goals are met. The purpose of this book is to introduce you to the *usability toolbox* and to give you a methodology for implementing the individual tools therein in a consistent way.

Depending on the corporate philosophy of our company, we may also have, as a principal design goal, making customer support easily available in order to strengthen customer loyalty and reduce the total number of dollars spent in technical support-line costs. (To the best of your estimation, how many companies clearly embrace this philosophy? Name two.)

Surfing, Known-Item Searching, and Task-Oriented Interaction

For many reasons, people will come to your Web site. They could be on their lunch break or, for shame, Web surfing on the company clock and just looking for amusement. They might have typed a keyword into a search engine that landed them on your site; they might be looking for a product or service that you offer. Or they might be on your site to get work done.

If we are designing a site principally for the purpose of getting users to surf and hang out on the site, we might not want to make things particularly efficacious for them. After all, if our users can quickly find what they are looking for, they may leave the site after finding it! This sort of reasoning has actually led some companies to produce sites that are purposefully difficult to use, just to keep users groping around the site a bit longer.

I don't advise that you take this approach; my point is that different styles of Web sites should have different approaches to user interaction. If you want your users to stay on your site longer, you need to cook up some clever magnet content that your users will want to hang around for. That, too, is outside the scope of this book, however.

Instead, we're primarily interested in the other two types of utilization: *known-item searching* and *task-oriented interaction*. Our goal is to actually speed our users through the successful completion of their errands so that they can get back to idle surfing and having fun.

The Web has brought an odd element to user interface principles. You can use the Web for both fun and business. You can do your banking via the Web. You can also watch stupid but oh-so-hilarious cartoons about a deranged donkey and his psychotic buddy (a Don Quixote for the Prozac Generation).

WHAT ISN'T USABILITY?

Usability Is not Accessibility

Two buzzwords in the field of Web design are often wrongly equivocated: *accessibility* and *usability*. Note that these are not the same thing. However, accessibility *is* a component of usability, and therefore I have devoted a chapter to this topic.

In a nutshell, the generally cited concern of accessibility involves making Web site content available to and usable by people with disabilities. For example, if a Web site is designed so that it is 100 percent graphic images (to make the site more visually appealing by forcing exact layout and control over font appearance), it considered not accessible to the visually impaired. If a visually impaired user encounters such a page, he or she will be clueless as to the content and unable to navigate or use the content of the site.

This outlook—that accessibility is needed only to accommodate users with disabilities—is myopic, however, because when a Web site is designed with accessibility in mind, people with disabilities represent only one group of beneficiaries. For example, Web sites that rely less on images to communicate are more accessible to automated search engines, are easier to index, and are more available to other browsing platforms, such as the stripped-down Web browsers embedded in personal digital assistant (PDA) devices and personal communication service (PCS) phones. This is only one nontrivial example of how designing with accessibility in mind benefits everyone, not just people with disabilities.

Usability Is Not Marketing Research

Usability science is also different from marketing analysis or Web server log analysis. The goal of usability science is not to increase awareness of a product, to entertain, or to make sure that the "user experience" guides a consumer through a carefully laid "entry tunnel." None of these areas qualifies as usability science, although arguably they are all important to the success of a Web site.

It is critical to note that usability is geared toward improving how easily users can use a Web site to accomplish specific tasks. This is completely different from the goal of entertainment or even "infotainment." Web sites that are intended to entertain have a very different philosophy than Web sites that are designed to get work done. Sometimes, a successful Web site will be a synthesis of both goals: to entertain and to accomplish a goal. Think of Amazon.com. As Jared Spool pointed out in his book, *Web Site Usability: A Designer's Guide*, likability—the degree to which a user likes a Web site—does not necessarily correlate with usability. In his book, Spool does a usability audit of several Web sites and finds that the most entertaining and fun (and most likable) site of the bunch—Disney.com—was considered to be one of the least usable.

Network Join Now | Free E-mail
Search Disney.com Family.com Go
Where to go
WHO DO YOU LOVE?
FTD.COM
CLICK HERE
Disney.com
January 31, 2000
Where the magic lives online!
DVD Bonus Offer!
DisneySTORE.COM
Zeether
Kids Click Here!
FUN!
GAMES
MUSIC
ACTIVITIES
CLICK OF THE DAY
WHAT DOES
SUPERBOWL
CHAMPION
Kurt Warner
DO NEXT?
DISNEY STORE
VACATIONS
CHAT STUDIO
DISNEY A-Z
CLUB BLAST
TV SHOWS
MOVIES & VIDEOS
PETS & ANIMALS
FUN for FAMILIES
Celebrates the Millennium
THE Tigger MOVIE FEBRUARY 11
family.com
CRAFTS, RECIPES, TRAVEL!

FIGURE 1.1 *Some Web sites simply are not designed to fulfill a critical role in goal-oriented tasks. They are designed merely to entertain. Some Web sites merge the two constructs, entertainment and functionality. This approach is generally quite successful. ©2000, The Disney Co.*

Note, however, that people concerned with marketing are also necessarily concerned with usability of the Web site because ultimately, no matter how well conceived the marketing ideas, an unusable Web site can shoot the marketers right out of the water.

Usability Is Not About "Crafting the User Experience"

Before you protest, read to the end of this paragraph! Clearly, the state of usability of a Web site determines whether the user will have a good or bad experience with your Web site. There is no denying this fact. However, a number of authors and well-known Web designers have spent much time trying to convince other Web site designers that they need to be concerned with channeling a Web site user's visit to their site into a type of orchestrated, electronic performance.

This kind of design works fine if what you're trying to do is create a piece of performance art, the access to which you can completely control. Furthermore, you should also be able to ensure that no one will gain entrance to your site through any page or search engine other than your carefully crafted entry portal. In the real world, however, we all know that there is no way of predicting how users will enter your Web site; it could be through bookmarks, search engines, or hyperlinks from other Web sites. In my humble opinion, this is an exercise in OCD[2] rather than UCD!

Usability does not concern itself with arbitrary coercion of the users' path through your Web site. It ensures that regardless of how, when, or where your users enter your Web site, they will be able to use it.

A BIT OF HISTORY

Not so very many years ago, a man named Tim Berners-Lee came up with a way for researchers all over the world to share scientific documents with their peers. The rest is history. The tool that Tim cre-

[2] Obsessive-compulsive disorder.

ated would soon turn into the fastest-growing technology in the history of humankind: the World Wide Web.

The first generation of Web pages was primarily made of very Spartan-looking documents, authored by scientific types. Most documents were almost entirely text, with an occasional splash of color here and there and the occasional image to illustrate a point. This type of document was really just that: a document, and of the static kind, at that. There was little to no "interfacing" that the end user had to do besides read it.

The second generation of Web documents saw a shift from simple text to a little more, when images became popular on the steadily growing World Wide Web. One major milestone in the growth of the Web happened somewhere in this era: people outside the realm of the slide rule and the atom smasher began to noodle with the Web. Ordinary people were starting to catch on to what the Web had to offer, and the boom that is still happening began. The use of enormous image files and the long download times associated with them caused the Web to become known as the "World Wide Wait."

The third age of the Web, which some could argue we are in now, saw the advent of Web sites not as mere curiosities but as tools for conducting business across great distances. Now a Web page is more than just something to look at; it is a means to an end. A Web page can be the thing that allows you, the busy technologist, to avoid going to the crowded grocery store after working a long day. A Web page could allow you to book that flight to Sydney for a lot cheaper than your old travel agent was willing to go. And of course, a Web site could allow you to make a small fortune in day trading. What a marvel of technology, this Web thing.

With all the excitement of a new technology comes the inevitable rush of pioneers who are willing to forsake common sense and good manners to attain precious gold. In the wake of the World Wide Web extravaganza, we are left with thousands—even millions-—of poorly designed Web sites and Web pages that don't serve any purpose well, except perhaps to annoy and baffle those who try to use them.

Many Web sites have been designed from the beginning with no real purpose, no guiding principle. The result? Unusable information that adds to the ocean of ubiquitous World Wide Noise.

One of the driving goals of Web site usability specialists is to increase the signal-to-noise ratio for our users. In other words, we should, through many different types of techniques, make it as easy as is technologically feasible for users to find the golden islands of information in the tumultuous seas of information noise.

At the current exponential rate of expansion of the Web, without intervention, the result will be a totally unmanageable mass within a few years. End users are frustrated enough at the inconsistency of transactional sites today; what will happen when things are *really* out of control?

A BIT OF JARGON

You might have seen the terms *usability, usability testing, human factors, HCI, CHI, UCD,* and so on, and wondered how they all fit together. As if all this complexity weren't enough, the authors of a recent Web site usability publication have coined the new term, *usage-centered design (UCD).* This book attempts to sort all these terms out bit by bit, but for now let's define the term *usability* thus:

> *Usability is the broad discipline of applying sound scientific observation, measurement, and design principles to the creation and maintenance of Web sites in order to bring about the greatest ease of use, ease of learnability, amount of usefulness, and least amount of discomfort for the humans who have to use the system.*

This broad umbrella encompasses the use of testing methods, casual observation, expert evaluations, and many other tools that are all useful in reaching the goal of a usable Web site.

Let's take a brief stroll through some of the terms and acronyms mentioned above, partly to define them but also to give a frame of reference to see where our field comes from in the first place.

HUMAN FACTORS

The field of human factors has its roots in the field of psychology, and in fact, many of the first specialists in this area were military researchers performing studies on how U.S. soldiers performed under varying types of stress and in varying environments. Since those early days, human factors psychologists have become part of many industries, including the automobile industry, the telecommunications industry, and many other fields that require humans to interact with an essentially nonhuman interface of some sort.

An example of the type of issues that human factors attempts to study is that of human vision, its limitations, and ways to leverage its strong points to enable humans to make better use of systems. As a Web usability specialist, you might find it very useful to know that selecting the color blue for text on your Web site will render many elderly users of your site unable to read it, due to certain types of degradation that occur in the human eye with age.

Some other examples of human factors at work involve studies on the nature of human memory, learning, and forgetting. Having an understanding of these areas enables us to design sites that leverage our users' abilities to use Web sites as well as be able to remember how to use sites over the long haul.

If, for example, we know that the principle called *interference* causes users to become confused on our Web site when part of our interface looks similar to another interface that they've used before but that works differently, we are more able to competently troubleshoot the problem and resolve the issue.

Although it is not entirely necessary to have a degree in psychology to become a Web site usability specialist, it certainly does not hurt; in fact, if you have a background in psychology, you will find the field a very natural fit for you.

Human/Computer Interaction

Human/computer interaction (HCI), which is sometimes also written *CHI,* is the field that seeks to apply the study of human factors specifically to the way humans interact with computer systems. HCI concerns itself with issues such as GUIs, the logic and functionality of the features the software provides, and the way that humans interact with the input and output devices. Another area of HCI, *ergonomics,* concerns the particular hazards that these devices can pose to humans and how we can avoid those hazards.

Much research has been done in the area of HCI. In fact, there is a Special Interest Group (SIG) of the Association for Computing Machinery (ACM) called Computer/Human Interaction (CHI). This SIG focuses entirely on the area of computer/human interface, and much of the literature in this area has been published in the journals of this group. If you have a budget for professional association membership fees, it would be wise for you to join the ACM and, in particular, the CHI SIG.

If this area of usability is of particular interest to you, you might also want to peruse the University of Maryland's HCI Web site *(www.cs.umd.edu/hcil/)*, which has many online publications and other resources of interest. Also check out *comp.human-factors* on Usenet.

By the time you are finished reading this book, you might take issue with the small semantic distinction between the wording of HCI and CHI. In the acronym CHI, the computer is put before the machine. This goes against the philosophy of UCD, as discussed in more detail in the next section.

Whatever you call it, HCI is a fairly scientific, empirical field that is usually left to the domain of the scholarly researcher with a lab, graduate student helpers, and funding to do the work. Nonetheless, we can certainly use HCI findings in our everyday, hectic schedule of Web site development.

User-Centered Design

UCD is both a philosophy and a methodology of product development that to be done properly, must necessarily permeate the entire infrastructure of an organization or a business. The simple idea is that no product, Web site, or software system matters—at all—unless there are users to use it.

Products and services that fail often do so for the simple fact that their designers never thought to ask the people who would be using the product what they thought they needed or how they currently performed their jobs with existing products. It's not quite the technical embodiment of "the customer is always right," because in reality this isn't always the case.

To provide a point of contrast, let's go back to the days before computers were mainstream, when they were still the mainstays of thick-glassed, pocket-protector-wearing types who loved to hack away at electronic and other gizmos. Many of the original minicomputers were designed to be programmed by flipping little switches up or down, depending on whether the bit you wanted to create was a 1 or a 0. This was not a very user-friendly interface!

I used to have one of these minicomputers in my office at the lab; to boot the operating system required flipping the levers in a mystical pattern that few people knew. If I had taken the computer to an average person's home and asked him or her to use it, he or she would probably have called the police! Clearly, the designers of the computer (in this case, a Digital PDP-11) were one and the same as the end users.

As computers became more and more mainstream, the user population began to change dramatically. Regular, nontechnical people began to use computers; accountants had to learn how to use one of the fancy new programs such as VisiCalc or become extinct. Today, the personal computer is ubiquitous; when Apple released the iMac not too long ago, even grandmothers bought them because they wanted to get recipes and stock tips over the 'Net.

Clearly, times have changed since the days of the minicomputer. But one thing hasn't changed much: the people who design microchips and computer systems are still just as technically oriented as they were 30 years ago. The beginning of failure is to let these engineers and programmers wholly design a product that is meant for use by the masses. Anyone who has ever been frustrated by a VCR has felt the bite of designer-centered design: products designed without thinking about the user lead to failed products, bruised reputations, and often, bankruptcy.

We'll talk a lot more about UCD as we go along, because it is the underlying principle that guides us, as usability specialists, toward our goals.

WHY USABILITY?

If you have ever been involved with the development of a software product, you know that a smart company spends a lot of time and money making sure that its software is easy and intuitive to use. You also know that smart companies make sure that in general the users of the software won't tend to make critical mistakes because of some poor design element. Usability testing and other usability tools are an integral part of the product development life cycle.

Why? Because, as mentioned, systems that do not perform up to users' needs and expectations usually fail. Take, for example, the Coleco company, which lost $6 million in 1983 on its failed Adam home computer product. I still have an Adam, and I still marvel at how good it actually was for the time. It was a home computer system, complete with printer, all of which sold for $600 retail. It had an innovative technology that provided secondary storage on a high-speed magnetic tape instead of a floppy disk drive. Floppy drives were very costly then, and tape cassette transports and media were relatively inexpensive.

The whole outfit should have done very well on the market, but the package had one fatal flaw: poor documentation that was too complex for the home users who bought the Adam. As a result, high returns from unhappy customers resulted in a failed product. Maybe, if the company spent more money in user-centered testing of the documentation, it could have averted disaster, and perhaps we'd all be using Coleco computers on our desktops today!

Take another example. In the mid-1960s, Honeywell created a very futuristic product: the H316 General Purpose Digital Computer, a.k.a. the Kitchen Computer—a computer for the kitchen. It was a $7,000 monster that had a built-in cutting board, looked like something right out of *The Jetsons,* and required the user to program the thing himself or herself in a language called BACK. Honeywell didn't sell very many of these, and it's likely that the project had never been market tested or designed with the user in mind. Who wants to write a program when they are sautéing peppers?

HOW THINGS END UP UNUSABLE

It is one thing to simply complain that a system is unusable; it is quite another to understand how systems can go wrong in the first place. The following list of reasons is by no means an exhaustive one. However, it will give you the general idea:

- **Reason 1.** All too often, the developers of a Web site focus on the site's features or its technical implementation while never paying any attention to the end user. This defies the first law of UCD: Know your user.
- **Reason 2.** The designers of Web sites are often highly technical people who possess skills in programming and other analytical areas. Unfortunately, the way these people think and act is usually totally different from the way the end user does. Assumptions these designers make simply do not generalize to the people who will actually be using the site.
- **Reason 3.** People who are in charge of the development of Web sites often give in to trends, assuming that incorporating the latest and greatest technology will give them the edge over their competition. In fact, this type of behavior usually works exactly the oppo-

site: it reduces the actual usability of the Web site, giving less state-of-the-art competition the edge. Remember, just because a feature exists does not mean that you are obligated to use it.

- **Reason 4.** Most people merely assume that good usability results from common-sense reasoning. Most people don't even think of usability as a discipline. In reality, you'll find that common sense is really quite uncommon. Highly usable Web sites do not happen accidentally; they're the results of iterative redesign and exhaustive testing.
- **Reason 5.** Unfortunately, people with little or no user interface design experience are making critical decisions about the look, feel, and logical model of Web sites.

In addition to these five broad areas, there are hundreds of other, smaller ways that usability problems can creep into your Web site design. One concept to take away with you after reading this book is the idea that virtually every usability problem can be traced back to the violation of one or more well-known principles of UCD.

Not Just a Gratuitous Moral . . .

Take, for example, the story of browser incompatibility and how two of my students created a Web site that caused a catastrophe. These two students worked for a division of the U.S. government. They were commissioned to create a brand new Web site for their department. Despite the fact that these two students were taking a HyperText Markup Language (HTML) course, where the dangers of using What You See Is What You Get (WYSIWYG) HTML editing programs is discussed, they used a very well-known, popular HTML editor to produce their entire site.

Unfortunately, this very popular HTML editor leverages several known bugs of a competitor's Web browser as well as several illegal HTML constructs to render its output unusable by the competitor's browser. The students assumed that this would never be a problem because their internal IT department allowed only the use of the "compatible" Web browser and, after all, they were designing the Web site for internal use within the department.

The students never bothered to check their Web site as viewed by the competitor's browser. After considerable taxpayer dollars had been sunk into the site, the deployment date was at hand. It was only then that the two found out that 50 percent of their users were, in fact, using the competitors' browser. Furthermore, these users were unable to use the browser for which the site was designed, because they lacked the staff to implement the new browser and support it.

We'll never know exactly how much pain these two students went through when they had to uncover all the proprietary, deliberate breakage in their code and fix it.

The moral of this story is that whether you are the designer or the usability expert, you absolutely *must* preview all your Web pages using all available browsers. That includes outdated browsers that you assume no one uses anymore. Read your Web server logs that record visitors to your site; you'll be amazed. If you fail to observe this simple rule of design, you will lose. Had these students done an initial on-site visit to get information from the users' perspective, they could have circumvented the entire calamity.

What You Need to Get Started in Web Site Usability

So far, so good. You've got this book, which is a start toward understanding usability. A common myth about usability is that you need a Ph.D. in psychology in order to be able to conduct usability testing, or any other sort of usability, for that matter. This is untrue, as is the myth that you need lots of money and a fancy laboratory. The fact is, all you really need is one or more people who are interested in making usable Web sites and a small area in which to do testing (this can be your office, a conference room, or even a janitor's closet![3]). You'll also need a decent stopwatch and of course at least one potted plant to improve the ambience. Because you will be testing the design of a Web site, you'll need at least one computer running an operating system comparable to the one your end users are using.

What you will find as you go along is that usability science can require very little material and fiscal resources, but you can also do much more sophisticated work if the budget allows. My guess is that your particular company might not be aware that such a thing as usability science exists, nor of the hidden costs of not integrating UCD into the core philosophy of your corporate Web site. Part of your duty as a usability specialist is to educate and inform; hopefully, by the time you finish reading this book, you will be able to make a case for integrating usability as part of your corporate philosophy.

Checklist for Getting Started

Here are the basics you need to get started in Web site usability:

- Digital stopwatch
- Computer workstation (similar to the type your users are using)
- Clipboard
- Web browser that your users are likely to use, plus any other browsers likely to be used to view your site
- Comparable operating system to what your users will be using
- Comparable Internet connection to what your users will be using
- Small, quiet room with minimal distractions

[3] The Chandra x-ray telescope, which was sent into space at 7:47 a.m. EDT on July 23, 1999, was operated from the Chandra Operations Control Center in Cambridge, Massachusetts. Most of the impressive hardware and control components for the center were housed in a janitor's closet.

- Two comfortable chairs
- Plastic potted plant

The first item, the digital stopwatch, is a critical piece of equipment, even if it does seem a little archaic. You need this piece of equipment when you are performing usability testing, which is one of the tools in the toolbox.

You need a digital stopwatch that is capable of displaying milliseconds, because in many cases, tasks that you will ask users to perform will take only seconds to complete. You'll also want a stopwatch that makes as little noise as possible; noise can be distracting to your participants and make them more aware of the time constraints of testing. Make sure that your watch is easy to reset and that the display is large and easy to read.

How do you know what kind of computer workstation your users are using? Hopefully, by the time you are doing testing, you will have amassed some statistics about your users by way of questionnaires or screening phone calls. Asking questions related to your participants' home and business computers is a pretty normal part of the process. This will help you get a general idea for how fast or powerful your testing workstation should be. Obviously, you don't want a computer that is so ancient that it can barely run a Web browser; on the other hand, you don't want to have the absolutely latest and greatest machine on the planet, unless all of your users have them as well.

As of this writing, the lion's share of the PC market belongs to the Wintel[4] platform. Therefore, you can assume that you need to perform usability tests on only that platform.

Careful—this line of thinking will get you into hot water! You can choose to believe otherwise, but there actually *are* other platforms that are widely used. The day is coming very soon that the notion of "platform" will change dramatically. Web browsers now include many types

[4] Windows and Intel—the two-headed colossus of 1990s computing.

of devices, including telephones, Web TV, Palm Pilots, and other non-Microsoft operating systems, like Mac, UNIX or Linux.

Therefore, you should remain open to the notion of testing your site designs on many different platforms and devices. In the rapidly approaching future, keeping up with all the new innovations in alternative Web browsing devices will be a full-time job and will become a much more critical role of the usability specialist.

You probably have noticed that the computer workstation, Internet connectivity, Web browser, and the operating system of your test machine should all be similar to what your actual users will be using in their real environments. It's critical that you match the lab setup as closely with the real-world environment as possible.

But You Can't Completely Replicate the User's Environment

So, you may wonder, is it necessary to replicate the entire environment of the user? If a user has a toy on the monitor, do you need to have a fuzzy toy on the test computer's monitor? The answer is no. Although the objective of a laboratory environment is to account for as many variables as possible that might affect user performance, you can't possibly replicate each user's unique environment. It isn't feasible.

What you do want to guarantee, however, is that during testing, each and every test participant gets the same, homogenous test environment. This at least ensures that the environment will equally affect the overall performance of participants. It also means that you don't have to take environmental fluctuations into account to explain variations in performance.

This approach has been criticized many times because a sterile lab environment does not necessarily duplicate the user's real environment. Nonetheless, it is important to control the environment in order to make sure that some random force isn't influencing users' performance. This way, if the lab environment itself has an effect on users' performance, we know that it should be approximately equal for all participants, therefore canceling out any random differences.

The rule of thumb is, the fewer things that go on in the test environment that you can't control (such as loud noises coming from a construction project outside your window or cold temperature one day and hot temperature the next), the more confident you can be in your findings. We look at experimental control in more detail in Chapter 7, "Usability Lab Setup."

A Word on the Scientific Method

This book is almost wholly adopted from a college course that I designed and teach. In the early days of the course, it included a vast amount of research design technique and even an entire module on statistics. I was determined to make my students observe traditional experimental research conditions and exercise the utmost in experimental control over confounding variables.

What I began to see was students' eyes glazed over during this part of the lecture and that the work they produced exemplified few to none of the carefully orchestrated research design methods that I learned in college. But one thing bothered me even more than the absence of control: the fact was, students still managed to uncover a wealth of usability problems, and after implementing changes, the end users were very happy. The end result was an absolute success.

At this point, I had to modify my concept of doing "good" usability work. A little usability is better than none.[5] In fact, I began to develop the notion of a continuum, on one side of which is the need for usability that adheres to classical experimental conditions and on the other side of which is the need for speed and thrift.

Let's look at a contrived example to illustrate the difference between the two ends of the continuum. Imagine that in the not-too-distant future, a Web site is created to manage the critical day-to-day functioning of a nuclear reactor. The Web site would be an application that the control operator would use to manage practically every facet of the reactor.

---

[5] See Nielsen's article, *Guerrilla HCI: Using Discount Usability Engineering to Penetrate the Intimidation Barrier* at *www.useit.com/papers/guerrilla_hci.html.*

Because, as we know, it is generally a really bad thing for a nuclear reactor to fail, the Web interface would have to be rigorously tested under every conceivable condition, all under absolutely precise experimental control.

The way test data would be accumulated and interpreted would have to comply with all known statistical measures used to ensure data integrity, reliability, and validity. Many millions of dollars would go into this project to ensure the safety of thousands of lives.

On the other end of the spectrum, we have a company that sells glow-in-the-dark yo-yos. The company has an annual revenue of $250,000. It is looking to do usability testing on its online store to make sure it works. For this company, a simple heuristic evaluation will suffice. The data collected can be distilled into simple percentages.[6] The vast majority of usability problems can be caught in a single day, and the budget for such an endeavor will be minimal.

In the real world, you will always be somewhere on this continuum. Your project might call for exacting measures because you'll need to replicate the test in many worldwide locations, or you might need to focus tightly on the effect of the presence of a new technology that has been recently incorporated into the site. Or you might simply need to repair a badly designed site as quickly as possible.

EDUCATING OTHERS ABOUT USABILITY

As of this writing, the number of people involved in Web site usability is relatively small—much smaller than the number of people who know

[6] In general, presenting data in terms of raw percentages has little use. A plain percentage is a very misleading figure because it cannot account for the element of chance. For example, if 50 percent of your test subjects cannot find a particular piece of information on your Web site, how much of that 50 percent is attributable to your design, and how much is due to random chance? Even a nearly perfect site design still presents problems to some percentage of users. These problems are due to chance, factors for which you cannot control. Statistical analysis allows you to figure out how much of the result is due to chance. This type of interpretation is not accepted by everyone, but keep reading.

how to crank out a shaded sphere in Photoshop or the number of HTML gurus; even smaller than the number of people making the critical decisions that forge the Web sites of the world.

Therefore, one of your responsibilities as a usability specialist will be to teach others in your organizations about the need for good usability. Because the whole idea of UCD and usability testing is philosophical in nature, people in your companies and organizations must understand the importance and embrace usability as not just some strange voodoo, but as a way of life.

Because the effects of good usability often are not directly observable—the way a flashy graphic or new look and feel might be—the results can be indirectly observed and usually translated into a language that the "higher-ups" can understand. You may opt to translate the results of good usability into a dollars-and-cents summary, as in "We estimate that last year we lost $125,000 in revenue from partially completed sales transactions on our difficult-to-use Web store interface."

Alternately, you may need to translate the absence of good usability into the accompanying negative consumer opinion of the business—for example, "In our survey, 85 percent of our respondents said that they thought our company was unprofessional because of our clumsy Web site."

You can also take a more optimistic approach and show the good results of the limited usability improvements that you can make with little initial investment, in the hope that doing so will propel the decision makers into funding more study. For example, "After performing a heuristic evaluation of the site, we were able to uncover 15 serious usability problems. Since we have located these problems and fixed them, our Web user satisfaction has risen 40 percent."

The approach that you must take to educate the decision makers in your own organization varies. The objective is the same, however: to help them understand the need for usability and how usability fits into the grand scheme of things. You must also make it understood that occasionally you must make decisions about usability that are contrary to what seems "cool"; decisions like these are always more compelling when they are backed up with solid data that you have acquired during usability testing. Otherwise, it's your opinion against another person's, and without backup, you will probably find that you'll lose in the end.

Approaches to Education

Whenever a Web design team from a major company approaches me to come on as a usability consultant, there is one step that I always take. I make a brief presentation to the decision makers to explain what usability is all about, how it is done, and what the return on investment (ROI) will be to the company, should it decide to implement it. If you are an independent contractor, you would be wise to develop just such a presentation for yourself.

Preaching to the Converted

Unfortunately, the people who are interested in doing the usability study are often not the people who have the authority to actually implement the changes you recommend in your final report. You'll need to overcome this hurdle by way of early education, before you expend any time and effort in developing a usability plan and executing it. Be sure to determine early on who is actually in charge; otherwise, you may be working hard to sell your ideas to people who can't actually do anything about them.

One of the worst feelings in the world is to design and run the perfect usability plan, only to have the client say "OK, great, now we've done usability stuff" and throw the results away. When this happens you can be fairly certain that no one really bought into the idea in the first place. This is not only a letdown—it also reduces the chance for an ongoing relationship with the client.

Prepare Your Material

To attain the goal of educating your clients (or your employer) about Web site usability, you can do several things to make things easier on yourself. The first action is to develop a presentation that explains what usability is all about: the philosophy behind it and how it ultimately affects an organization's bottom line. The CD-ROM that accompanies this book includes a PowerPoint presentation that is covered under the GNU public license. You can use the presentation free of charge. You can modify it, and you can even distribute it as long as you distribute it in its entirety (including any modifications that you make) and include the same GNU public license conditions that I have. Please refer to the CD-ROM "README" file for more information.

Case Studies

Another great tool to use is the case study. As you develop a portfolio of clients, you can obtain permission from them to use their results as part of a case study. When you present your client or employer with concrete facts about other, similar businesses that have had good success in implementing usability studies, it becomes easier to sell the idea. It also helps crystallize just what it is they can expect of you and the service you will provide.

Public and Private Seminars

If you are a consultant, it's a great idea to offer public seminars on usability (at a local hotel or conference center) and invite local companies to attend for free or for a minimal charge. This way, you get to educate your potential client base while you do some self-promotion.

Depending on your goal, you could place ads in local computer circulars, post the conference details on Usenet, or use any of a variety of other techniques to get the word out. For a minimal investment, you will be spreading the word about usability and developing a network of potential clients at the same time.

CHAPTER SUMMARY

- The point of Web site usability is to make Web sites perform the function for which they were designed, with the minimal amount of user frustration, time, and effort.

- Web sites that exist primarily to entertain are very different from sites that exist to fulfill specific user needs. In this book, we are concerned with the latter, not the former.
- One of our primary responsibilities as Web usability specialists is to educate others about the need for Web site usability.
- It is critical to understand the purpose of a Web site, since no other usability study can happen until it is determined.
- User-centered design (UCD) is a keystone of good Web site usability.
- Human factors psychology is in many ways the roots of how we study usability.
- Designs that are not based on user input are doomed to fail.
- It's important to be as scientific as your circumstances will allow, but in reality, the nature of our field restricts how sterile we can be.
- Some usability is better than none.
- You don't need much to get started in usability.

HANDS-ON EXERCISES

Take a look at the slide presentation included on the CD-ROM. Begin to think about how you will customize it for your own use.

1. What is the purpose of your Web site? Talk to the people involved with the Web site in your organization, and write down the important goals for the site. Then write a paragraph or two that captures the essence of the site's *raison d'être*. This material will become the foundation for your usability plan.
2. Do you have a record of user feedback on your site, such as e-mail to the Webmaster? Amass all the input you can, for starters. What trends do you discern in the feedback?

DISCUSSION TOPICS

1. What were your preconceptions about Web site usability? Do you think differently now that you have read the chapter?

2. What are the 10 things you hate the most about the Web?
3. What are the 5 things you love about the Web?
4. What are your favorite products out of those you have used, and why were they your favorites?
5. If you had to make the decision to perform a comprehensive usability plan on the Coca-Cola Web site or the Microsoft Web site, which one would you choose? Why?

CHAPTER

2

USER-CENTERED DESIGN

Make everything as simple as possible, but not simpler.

—*Albert Einstein*

WHAT IS USER-CENTERED DESIGN?

Your mantra for the rest of this book, and, indeed, hopefully for the rest of your career, should be "Know Thy User." This mantra has meaning on several levels beyond its "common sense" meaning. In Chapter 1, we discussed how early computers were designed by engineers, for engineers. The designer and the end user were usually the exact same sort of person: highly technical, with a true hacker[1] spirit.

---

[1]I use *hacker* in the Massachusetts Institute of Technology (MIT) sense of the word, not the vulgar sense. In the MIT community as well as several other technical communities, a hacker is a person who delights in understanding the inner workings of a computer, or a program, or a machine, or anything that is normally incomprehensible to the layperson. Going to great lengths to understand how an arcane piece of computing machinery works is seen as a challenge to the keen hacker. The general public's use of the term *hacker* to denote a 14-year-old computer criminal is both misinformed and unfortunate. The hacking community calls these types *crackers*, since they seek to destroy, not to make the world a better place. See Steele, 1992, for more information.

Because the computer user community has been radically transformed into primarily nontechnical types, a new approach to design has been needed. "RTFM"[2] is no longer a valid response to a bewildered user who cannot figure out how to use your Web site. The bottom line is that you, as a Web designer, must ensure that your site is self-explanatory enough that users in your target population with the least amount of experience can use it with little or no distress.

User-centered design (UCD), then, is both a technique and a philosophy that puts the user's needs ahead of anything else. UCD is *typified by early and frequent interaction with the real user community to solicit feedback and to gain foresight into the future of the design.* It is a philosophy, because every part of the design process and other processes that touch it are necessarily touched by it.

Ask

UCD involves interviewing potential users of your site (or the revision of an existing site) before a single line of new HTML has been written. The goal of this effort is to determine users' likes and dislikes, hopes and expectations, as well as to find out how they currently interact with existing tools. The usability expert knows how to systematically assemble such information gathered from potential users and assemble it into concrete suggestions for the site designers.

There are several tools that you can use to obtain user information, but the things you are interested in finding out can be broken into several common categories:

- **Minimal required functionality.** What, minimally, does the user need to be able to do with the site? Remember that adding tons of features initially may be the wrong approach. The more you add to an interface, the more complex it becomes and the harder it is to use intuitively. Focus on what the users really need to work initially, then add features gradually, as you become more comfortable with

[2] *Read the fine manual,* depending on whom you ask.

troubleshooting. This approach also allows users to become familiar with the interface gradually.

- **User constraints.** What sorts of limitations do your users have? Common constraints include bandwidth limitations, browser type (not just Netscape Navigator versus Microsoft Internet Explorer, but also new types of Web browsing devices such as PDAs and information appliances such as WebTV, hardware, plug-ins, and platform. Additionally, you must consider Web accessibility constructs to enable all of your audience to access your content.
- **User preferences.** How do your users want their Web site to act? Do you have savvy users who want lots of time-saving features, or do you have primarily novice users who want very self-explanatory, although perhaps less efficient, interfaces? Do your users have "cookiephobia"?[3] Are your users fans of elaborate graphics (possibly because they surf at work, where the bandwidth is plentiful and free), or do they prefer tight, simple pages with minimal graphics (home use over a 56k modem)?
- **User habits.** How do users currently carry out tasks? Do they use a competitor's site that they like or hate? Are there actions that they carry out "in their sleep" on existing sites that you can incorporate into your design? Any existing habits can be transformed into time savers for your users when approached in this manner. Learn to look for these habits and catalog them well.
- **Existing systems.** What kinds of systems are users currently using to carry out actions? "System" does not necessarily refer to a computer system; it could be a toll-free telephone number (for sales and customer support), paper forms (for membership application or financial reporting), mechanical systems (such as punch-clocks or fire alarm control panels), or basically anything else that might be used to accomplish the tasks that you want to enable with your design.

---

[3]"Cookiephobia" is the fear that allowing Web servers to set and read cookies on users' computers will somehow greatly reduce users' anonymity or allow companies to get access to otherwise private information. In context of recent events, this may be a far more realistic fear than a phobia.

- **User dislikes.** What do your users hate about the existing site or comparable sites? This list can include general sorts of Web peeves (slow server response times or clumsy graphics) or very site-specific complaints ("This site is poorly organized. I always look for the commercial banking information on the wrong part of the site!"). Pay close attention to these dislikes; you won't want to repeat any of the faulty design in your new version.
- **Personal data.** Most important, who are your users? How old are they? What's their level of Internet know-how? How educated are they? What sites do they use the most? Are they current customers or potential customers? Where do they live? How many computers do they have at home, and on what platforms? The list of possible questions goes on and on, but the general idea is to gather as much information as you can about your users as people. This demographic data will enable you to better categorize your user base and focus your site to meet their needs.

Test . . .

UCD extends into the midlife of a site design (or redesign) in the form of user testing. Once you have assembled initial user input and made at least a prototype of the site, it's time to get real users to try it on for size. What you will probably find is that you misinterpreted something users said or took a concept too far. The feedback from your users at this point will propel you into the final stages of design.

User testing can occur at any stage in the design life cycle, and it should happen as often as possible. In addition to classical usability testing, in which you assign users tasks such as searching for information or completing a transaction, you can also use tools such as focus groups to gather user opinions.

And Retest

Nearing the end of a design or redesign, just before the site "goes live," your users should be involved again, for a phase of testing called *valida-*

tion. This phase is a last-minute sanity check that buys you the peace of mind of knowing that the site lives up to user expectations and that there are no serious, undiscovered usability problems.

But Users Aren't Designers

If you have ever watched the TV cartoon *The Simpsons*, you might have seen the episode in which Homer (the father of a dysfunctional family) meets his long-lost brother. His brother turns out to be the president of a major car manufacturer. The company's sluggish sales prompt Homer's brother to offer Homer, an "ordinary American guy," the chance to design the company's new flagship vehicle. The idea is that since Homer is exactly the type of person the company is trying to reach, surely he will design an automobile that will be wildly successful.

As you can probably imagine if you're familiar with these characters, Homer comes up with one heck of a car—or, rather, a hunk of a car. The car is riddled with features that only Homer would ever want, and the car is a massively expensive flop. The moral of the story is, because the company put a regular user in the role of a designer, things fell apart.

Whether you watch cartoons or not, one thing is clear: Users are not designers. They lack the essential skills to understand design implications and to implement changes in a sound, scientific fashion.

USERS DON'T ALWAYS KNOW WHAT THEY WANT

Another job of the skilled designer is to divine what, exactly, a user truly wants—not just what the user says he or she wants. A case in point is the research done by Bell Research. Henry Dreyfuss began work as a consultant to Bell Telephone Laboratories in 1930 and was commissioned to perform a minor cosmetic facelift to the classic, heavy phone of that era. He ended up completely redesigning the phone into the lightweight phone that is the model for phones we still use today.

Dreyfuss believed that machines that were adapted to people's physical requirements would be the most functional and the easiest to use.

Toward this end, he measured 2,000 sample faces from mouth to ear. He ensured that the hand grip wouldn't slip in the user's hand, and that the instrument could be easily handled by a variety of sizes of hands under different environmental circumstances. Through his collection of data on the human body's proportions and capabilities, Dreyfuss helped establish the science of ergonomics.

During some of the research performed by his team, Dreyfuss found that telephone users reported that they were completely satisfied with the weight and feel of the old-style handset; it was heavy, and weight imparted an image of quality. However, when prototypes of a newer, lighter handset were given to users to try, they changed their tune quickly and became attached to their new, lighter, easy-to-cradle phones.

The moral of the story is that your job as a usability specialist is to present choices in a scientific fashion to your users to best determine what the user "really" wants. This is not an endorsement for design fascism, however. The designer doesn't always know what's best until thorough testing has been done.

THE USABILITY LIFE CYCLE

In the phases outlined above, it appears that there are exactly three phases to your work, and no more. But the fact of the matter is that a Web site is never truly completed; revisions happen frequently. That's a fact of Web life! Hence, the three phases of UCD are actually just segments of a closed loop, one that you will cycle through an indefinite number of times in your career—or at least over the lifetime of your Web site.

This cyclical design concept is called *iterative redesign* and is a key notion in UCD and usability. The fact is, the job is never done, and the site will become better the more that UCD principles are applied to it over time. Furthermore, never forget that your audience is bound to change over time; and if you stop the cycle of regeneration, your site will "die."

The tools and techniques that you use at each phase of testing can vary. Some tools are best suited for use in the first phase; others work well only in the middle phase. The whole plan that you will create for the lifetime of your site is a blueprint for development. Called a *usability plan*, it is the cornerstone of what you will do as a usability specialist.

Be as Impartial as Possible

It is important to note that in most cases it is inadvisable for the usability specialist to be a member of the Web site development team. If a person has invested his or her own design ideas and habits into a site, that person is much, much more likely to let his or her interpretation of user data to be skewed in his or her own favor. This happens, regardless of how secure you believe your own ego to be, so the best plan is to avoid this kind of a dual role entirely.

It is not always possible to have a separate usability specialist, though, and that's understandable. Often, the Webmaster for a small site (and even some large sites—scary!) is a one-person show. It's not uncommon for one person to be a graphic designer, marketing specialist, HTML coder, and programmer all in one. If you are in this unenviable position, you might just be stuck with the task of critiquing your own work.

The Frame

The Zen-like state of being that the moderator must adopt is called the *frame*[4]. Whenever I refer to the frame with regard to participants, I am talking about the state of being that facilitates the study process, yet maintains a warm, comfortable state for the participant. As a moderator, one of the greatest tasks you must learn is how to be warm and comforting to participants who will likely be stressed out by being in a test

[4]The term *frame* comes from the field of psychotherapy. The frame is considered the state of being in which the therapist (in the case of Web site design and usability studies, the moderator) is in control of the situation and clearly is not a peer to the patient (in this case, the participant); yet is not harsh, sterile, cold.

session, while still remaining neutral and having the same effect toward every single participant.

As you might anticipate, this can be hard to do. It's important not to become "chummy" with your participants, since any impression that you leave on them invariably will influence the way they perform tasks. For example, if you are harsh and cold or if you lack basic human empathy, your users are going to freeze up in fear and probably perform poorly. On the other hand, if you try to be the participant's best buddy, you will find that you waste a lot of time talking about sports scores, the weather, or other extraneous topics that only hinder your study.

Therefore, the right stance to take is a precarious one that gets easier with practice. You need to be supportive, urging participants to try for just a little longer when they seem to give up "too quickly" because they are probably giving up due to the pressure of being observed.

The Disease of Familiarity

One of the gravest disabilities that can plague a designer is the "disease" of familiarity.[5] That is to say, designers often forget what it was like before they became completely knowledgeable of the system they have designed; they lose the ability to "see through new eyes" and forget what they didn't know when they first approached the site. What seems like common sense to the designer is really a quantum leap for the uninitiated—and sometimes the leap is just too much for even a savvy user to make.

As a usability specialist, you must "learn to unlearn" and to see the interfaces as an outsider sees them. You cannot assume that the user knows how to do anything beyond rudimentary navigation. You probably take for granted thousands of bits of information about Web design and use that the average user simply does not possess.

[5]The term dis*ease of familiarity* comes from distinguished author and information analyst, Richard Saul Wurman, whose classic work *Information Architects* is a must-read.

For this very reason, you must never attempt to do budget usability using your coworkers, especially people who actually helped create the site, as test subjects. They have knowledge of the site that the average user does not have, hence they are simply not the right people to test the site. However, it is generally considered acceptable if you run through your usability tests with a coworker before you use the plan with real participants. Obviously, you cannot use data acquired from your coworkers (although they may turn up some important usability flaws anyway!), but doing a dry run with them helps you adjust task length and find serious problems with your test plan.

The Other End

Contrast UCD to the opposite end of the spectrum, feature-centered design,[6] in which the end user is rarely (or never) taken into consideration; features are added to a product to enable the marketing department to wage a totally artificial war against the competition, hurling spears of buzzwords and specifications. In this sort of design, everyone who actually matters loses.

There are many examples of this type of design in the real world, and they are the hallmark of a company that has no real advantage over a competitor and so needs to manufacture one. The end user is the victim of this kind of myopic behavior.

POPULATION VS. SAMPLE

If you are concerned about how usable your site is, you must have at least some notion of who might be using it or who you'd like to see using it. The collective of people in the whole world who are potentially your site's users is called its *population*, which we will discuss in detail shortly.

---

[6]The result of which is usually *creeping featuritis*, a terrible disorder of a product that can result in partial or complete insanity of the end user, the programmers, or both. Also see Steele, 1992.

Unless your target audience is small and known (such as the users of your company intranet), you can never hope to acquire data from every single user. Fortunately, the magic of statistical analysis help in this regard. It is possible to do a study involving a fraction of your population that will yield results that are almost as accurate as studying the entire population. There are some constraints on how you may select the fractional group of participants, but the methods for doing this are well known (we'll discuss how to do this later). This fractional group of people, drawn in a random fashion for your population, is called the *sample.* This is the group of people who will be your participants for any given test.

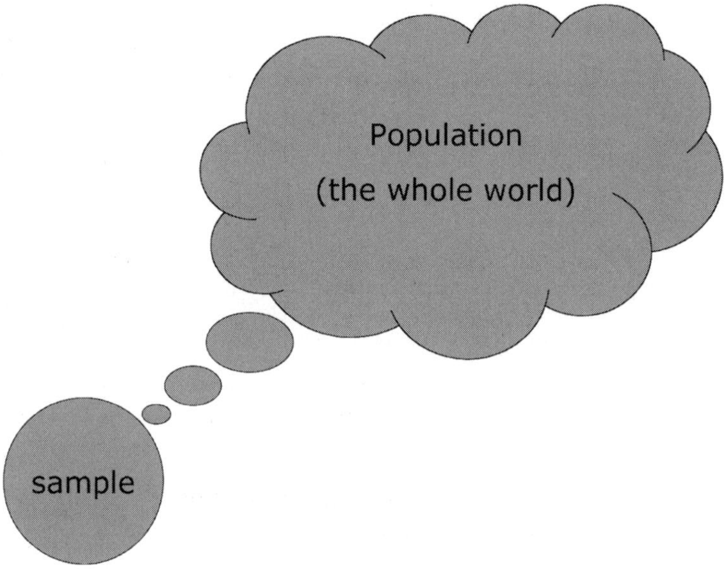
Population
(the whole world)
sample

The Participant

One thing to keep in mind is that the participant is a major part of your *raison d'être:* without participants, you can't really do anything! A major part of usability science is recruiting and interacting with participants; these participants are carefully selected people who are good representatives of your total user population. The participants are human, of course, so you and your team need to consider many interpersonal and ethical issues.

"It Must Be My Fault!"

You will quickly realize that humans tend to blame themselves for failing to perform a task, such as finding a piece of information on a poorly designed Web site. Although this tendency seems to be influenced by age and region of habitation, it is still prevalent enough to be a major concern for you, the moderator. Even in light of the fact that a Web site might be terribly designed, with broken links, tar pits, confusing frame sets, and distracting animations, a participant is still likely to self-deprecate to some level.

This fact means that you have special responsibilities to ensure that the participant understands that there are no right or wrong answers and that he or she is not being evaluated for his or her performance, but rather that the Web site itself is being tested. This is a hard thing of which to convince a participant—it's like telling a punished child, "This hurts me more than it hurts you!" It is something that is often said and rarely believed.

The important key to making your participants feel at ease is your disposition. If you are cold and analytical, participants will likely view you as a harsh authoritarian and feel even more uncomfortable. By being human, empathic, and warm, you will make participants more relaxed, more receptive to continue, and, in general, less anxious. But note that there is a fine line between being warm and trying to be every participant's best friend! If you try to chum it up with every participant, you will waste a lot of time, and you may risk invalidating your results.

Compensating Your Participants

You should always compensate participants for taking part in your usability studies. The amount or type of compensation will vary. If you are doing a usability study within your own company, the compensation might range anywhere from a free brownie or a coffee mug to a free vacation day.

If you are recruiting participants from a pool of your existing clients, it could be appropriate to offer them free services or goods. If you have obtained participants from a recruiting firm, their compensation might be built into the fee you pay the firm; or you might need to compensate them yourself. You can read more about this topic later in the book.

You need to have a pretty clear policy on compensation well ahead of time. What do you do if someone comes in a half-hour late and demands to be paid? You need to decide ahead of time how you will handle exceptional cases. I have had people come in hours late and still demand to be paid. I've also known people who have complained that they weren't being paid enough to participate (after they had willingly signed up for the session, knowing full well what the compensation was!). Be prepared.

For some examples of how Microsoft compensates its participants (about 750 people per month, if that puts the importance of usability in some kind of scope), see *microsoft.com/usability/gratuity.htm.*

Ethics

Another thing to keep in mind is that participating in tests and other types of interviews is often intimidating and stressful for participants. You are ethically bound to make sure that your participants do not suffer as a result of your usability work. You are responsible to advise your participants that they are under no obligation to participate, that their actions are totally voluntary, and that they do not need to perform an action if it makes them feel uncomfortable. You also need to let them know that they can leave at any point throughout the proceedings.

The Milgram Study

It is important to understand why it is critical that your study participants not feel trapped, as though they must complete tasks. Here we briefly recount a famous 1965 experiment by Stanley Milgram, who was with the Department of Psychology at Yale University. The experiment used deception and a form of coercion to keep participants performing actions long after they became uncomfortable doing so.

In this experiment, three people were involved: the experimenter, a confederate (someone who was "in on" the experiment with the experimenter) who behaved as a "learner," and a participant (who was deceived into believing that he was, in fact, a confederate) who acted as a "teacher." The teacher was informed that his sole purpose in the experiment was to teach a list of paired words to the learner. The learner was hidden from sight and supposedly attached to a machine that delivered an electrical shock when the learner made an error.

The participant (the "teacher") believed that the intensity of the electrical shock increased in voltage as the experiment continued. The machine, which administered the "pseudo-shocks," was clearly labeled, indicating the increasing levels of shock intensity being imposed on the "learner." The experimenter was present and used only four statements to encourage the teacher to continue with the experiment:

Statement 1: "Please continue" (or "Please go on").

Statement 2: "The experiment requires that you continue."

Statement 3: "It is absolutely essential that you continue."

Statement 4: "You have no other choice, you must go on."

Milgram found that the majority of the "teachers" complied with the demands of the experimenter, even though it was apparent that they felt conflict of emotions and uneasiness. Some participants actually proceeded with delivering the "shocks" when the "learner" was howling with pain; at least one participant proceeded when he or she thought that the "learner" had died as a result of the shocks.

This experiment shows that clearly, people who are perceived as being in a position of authority can have a vast power over others. This form of power has manifested itself in many places. Take, for example, the college classroom, in which eager students are willing to give erroneous answers if they know that the erroneous answer will please the professor.

The point of all this discussion is to point out that participants can often feel coerced into giving answers that they feel will please the test moderator, even if the test moderator has made no outward or conscious effort to coerce them. Therefore, you must always be mindful of this possibility when conducting usability tests.

The other critical lesson to learn from this study is that full disclosure is an essential feature of well-designed research. Full disclosure does not mean that you need to tell your participants absolutely everything about your research; it does not mean that you need to tell them exactly what you plan to do with your findings. It also does not mean that you must share with them your suspicions about the Web site design in question.

It does mean, however, that you must not use deception of participants as part of your test plan. Even a simple ruse could quickly devolve into a very unethical situation; major research organizations and universities utilize a very strict peer review and special ethics committees to weed out unethical research designs.

To make this point very real, you should, for example, not inform a participant that he or she is simply being observed to see which navigation links the participant prefers, when, in reality, the participants are being subjected to a series of deliberately frustrating designs intended to incite rage!

Generally speaking, you are expected to cover all these bases before you ever begin any sort of participant testing or other activities involving participants. Although we discuss the test plan in great detail in a later chapter, for now you should know that you usually make a point of full disclosure and let the participants know that this activity is fully voluntary during the part of a test called the *orientation*.

The orientation gives participants the chance to opt out of the activities if they feel uncomfortable or even if they were misled regarding the nature of the activities. Regretfully, sometimes recruiting agencies deliberately deceive potential participants because each recruited participant represents a dollar amount to a recruiter.

You may be thinking that you'll never design an experiment like the one described here and that anything that you do will clearly be an exception to the rules of ethical research. Think again! In a litigious society, this point should not be ignored.

Ethics in the Workplace

Another area of concern is the participant's workplace. If you are performing a usability study for a company, perhaps your own, it is critical that if you use participants from the company, you make the results of your sessions totally anomymous.

Otherwise, you could end up in a really sticky situation, so you need to lay down the law from the start, long before you begin the test sessions. Institute a well-known and accepted policy that the participants have a right to privacy and that your study has the requirement that "the show must go on."

If the client insists on observing the participants or seeing "anonymous" results, the ethically right thing to do is to refuse the job.

To wrap up this section on ethics, always remember to observe and make clear the following in all of your sessions with users:

- Participants are not obligated to stay in the session and may leave at any point if they feel uncomfortable.
- Participants are not required to perform a task if that task makes them uncomfortable.
- Participant data will never be shown to superiors unless it is in a totally anonymous format.
- Participants should never be deceived during the course of a study.
- Participants should be allowed to ask questions at the end of the session during a "debriefing" session to help minimize any discomfort they might have.

KNOWING YOUR USERS

Like any other well-laid plan, there is a definite process to UCD. The principles are constant throughout industries, but since this is, after all, a book on Web site usability, this section remains focused on that aspect. The first step is, as noted, "Know Thy User." Let's discuss what exactly that abstract concept means to us in the very real workplace.

What's the Site's Purpose?

The first step to good usability is to decide the true purpose of your Web site. What service are you providing to your users, or what services do you hope to provide? Too many Web sites are devoid of purpose, often reflecting the inherent lack of direction of the site's sponsoring company. If this is the case with your company or organization, no amount of good usability techniques can help you: without a purpose, all is for naught.

Hopefully, your organization has some modicum of direction, and a corporate vision will be clear. You'll need to understand the company's direction to some extent to be able to continue. You may, for example, determine after meeting with the executives of your company that the company's Web presence vision is directed toward three main goals:

- Provide technical support for current customers
- Provide product information to prospective customers
- Provide investor relations information

With this concrete list of corporate goals in mind, you can begin to divine the nature of your user population. From looking at the list of goals, it becomes apparent that there are at least three main categories of users of the site: potential investors, potential customers, and current customers. We don't know an awful lot about these people yet, but we have a baseline to begin with.

You may already be in charge of an existing Web site—not an unlikely case nowadays. Perhaps it's a Web-based application that you offer, such as an image-retouching service or stock quotes. Perhaps you offer a news service or consumer information about your brand.

Whatever the case, there is a target audience for you,[7] and your job is to recognize who makes up that audience and to refine your picture of them so that you can better serve them. This effort will, of course, result

[7]This is true unless your service is so totally obscure that no one could ever possibly want to take part in it; but that is very hard to believe possible, given the proliferation of oddities on the Web.

in everyone winning; you'll do more business, and the end user will have a better experience.

If you are creating a Web site from scratch, perhaps for a startup company or one of the 24 businesses left in the world that don't have a Web site, you also have a target audience. You may have less to go on than the people in the case detailed previously, but there are clues for you nonetheless. At any rate, the goal is the same: to find out who uses your site now and who might use the site, either in the future or in the present. We know that the World Wide Web is open to the world; but limiting our potential group of users to "the world" doesn't narrow it down much, and in fact it can hinder development, since you simply cannot design a single Web site that appeals to the entire world. We must settle on some arbitrary chunk of the world as our user population.

Who Makes Up the Population?

We call the total aggregate of your potential users the *population*. The population represents every single person that fits your market's demographics who might be a potential user of your site. This group might be limited to people within your company, in the case of an intranet. It might be limited to first-time car buyers who live in the Boston area, and so on. Your target population will have certain common characteristics; you must determine what they are.

Of course, it is normal for individual users of your site to fall outside of the "norm" at which you arrive. In fact, you will find that it is usually advisable to include at least one participant in your studies who has an almost complete lack of skill or experience. This user, often called the *least-competent user (LCU),* is the acid test of your design. The belief is that if this user can manage to get most of the tasks in your test plan accomplished, any "real" user will be able to as well. I personally find the LCU label offensive; imagine if you played this role in someone else's research! I offer the term *ultra-novice* as an alternative.

Unless your Web site is an intranet for your company, it is very unlikely that you will be able to know every single user by name or know all of their hopes, expectations, dislikes, and so on. What you must do instead is form a model of the general population based on some sleuthing we'll explore next. This way, you'll avoid the pain of going out and polling every single user in the world, but you'll still get the general idea. The magic of statistics will be our ally.

If your site already exists, there is a good chance that your marketing department has information about your target audience. What you find might shock you: in many cases, a company's Web site is geared almost totally to a part of the user population that is by far the smallest group.

In some instances, the site does not adequately address the needs of any significant portion of the user community. If you can get access to this information, make a table for yourself that synopsizes the types of people in your target audience. You will find this table invaluable as the cornerstone of your usability plan for your site.

Starting from Scratch

What if you don't know who makes up your target population? Perhaps you are in a startup company or your organization is using the Web as an outreach mechanism to gain a foothold in new, previously untapped terrain. In this case, you still have several options.

One option is to obtain marketing research conducted by your company's founders. Unless the business was built in an utterly ramshackle fashion, there must be at least a little information about the original target audience.

Another option is to look at information derived—at a price—from marketing research companies you can hire. These companies can typically reveal to you user trends from competing Web sites; although your brand or service is hopefully better than the competition's, you can still create a baseline for yourself with this "borrowed" information.

Finally, some organizations have been successful in launching pilot Web sites that are designed to gather information from potential users long before the actual site is scheduled to go live. For example, you might have a Web site featuring prizes of technological goodies or cash for random participants in your survey.

The key to success here is to keep the usability survey as short as you can and to make the lure of winning strong enough to keep participants going as they fill in information.

Finding Participants for Your Sessions

Once you identify your key audience(s), you need to recruit participants for the usability sessions that you will be designing. There are several ways to locate willing participants; the method that you should choose depends on your particular company or organization.

If you have a known group of users—for example, if users of your site are required to sign up for an account to use it—you already have a well-defined audience. You can recruit participants from the list of enrolled site users.

If you're not so sure about your users, you could need outside help. Two common places to look for participants (at a price, of course) is through marketing research companies (perhaps the same one that helped you refine your potential audience), recruiting firms, or temporary agencies. Each of these groups can provide a pool of people for the selection of participants.

Beware of Best-Testers

Unfortunately, if you choose to go with a firm to locate your participants, you will not get a truly random selection of people. In fact, you will get a group of participants who share a certain set of unique qualities that make them unlike the average person.

Many people included in the databases of recruiting firms are veteran product testers. In many cases, they make a full-time living participating in tests, and they have learned how to "perform" to get them in and out of the sessions as quickly as possible. They are probably experts at whatever they have agreed to test, which isn't what you want!

The potential for recruiting these "best-testers" does not mean that you should never use recruiting agencies. It just means that you need to know how to spot a best-tester, since combining their data in with the rest of your data will poison your results. To facilitate the recognition of a best-tester, here is a list of top ways to spot one:

- The participant has a gold-plated Web-surfing thimble.
- The participant brings a special mouse to the session.
- The participant wrote the code for the browser you are using.
- The participant asks to be compensated in Amazon.com gift certificates.
- The participant spikes the mouse and yells "Yessss!" after each task.
- You greet the participant, who responds "Hello" back to you—in binary.
- The participant views the source of your site and rewrites the HTML on the spot for you.
- The participant uses keyboard shortcuts instead of the back and forward buttons to navigate.

- The participant asks you if you've got anything more challenging to do.
- And finally: You end up behind the mouse with the participant telling you what to do!

Learning More About Your Users

Once you know the general groups, or *profiles*, of users of your site, you need to begin to flesh out your picture of them by gaining more specific information.

However you acquire user information, there are certain universal bits as well as certain product- or service-specific items that you will need. User information can generally be broken down into the following categories:

- **Concrete data.** This is data that is easily quantifiable, not typically subject to interpretation. Examples: age, gender, education level, years of computer/Web experience, application experience, Web browser most commonly used, operating system experience, household income, Internet connection speed, and so on.
- **Preference data.** This is data that is based solely on the user's reported preferences. Examples: favorite browser (note the difference between "favorite" and "most often used"), cookies/no cookies, Java/no Java, reasons the user uses the Web (surfing for fun, hunting for solutions, and so on).
- **Self-reported data.** This is data that indicates a user's status in a way that you might be charting, but it comes from the user rather than testing. Care must be taken in interpreting this kind of data because it is usually at least a little inaccurate (why?). Examples: experience level with the Web (novice, intermediate, advanced),[8] experience using competitor's sites, and so on.

[8]In one study that one of my students performed, a user reported himself as an "absolute expert" yet did not realize that you could just click on a hyperlink to follow it; he had been right-clicking on the link and selecting "follow this link."

Getting all this information about your users can occur via one or more methods. Generally, you, the usability specialist, need to construct a questionnaire to collect user information. This questionnaire can be deployed via the following methods (this list is not exhaustive):

- Via the existing Web site (thus giving existing users the chance to impact the new design of the site)
- Via a recruiting agency (more on this later) or your human resources department (if you are working on your company's intranet)
- By placing an ad in a specifically targeted area (for example, in the local university's student center, if your user population consists primarily of college students)

What Questions Should You Ask?

Initially, you'll need to gather enough information about your users to be able to classify them appropriately. The information you are looking for may vary depending on your current usability goals. For example, you might decide that you need to gather information regarding your users' experience with an existing Web database interface that you are planning to upgrade.

Obviously, this particular chunk of information might not be applicable to other testing sessions; however, a basic template for your questionnaire can be used as a starting point. You can add to this template or subtract from it as the need arises.

The Screener

You could use a slightly modified version of the questionnaire as a telephone screener for potential participants. For example, if you choose to hire a recruiting agency to gather your participants, the agency will need some criteria for selecting who to get on board. A questionnaire can be modified to fit this need.

Normally, as per the term, a screener is designed to filter out people you don't want to participate. You may have determined that males of age

18–35 are not in your audience; hence you don't want to waste time and money recruiting and testing men in that age group.

Likewise, you probably want to filter out people who do Web site design for a living, since they will perform very differently from the average user. In short, you need to decide on the criteria for allowing a candidate into your pool, and you must formalize these constraints in a document that you give to your recruiting agency.

User Profiles

After a bit of research, you may find that your original three groups of users have mushroomed into five, or seven, or more. Often a single main population will contain many subgroups that can be classified along various lines of attributes.

The fact of the matter is that you cannot expect that one Web site design will appeal to every single user. However, by developing well-researched user profiles, you have a much better understanding of your user population.

It also follows that testing the effectiveness of your site is more fluid with regard to each category of user. As an example, if we identify the fact that 60 percent of our site's users are administrative staff, 25 percent nurses, and 15 percent doctors, we can identify a much more exact route to restructuring a site dealing in health care.

You will want to take special note of the various profiles that constitute your overall population. These details enable you to understand performance trends in your usability tasks; they also prepare you for the possibility that your user profiles might be so divergent that you'll need to prepare separate "flavors" of your site for each group.

THE ITERATIVE REDESIGN CYCLE

Remember those completely annoying "Under Construction" signs on sites that hadn't been modified in months—or years? The truth of the matter is that *the whole Web is always under construction; every Web site is understood to be a work in progress*. No cute animations of stick people shoveling digital dirt are needed; people understand that the entire Web is "in flux," and all too often, the notion of a site being "in progress" is a cop-out that really means "we're too lazy to put content here!" (See Figure 2.1.)

With that said, it's important to also embrace the fact I mentioned earlier, that the entire lifetime of a Web site is a cycle—a loop that has distinct phases but no starting point and no ending point, much like the

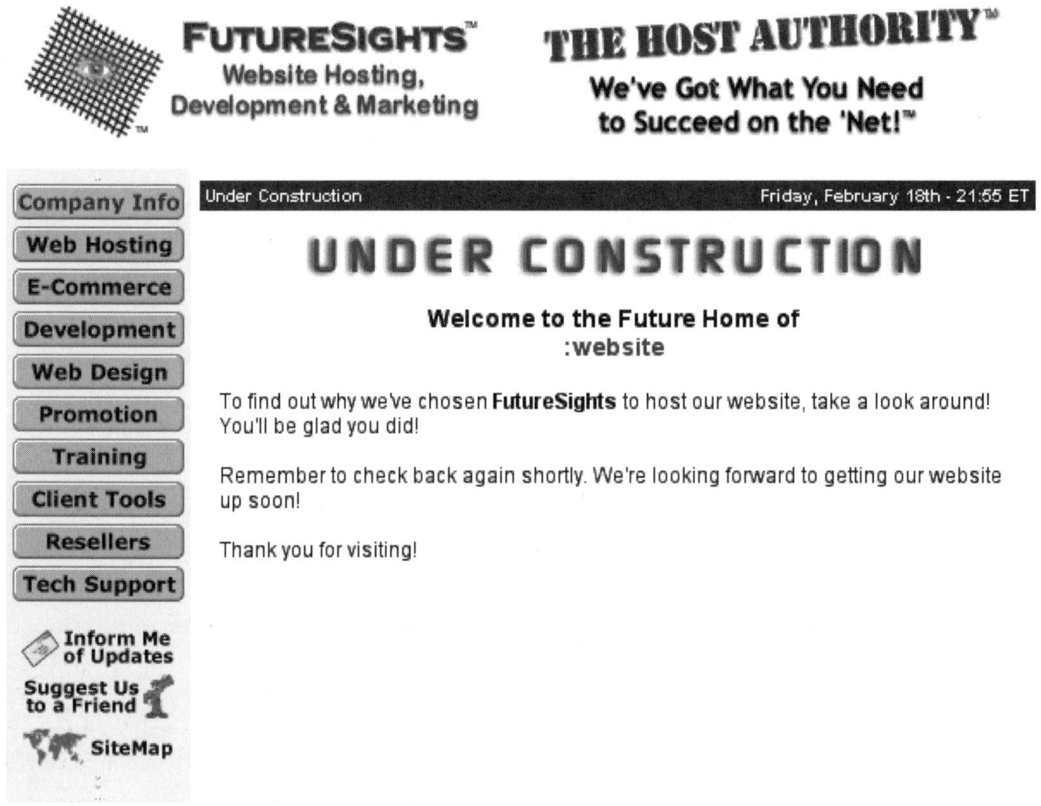
FUTURESIGHTS™
Website Hosting, Development & Marketing
THE HOST AUTHORITY™
We've Got What You Need to Succeed on the 'Net!™
Company Info
Web Hosting
E-Commerce
Development
Web Design
Promotion
Training
Client Tools
Resellers
Tech Support
Inform Me of Updates
Suggest Us to a Friend
SiteMap
Under Construction
Friday, February 18th - 21:55 ET
UNDER CONSTRUCTION
Welcome to the Future Home of :website
To find out why we've chosen FutureSights to host our website, take a look around! You'll be glad you did!
Remember to check back again shortly. We're looking forward to getting our website up soon!
Thank you for visiting!

FIGURE 2.1
Oops! We've hit road kill in the Information Superhighway. Everyone knows that a Web site is always a work in progress. Iterative redesign means insulating your users from encountering this. Copyright 2000 Future Sights.

seasons. A major principle of UCD is that users should be involved in some capacity in all the phases of the redesign cycle.

"Work in Progress" not an official endorsement of Web site neglect. One of the most often cited user complaints about Web sites is that links are "broken" or out of date. Just because it's understood that your site is always under development is no excuse for you to be sloppy.

The Phases of the Cycle

Many people have interpreted the phases of redesign differently, so there are several "road maps" for the overall process. What really matters is that you have some way of envisioning the abstract concept of a design cycle. The labels that you use aren't important. Some observations of the cycle follow:

Phase 1: User Needs Analysis

During this phase, the usability specialist communicates extensively with users, in the form of interviews, field studies, and other techniques, in order to gain a thorough understanding of current system limitations, areas of improvement, and user needs.

Areas of focus for the usability specialist include user work environment, existing Web systems and applications, traditional workflow methods, traditional media used to accomplish tasks, user "jargon" (natural user language), and competitor techniques.

Phase 2: Operational and Conceptual Design

The usability specialist coordinates with the design team to translate the user needs analysis into concrete terms that become the blueprint for the site design or redesign. User needs and requirements are formalized into a set of design requirements—a set of concrete guidelines that specify the priorities for the site. For example, a design requirement might be that the site must provide two different views of a particular Web application: one for people in one department and another for people in a different department.

These design requirements need to be formally stated so that all team members share an unambiguous view of the design plan.

Once the design requirements have been formalized, they should be echoed back to the original users to make sure that the usability specialist understood their original intentions. If the requirements are valid, the team can move on to the conceptual design and initial prototyping of the site.

Phase 3: Development and Testing

Once the initial prototyping has been done, the design team may begin to create the site in a fully formed fashion. Along the way, at strategic points (which will vary, depending on the individual project), the usability specialist should involve users in usability tasks and other usability sessions to get a baseline for the usability of the site. Initial benchmark times for task performance can be established at this point; these times will serve as beacons for the usability team in subsequent redesigns.

Frequent user participation during this phase is critical for discovering usability and conceptual design flaws. Remember, the earlier you catch a problem, the less likely it is to be a "critical stop."

This is also a good time to test parallel designs that you may have developed in order to determine the "best" design.

Phase 4: Validation

This period occurs just before deployment and is designed as a "flight check" before the site goes live. This period allows the usability specialist the opportunity to validate everything that has been done so far. This usually means one last round of user task sessions focused on the most critical elements of the site. Unfortunately, many organizations do any kind of usability testing only at this point, when it is usually too late to implement all but the most trivial of changes.

Phase 5: Deployment

The site goes live. This marks the time to start over at Phase 1 for the next site generation.

Repeat forever . . .

CHAPTER SUMMARY

- User-centered design is the key to a successful Web site. Period.
- UCD is typified by early and frequent interaction from real users in order to solicit feedback and to gain insight into the design of your site.
- UDC does not mean that you let users design your site for you.
- As a usability specialist, you must design a comprehensive usability plan for your site. It will be the overall blueprint for how you will measure and redesign your site over the entire life span of the site.
- The *frame* is the state within which the interaction between the moderator and the participant must remain.
- Humans are quick to assume that if they fail to accomplish a task, it must be their own fault, not the fault of poor design.
- Watch out for "best-testers."
- A good test moderator keeps the participant from being self-deprecating and helps the session move smoothly forward.
- You have the obligation to practice in a fully ethical manner. This means no deception; you must adhere to full disclosure and give the participant the option to leave.
- Know thy user.
- In order to know thy user, you must gather information through screeners and questionnaires.
- You can also get information about your user from other sources, such as existing client databases.
- Your entire user population is likely to consist of multiple user profiles or groups of people with similar characteristics.

- The life cycle of a site is divided into various phases, each of which requires user participation and interaction.

HANDS-ON EXERCISES

1. Find out who your users are. Find out if your company has market research data about your potential users. Also determine if your company has existing databases of client information that you can use as a foundation for your user information.
2. Determine your user profiles. Make a detailed analysis of your user characteristics, and figure out if there are multiple profiles in your population. Give each profile a label (name the profiles) for future reference.
3. Decide how you will recruit participants for your usability sessions. Remember that you can generalize your findings only to a population that can be represented by the sample you choose.
4. If you will use a recruiting agency to acquire participants, who in your area provides this kind of service? Place some calls to establish a working relationship with one or more agencies.

DISCUSSION TOPICS

1. Was the Milgram study justified because of the discovery it uncovered?
2. What other potential problems can you think of with regard to selecting participants from within your own organization, besides the possibility of their supervisors finding out how they performed?
3. What happens if a participant shows up and you know him or her from "real life" (from outside the context of usability testing)?
4. What do you do if a user begins giving you instructions on how to design your site during one of your sessions (assuming that you haven't asked the participant for this information)?

CHAPTER

THE USABILITY TOOLBOX 3

Beware of programmers who carry screwdrivers.

—Leonard Brandwein

IT TAKES MANY TOOLS TO "DO" USABILITY

Once you have determined your target audience, you can begin the task of making your Web site more usable. Remember, without a clear purpose and without knowing who your user is, you can't really move ahead.

Many tools, techniques, and tips comprise a usability specialist's arsenal. Collectively, I like to refer to these elements as the *usability toolbox.*[1] Some of the tools in the toolbox are complex; others are quite simple. You will find that they each have strengths and weaknesses, and only experience and trial and error can teach you which tool to use in any particular set of circumstances. Just as a master carpenter begins by learning how to drive a nail perfectly, it's critical that you learn to use

[1]Since I began writing this book, I have noticed that at least one other person uses the term *usability toolbox* to describe the set of techniques employed in usability work. James Hom maintains a Web site, *www.best.com/~jthom/usability/usable.htm,* which is an excellent synopsis of techniques. After one of my students pointed this site out to me, I initially decided to try using a different term, but everything I came up with sounded contrived.

each tool before you begin to assemble a comprehensive test plan for your site. The goal of this chapter is to familiarize you with a plethora of tools.

Here we look at several techniques and discuss where each tool might fit in a comprehensive plan. In Chapter 10, you'll see how the tools are put together by a fictional software company to create a comprehensive usability plan.

Please note that the list of tools described in this chapter is not exhaustive. You probably know of or use a technique that isn't listed here. This does not mean that unmentioned techniques (such as journaled sessions and cognitive walk-throughs) aren't valuable in some context. It just means that in my opinion, you won't find them immediately useful; we'll focus on a smaller set of tools.

Some of these tools are complex enough that they merit their own chapter in this book. The other tools are covered in some depth in this chapter.

TECH-CO

Some Useful URLs

To begin with, several Web sites you should know about provide a vast array of usability resources.

- ***www.useit.com.*** This is the Web site of Jakob Nielsen, who is usually regarded as the "father" of Web site usability. You'll read more about him in this book; he has an extensive section in the bibliography. His site is primarily a collection of his own writings, essays, and periodical Web columns entitled "Alertbox." There is a mailing list to which you can subscribe to get notifications of new "Alertbox" columns.
- ***www.usableweb.com.*** This site, maintained by Keith Instone, is the best collection of usability links that I have ever found. Here you can find links to virtually every usability Web page on the planet.
- ***www.usablesites.com.*** This is the official Web site for this book, which I maintain with the help of my students. Here you can subscribe to the Web usability majordomo mailing list as well as participate in multithreaded discussion groups that are all related to some aspect of Web site usability. You can also find links to other resources that will assist you in your endeavors.

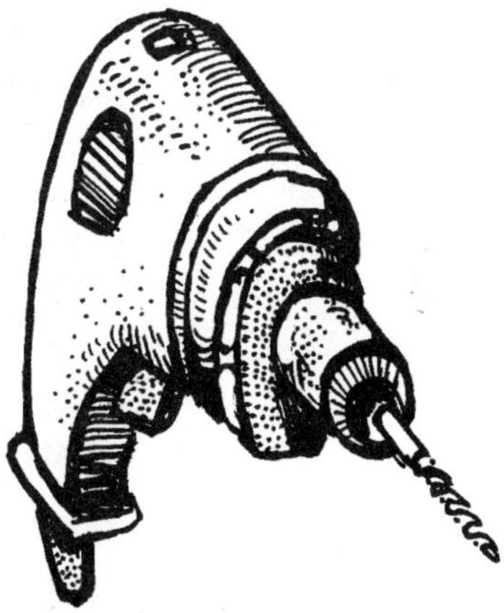

Part of a Well-Balanced Plan

Whenever you set out to survey the usability of a Web site, you need to create a comprehensive plan for how you will proceed. The tools that you will read about in this chapter are individual components of such a comprehensive plan. Normally, when you set out to begin a usability study of a site, you need to set up an initial consultation with the client to determine their usability needs. You should allot as much as a day for this initial visit. Perhaps you are conducting this usability study for your own company, in which case, making time shouldn't be too hard.

You should come to this visit equipped with several questions to help determine the course you should take. Here are some examples of questions you might ask your client:

- Why have you decided to begin a usability study of your site?
- What do you hope to accomplish with the results you get?
- What time frame are you planning on for the total study?
- Will you be able to implement changes that are suggested?[2]
- What is your budget for this usability study?
- Is your Web site a stand-alone site, or does it contain content that you don't control?
- Are there corporate design standards that must be observed?
- What information do you have regarding your user base?
- Who, if anyone, is your competition?
- What previous usability efforts, if any, have you made?
- Is anyone else working on the usability plan for this site?

Once you have determined what the client is hoping to accomplish through a usability study, you can begin to assemble into a usability plan the individual components described in this chapter . You will need to include scheduling information, such as the following:

---

[2]Sadly, you have to ask this question because, in some cases, the department that asks you to do testing isn't the one that will be able to implement the changes.

- Project begin and end dates (projected, of course)
- Critical dates for the various sessions that you include in the plan
- Budget information, including the following:
  - Equipment purchases or rentals
  - Location scheduling and rentals
  - Participant compensation
  - Your fees
- Any other pertinent details that you want to make explicit to everyone who is working with you on the study

NOTE

(Note that this usability plan is not the same as a test plan, which is the blueprint for a classical usability test. That is the topic of Chapter 8. The test plan is just another component of the overall usability plan. An example of a comprehensive test plan is given in Appendix A.)

THE TOOLBOX

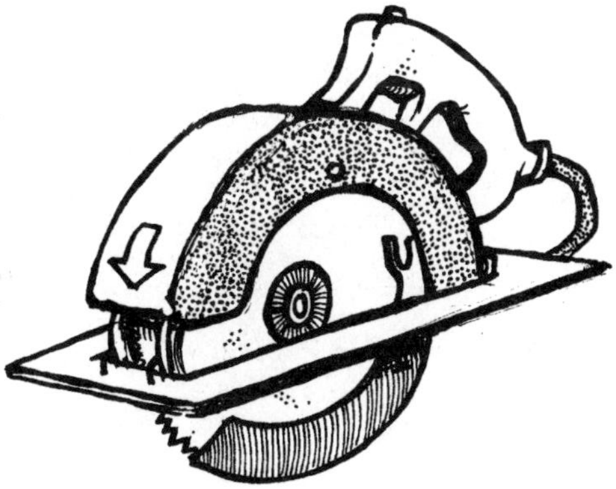

The Card Sort

The first tool we talk about is one of the simplest yet most useful. It requires few resources, needs little time to complete, and gives you quite a bit of insight. You should use it when you are having trouble determining where particular pieces of information should go on your site.

For example, you might feel confident that you have the right top-level headings for your home page. For example, your navigation guide from the home page could include the following top-level heading links (See Figure 3.1):

- Products
- About Us
- Investor Information

Guitar Center .com
musician.com
vintageguitars.net
rockwalk.com
guitar.com
FREE tech support
FREE subscriptions
FREE music links
FREE musician's search
about guitar center
locations
events & promotions
guarantee & financing
career opportunities
investor relations
press releases
feedback
the Guitar Center Story
selection
vendors/ manufacturers
hear the radio spot
SLOW MODEM? click here for quicker site
the best deals on gear

FIGURE 3.1 *This is an example of a site that clearly has established top-level headings (and a lot of them!), but where would you put product information? How will users know what kind of synthesizers the company sells? © 2000 GuitarCenter.com.*

- Technical Support
- Solutions

These headings might be well known by your users and might be intuitive enough. However, you might be at a loss for where to put information on optional extended warranties; should it go under Technical Support, or should it go under Products? It seems as though it could go under either.

Since humans naturally tend to use preconceptions about a site, coupled with their habits picked up from using other sites, to find information, your site's visitors will naturally tend to look in certain places first. The *card sort* helps you understand where your users are likely to look first. You can leverage this information to build a more intuitive navigational hierarchy.

When to Use the Card Sort

The card sort is best used when your participants have never seen the site you're testing or when you are heavily redesigning the site. Additionally, you might use the card sort when you are adding items to your site that are unlike other things already on the site. Such "orphan" items are often hard to locate on a site because they were arbitrarily stuck someplace with the attitude that "Users will find them somehow!"

Methodology for the Card Sort

The objective of the test is to see if your site architecture makes sense to the user. A generally accepted architecture rule of thumb is that the site's navigation system should include several broad, top-level categories of information. Each heading should have a hyperlink on the home page of your site; such links will probably also exist on a consistent part of the page design (a navigation bar along the top or at the left-hand side of the page).

When you are creating clusters of information for the first time or when you add a new piece of information to your site, it is not always obvious where the items should go or under which top-level heading they should be categorized. You could be perplexed about where to put information about a service that your company offers: individualized consultation for small businesses to create a computing environment that best suits their needs. Let's say that analysis of your site logs shows that very few people are looking at this part of the site, but your marketing information says that people really want this kind of service. This should be a warning flag to you that something is wrong with the navigation design of your site.

Often, the problem is simply that you have classified the information under a heading that doesn't make sense to the user. For example, your users might not anticipate finding information on this service under the heading "Solutions," although that is where many designers put such information. Instead, your users might expect the information to be under "Products"; after all, a service is just another type of product.

On the other hand, users might erroneously go to the "Solutions" section seeking free technical support. Why? The word *Solutions*, from a user perspective, is something that fixes a problem they are having right now. One of the great Web design principles is to always use labels that come from the user's natural language, not from some industry-derived jargon that makes perfect sense to engineers and designers but not to the poor end user!

The card sort is the answer to this dilemma. (See Figure 3.2.)If you want to find the most sensible arrangement for informational items on your site, you can follow the following formula:

1. Get two packs of 4″ x 6″ index cards. One pack should be plain white, the other colored.
2. Write the name of each major heading (About Us, Products, etc.) on a colored card. On the back of each of these cards, inconspicuously write a unique identifying number.
3. Find informational items that are inside your site, such as individual product information or, in the case of our example, individual small business consulting, and write a short description of each item on a white card.

4. Pin the colored heading cards on a bulletin board or arrange them on a table so that they are side by side, with the ID numbers hidden.
5. Shuffle the deck of white informational item cards and hand them to the participant.
6. Ask the participant to sort the cards and put them under the headings that make the most sense to him or her.
7. When the participant is done, record which informational cards the participant sorted under which heading cards by noting the ID numbers you wrote on the backs of the colored cards.

The point of this tool is that the user tells you under which headings he or she expects to find information. You could consider including a "Miscellaneous" heading under which participants can put cards that they cannot identify as belonging to an established group. If a lot of cards end up in this pile, it's usually a sign that your headings are inappropriate or unhelpful and that you need to dramatically rethink your categories.

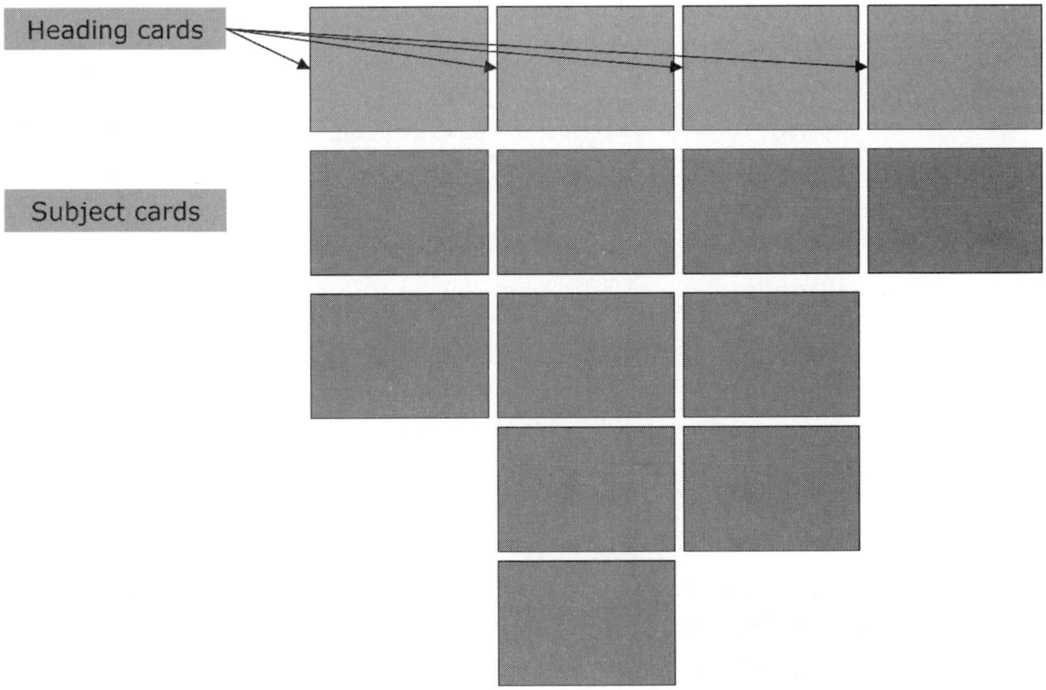
Heading cards
Subject cards

FIGURE 3.2 *A card sort with predetermined headings.*

If an informational item repeatedly shows up in a category other than the one to which you originally thought it should belong, the users are telling you where it really should be placed.

Unfortunately, corporate politics can often interfere with a perfectly logical design, and you might encounter resistance to reclassifying the informational item. In this case, at least try to compromise by cross-referencing the item (creating a link on both pages to the same item).

When all your participants have finished the card sort, you'll have a mass of raw data of headings and the informational items that were lumped under each. By looking at the trends, you can begin to see the most likely structure for your site.

Note, however, that this approach to the card sort assumes that you have come up with appropriate main headings for the site. What if you are designing a site from scratch and have no clue how to begin lumping stuff together? What if you have *no* headings?

A Card Sort Without Heading Cards

You need to modify your card sort only slightly. In fact, all you have to do is eliminate the heading cards and have the participant lump cards together in as many or as few piles as makes sense to him or her. The piles that result represent the groups that the user perceives naturally exist within the information on your site.

Once you know what the groupings are, all you need to do is come up with sensible headings, derived from the user's natural vocabulary (and not from your trade jargon) to describe them. These labels then become the blueprints for the architecture of your site.

One thing we should note about the second method for using the card sort tool is that a good way to tabulate the data acquired hasn't been found. Since there are no pregenerated headings and since each participant could technically have a different number of piles, the process of best representing these results is not trivial.

I have experimented with a statistics technique known as Cohen's Kappa, which is designed to show strength of subject agreement on a given topic (here participants are agreeing or not agreeing on the lumping of informational items into categories), but as of this writing I have not solved the problem. (See Figure 3.3.)

FIGURE 3.3 *A card sort without predetermined category headings. Remember to always allow for an "orphan," or miscellaneous, pile.*

The Interview

This is essentially just what it sounds like: a person-to-person dialogue about the web site or specific parts of the site. The interview is generally semistructured, driven by a set of questions or topics provided by the test moderator.

However, the interview is spontaneous in nature, and many nuggets of valuable information that you might not have planned on could result.

Don't be too rigid in your use of the interview or you'll miss out on a great deal of useful information.[3]

When to Use the Interview

The interview is expensive in terms of finding and paying for participants and the test moderator. However, when you are trying to get initial information from the user community about a particular topic, nothing else will do. In addition, if you are ever stumped about a particular type of error that keeps cropping up on your site for no apparent reason, the interview is a very valuable tool for resolving the issue. The interview has a wide range of applicability, but here we focus on two common times it is used:

- During the debriefing of a usability test to probe the participant for more information about a particular error or behavior
- During the initial contact with your users to determine current behavior, requirements, annoyances, and the like

Methodology for the Interview

The objective of the interview is to gather information about user's expectations, needs, thoughts, past experience, and other information related to the site in a semiformal format. The format of the interview needs to be thought out in advance; you should have an ample supply of questions to ask participants in case they have a hard time keeping the conversation going.

Don't forget that the best parts of the interview are the ones you can't plan. You should always schedule a little extra time for each session, just in case one or more participants have a lot of information to give you.

---

[3]Also be prepared to hear potentially, well, anything! A participant in a test I conducted once interrupted me in mid-sentence to tell me an elaborate story of his own invention that detailed the formation of the company whose site we were testing. It was quite fantastic and reminded me a lot of J. R. R. Tolkein's book *The Silmarillion.* The tale had almost no context and seemed to come out of nowhere.

A video camera can be a very valuable tool for use in interviews, for a number reasons. First, you'll probably want to have a video archive of all your testing sessions for the simple reason that you can't possibly catch everything in every session the first time through. Having a video archive allows you to review the video footage to see if you missed any really crucial pieces of information. Furthermore, as a test monitor, you may get so wrapped up in the moment that you overlook some important facial expressions or points that your participant may make. Of course, to use video cameras in your sessions, *you'll need to get permission from your participants.*

Typically, you ask participants to sign release forms for video and audio interviews. Your company might already have such a form on hand; otherwise, you need to come up with your own template for use in your sessions.

Another reason to videotape interviews is that you might need to use them to persuade the higher-ups in your company to implement the change that you ultimately suggest. Your CEO may not be convinced that some of your suggestions for change really need to be implemented unless she or he witnesses a participant complaining.

The Questionnaire

This technique is powerful because it allows you to gather all great deal of information from a large number of participants very cheaply. Your initial investment lies in designing the questionnaire so that it uncovers answers that you're looking for.

Often, tabulating questionnaire results can be an automated process, through either an optical reader or Web automation. However, the questionnaire should never be regarded as the sole tool for Web site usability work for the simple reason that it minimizes the amount of human-to-human contact.

When to Use the Questionnaire

Questionnaires are usually the most useful as pre-session screening devices. You can develop questionnaires that will gather demographic information about your participants; you can then use this information to help refine your user profile or to ensure that your participant selection process has been relatively accurate.

There are two basic types of pre-session screening devices that you can use. The first sort is used by recruiting agencies or your internal staff who are recruiting participants and weeding out ineligible people.

Typically, in this sort of phone screening, you are required to design questions that will help pick out people you do not want participating in your study. For example, a common question to ask in a phone-screening session is, "Do you currently work in the field of Web site design?"

Unless the target population that you're trying to generalize to consists of Web designers, you probably don't want these types of people in your sample. Because they possess uncommon knowledge of the inner workings of Web sites, these folks could have an edge over the average user, thus skewing your results.

You probably also want to ask questions that will help categorize each potential participant into one of your user profiles. It's common to ask questions relating to a potential participant's amount of Web experience, amount of overall computer experience, education level, household income, and so on.

You might need to develop other types of questions for your phone screening that help you classify participants according to your own particular needs. For example, if you are developing a Web site that is targeted toward purchasers of office supplies, you might need to develop a question to help determine whether a potential participant is an office manager, a CEO, or an administrative assistant. You might need to know this piece of information because your marketing research shows that different approaches are needed for these different positions.

The other type of pre-test questionnaire is a more open-ended, preference-oriented one. Typically, you might want to develop a questionnaire to probe the participant for previous experiences with products, services, or Web sites similar to your own. This sort of qualitative information can really help you understand where a potential user stands regarding likes and dislikes, which will enable you to make suggestions to improve your site.

Methodology for the Questionnaire

The questionnaire is probably one of the oldest formats for gathering quantitative information from a participant. The questionnaire can be either a very low-tech or a very high-tech solution, ranging from pencil and paper to Web-based interfaces.

Regardless of the method of delivery, the end result is the same: gathering self-reported data from multiple participants who have been asked the same questions.

Classic Usability Testing

This tool is so large and so useful that it merits a chapter of its own (see Chapter 8). Based on classical software usability testing, the technique of classic usability testing is truly the most powerful, most complicated, most expensive, and most rewarding tool in the toolbox. It is very expensive in terms of money and resources, but the payoff is big.

This tool requires a team of knowledgeable people to design and carry it out. You can rest assured that any of the major, highly successful, trend-setting Web sites use this tool to ensure the quality of their sites.

Full details on usability testing can be found in Chapter 8.

When to Use Testing

Whenever you are designing a comprehensive test plan for a site, you should include at least a touch of this tool to test the functionality of critical areas of the site. For example, if your company is relatively small and your Web site sparse, you might want to dedicate usability testing to the product-ordering section of the site. Since selling goods or services is your life's blood, you want to have 100 percent confidence that the electronic commerce component of your site is easy to use. Otherwise, you'll go out of business pronto!

Usability testing allows you to empirically test the usability of specific portions of your site. Therefore, this tool is the most useful when it is applied to critical types of transactions on the site, such as making a purchase, signing up for membership, and so on.

Note, however, that usability testing isn't just about testing transactional-style components of the Web site; it also concerns such things as navigation and general information finding.

For example, you may be concerned that your toll-free phone line constantly gets phone calls from clients asking about a particular service or product, saying that they couldn't find any information on your Web site. You may know exactly where the information is that your callers are seeking, but why aren't *they* finding it? Usability testing lets you flush out the source of these kinds of problems, including severe problems called *critical stops.*[4]

---

[4]A *critical stop* is a problem on a site that is so severe that it completely impedes the user from accomplishing his or her goal. It can also be a problem that causes destruction of

Methodology of Testing

Usability testing is the most advanced tool in the toolbox and as such requires a good deal of preparation and lots of hard work. Although a highly detailed explanation of the tool is given in Chapter 8, this section presents a synopsis.

The most important document in usability testing is the *test plan*. This document is a blueprint for the entire testing process; it acts as a means of communicating what is to be done throughout the testing process, and it makes the procedures operational. Most test plans have a common structure, which we discuss later in this section.

The first step in creating a usability test plan is to answer the question, "What is the purpose of this Web site?" In other words, what does the site aim to do? What is the corporate vision for the site? The answer to these questions can usually be summarized in one or two paragraphs, which cover the main points of the reason the site exists.

As you look at this description of your site's purpose, it will be more or less obvious that the purpose emits some number of problem statements—that is, slightly more concrete rephrasing of individual goals. There are usually anywhere from 2 to 10 problem statements.

For example, if our company is the Wonder Widget 2000 Company and our goal is to sell our product over the Web as well as provide support for current customers and inform the public about our human-interest activities, we can reframe our problem statements thus:

- Can our existing clients find the technical support information they need to solve Wonder Widget-related problems on our Web site easily and quickly?
- Do potential new clients find our online ordering system intuitive and easy to use?

---

data or a crashed browser. Critical stops are the worst kind of usability problems. Unfortunately, they are often also the most obscure problems and thus escape the net of less accurate tools such as *heuristic evaluation,* described later in this chapter.

- Can nonclients easily find information about the things that we do in the common interest?

With these three problem statements made a bit more concrete, we can begin to form them into even more atomic, operational tasks that will become the usability tasks that our study participants will perform. From each problem statement will radiate some number of usability tasks that we design. For example, to test against the second problem statement above, we might come up with the following quantifiable tasks:

1. Using the PRODUCT SELECTOR tool on the Wonder Widget home page, please locate purchase information on the model 2000 X26.
2. Now that you have found the purchase information for the X26 Widget, please use the CUSTOMIZE feature of the PRODUCT SELECTOR to add a Frodis Modulator to the base widget.
3. Now complete this transaction by checking out and finalizing the transaction.

We would also have some pretty concrete criteria for scoring the participant's responses to the tasks. We want to make sure that we can tell when a participant has successfully completed a task, as well as whether the participant has completed it under acceptable conditions (time limits, number of clicks, or the like).

Heuristic Evaluation

Pioneered by Jakob Nielsen and his colleagues, the *heuristic evaluation* technique is a very valuable tool for the initial assessment of the usability health of a Web site. A *heuristic* is a rule–of thumb; a heuristic evaluation is performed by an expert who analyzes a site and ranks it based on a standard list of usability heuristics. This tool can be implemented for relatively low cost and with little preparation, since the list of usability heuristics remains constant for all sites.

The catch is that you always need more than one usability expert to make heuristic evaluation a valuable tool. Nielsen explains in his article,

"How to Conduct a Heuristic Evaluation,"[5] that the number of evaluators correlates to the number of usability problems found—up to a point. It seems that about five evaluators constitute the right number for a job.

One thing to note: Evaluators should probably perform their assessments in isolation, not in a big room with one another. The reason? Any time a person is an "expert" on a topic, there is a good chance that the person will have a healthy ego and/or a persuasive way of changing other evaluators' minds. Clearly, this kind of influence is detrimental to your study, so it must be eliminated.

When to Use Heuristic Evaluation

In my opinion, the heuristic evaluation is very useful when you are performing an initial assessment of a site for its overall health. You will be able to catch a great number of usability problems with this tool; according to Nielsen—about 80 percent, if you perform the evaluation correctly.

This tool is a good part of a balanced test plan. However, I tend to believe that it should be the only tool used, because it simply cannot do the same job as user testing. There is no predicting what random users will do; only they can create situations of complete functionality breakdown—situations I as a Web usability specialist would never have discovered on my own.

One thing to remember is that even if heuristic evaluation catches 80 percent of your site's problems, lurking in that remaining 20 percent could be the critical stops that might render your site unusable in some context you haven't thought of—but rest assured your users will find them!

You can certainly perform a heuristic evaluation at any point in the life cycle of a site. Any time there have been major infrastructure changes, graphical facelifts, or any other perturbation of the site, it's probably a great time for heuristic evaluation.

---

[5]You can find this article at *www.useit.com/papers/heuristic/heuristic_evaluation.html.*

Methodology for Heuristic Evaluation

We cover this tool in great detail in Chapter 6. Briefly, the idea is that you and a panel of other expert evaluators perform assessments of the site being tested. This essentially means that you, to the best of your ability, navigate the site, use functions, and generally do the types of things that a "regular" user would do. You rate the site using a scoring sheet that has a row for each heuristic (a complete listing is contained in Chapter 6) and a column for a score.

Once each evaluator has turned in the scoring sheet, the scores are tallied and the comments about violations of these heuristics are compared. Although most evaluators find many of the same problems, each evaluator stands a chance of finding a usability problem that everyone else overlooked.

Traditionally, heuristic evaluation that has been applied to GUI software has not been very concerned with actually using the system; rather, it's objective is to observe the system and look topically for problems. Heuristic evaluation has even been used on prototype systems, even including paper mockups of software. In my opinion, there is little need for paper mockups of Web sites. I once did testing for a client that had a large budget. The client hired a graphic layout company to mock up the proposed site using desktop publishing tools such as Adobe Illustrator, then expected me to use the printouts of the pages to do user testing. I think it would have taken less time to actually implement the site in HTML than to do a paper mockup. My participants were pretty confused about using the mockups. How do you "click" on a piece of paper?

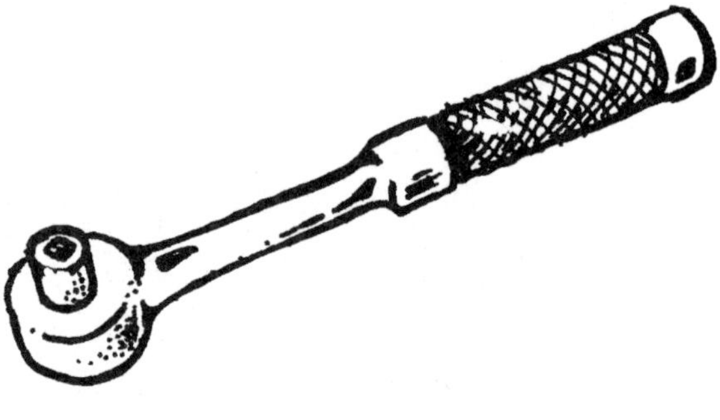

Prototyping

Now that I have convinced you that using prototypes and mockups is a bad idea, let me try to convince you that sometimes it's actually a good idea. A *prototype* is a semifunctional mockup of your final Web site. It's usually a good idea to begin doing some user testing long before the final version of your Web site is completed. Using this partially finished version of the site is a common way to do some usability testing in the early phases of the site's life cycle. (See Figure 3.4.)

An important point to note is that developing GUI-based software applications using traditional programming tools is very different from creating a Web site. Programs that are written in C++, Visual Basic, or other programming languages are far more complex than a Web page. The hours of programming time needed to develop even a simple user interface in one of these environments vastly outweighs the development time of a moderately complex Web page.

The use of prototypes for traditional software applications has been quite common for some time. It's a lot easier to mock up the look of the user interface on paper, or even to develop the GUI with no functionality underneath, for testing purposes. This is not always true with Web site design.

As discussed in the preceding section, it often takes just as long—or in some cases, even longer—to mock up a site using desktop publishing layout tools or even to just draw the Web pages on paper. It can, however, be quite useful to develop just the skeleton of the site and to fill in functionality in either the horizontal or vertical direction. This way, you expend a minimal amount of effort in design and content creation while still getting the benefit of early usability testing.

When to Use Prototyping

The best time to use prototyping is early in the design phase of your site (or of a major revision), before it is practical to fully develop the entire site. Often a prototype can serve as a proof of concept.

Methodology for Prototyping

Prototyping usually involves a mockup of the site under development. A prototype can be anything from a paper-and-pencil drawing to a partially "HTML-ified" version of the site. However, drafting the site in a page-layout program such as Illustrator may be ineffective.

Horizontal vs. Vertical Prototypes

A *horizontal prototype* is one in which all of the top-level functionality of the site has been designed and enabled. This structure allows you to test the overall organization of your site. For example, if you lay out the entire home page of the site and make sure that everything on it works (even if only to go down to a next "dummy" level), you can begin to test the site to make sure that you have gone down the right path in choosing the top-level architecture of your site.

Let's say that we want to make sure that our new revision of the Wonder Widget 2000 site has an intuitive navigation structure. We might design the home page, complete with all of the top-level headings, and make sure that each link on this page links to at least a minimal Web page.

We can now test the intuitiveness of our top-level headings. Perhaps these top-level headings are the ones that you derived using the card sort, and now you want to double check to make sure that they are truly intuitive.

A *vertical prototype* is one in which all functionality of the site is constrained to one set of activities on the site; usually this means some sort of transaction. For example, in our new revision of the Wonder Widget 2000 Web site, we might be primarily concerned with electronic commerce portion of the site.

Therefore, we create only the Web pages and back-end programs that pertain to locating and buying a product. That way, we can test this activity to completion. We haven't wasted any time developing any other parts of the site, so we can pool all our resources into this one task.

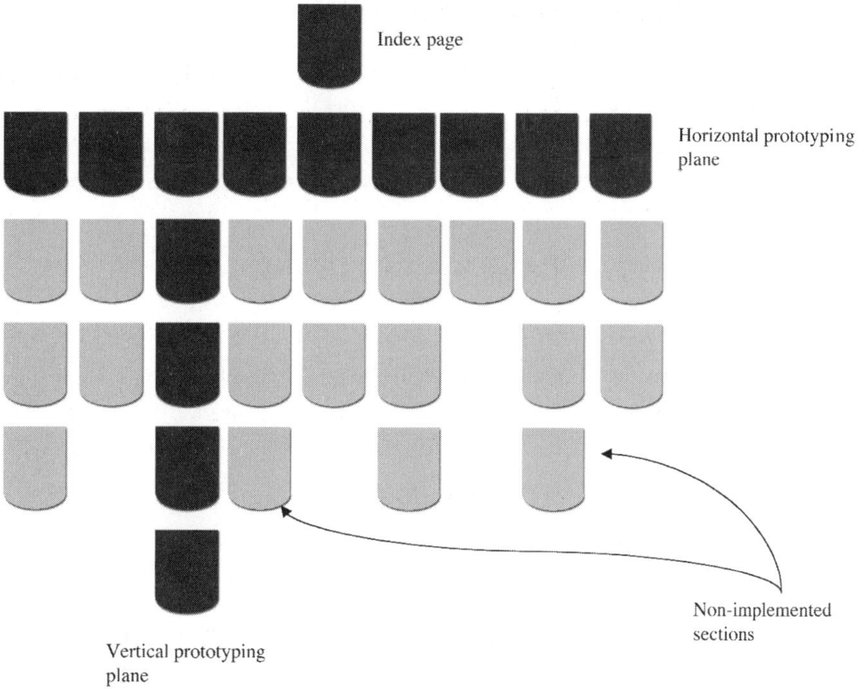
Index page
Horizontal prototyping plane
Non-implemented sections
Vertical prototyping plane

FIGURE 3.4 *An example of a prototype layout for a Web site.*

The Field Study

Although this technique originated in the field of anthropology, it certainly has applicability to Web usability studies. A *field study* is a semi-structured period of observation of users in their natural environment. For example, if we were designing a site for use by human resources staff members at our company, we'd need to initially spend some time in the office with the people for whom we are designing the site.

During a field study, the usability specialist observes the users carrying out the tasks that they normally do from day to day. It is important for the observer to be as unobtrusive as possible while still attempting to gain an understanding of what's going on. People who are being observed—and know that they are being observed—tend to behave differently from the way they do when they are not being observed.

For example, if a common HR task normally requires filling out many redundant pieces of paperwork, which the employees normally skip when no one's looking, the same employees might fill out all the paperwork to completion when they are being observed. This practice may incorrectly lead the usability specialist to base the design of the new site's functions on this behavior.

When to Use the Field Study

This tool is almost invariably used at the beginning of the design process. During this critical period, the usability specialist can gather information about workflow process, user habits, and user "lingo" vis-à-vis natural language, as well as gaining an understanding of current limitations and areas for improvement.

Methodology for the Field Study

You begin a field study by arranging a day and time window with the supervisor in charge of the department or office you want to observe. All the potentially observed participants should be notified well in advance and given the option not to be observed. Your job is to help, not to hinder, the end user. Therefore, you may encounter people who are steadfastly unwilling to participate, despite the potential benefit they may get as a result.

You need an agenda for observation, and you should also generate a list of questions you want to ask people. Pay special attention to the way people utilize their existing resources. Watch how they enter data into existing applications. Note any habits that seem consistent among users, especially if the habits are not what you might have expected.

You may want to take along a tape recorder and plenty of audio tape; even consider using a digital camera or unobtrusive video camera to help in note taking. Write down the time and location of each observation you make. It's a bit like being on safari!

You may opt to interact with participants. Be careful how much you do, though, for several reasons. First, you want to minimize your presence as much as possible because, as mentioned earlier, people behave differently when they are being observed. Second, you don't want participants to feel they have to entertain you; they should just work as they normally would. Don't make participants miss a deadline because you are chit-chatting with them.

Once you have finished your day's worth of observation, you should make a short report based on what you discovered. You might determine, for example, that everyone complains about a specific limitation of the current application ("When we enter a purchase order, we want to be able to recall the information for the PO by either typing in the PO number or the date. Right now we have to know the PO number! What a pain!"). This report will become a baseline for you to begin the next phase of design.

The Automated Session

The *automated session* is essentially a software-driven, self-scoring application. It can come in the form of a modified Web browser, a nonbrowser-based questionnaire, an interactive CD-ROM, or several other forms.

The automated session's strength lies in its capability to be deployed en masse and for a relatively low cost. Since the application itself usually generates the scores, little in the way of human effort is needed to tabulate data.

Even though it is an easy-to-implement tool, the automated session has some serious drawbacks that can be overcome only if it is used in conjunction with other tools to create a well-balanced plan.

When to Use the Automated Session

Automated sessions can be handy during almost any phase of the iterative redesign cycle. This tool is great for getting a large sample of data for higher levels of confidence in a particular area. You might use an automated session to measure the usability of the login feature of your site, for example. You could also use the tool to gather preference data from a vast quantity of users to best determine which of two parallel designs to use for the final site.

Methodology for the Automated Session

As of this writing, no off-the-shelf, commercial solution is available for automated Web site usability testing. Therefore, if you choose the automated session tool, you will have to "roll your own."

Typically, the automated session comes with a set of instructions or tasks for the participant to follow. The program usually logs several common items:

- The click path (the links a user takes, in the order the user selected them)
- Time between clicks
- Total number of clicks per task
- Total elapsed time per task
- Success or failure (based on a time limit or upper acceptable number of clicks)

Several commercial sites function solely to test the usability of other sites. These sites can be powerful tools. They are generally not free to use, however. You might consider using an existing site as opposed to expending the time and effort to develop your own solution.

Caveat emptor: Automated sessions remove the critical element of interpersonal dialogue that can reveal the most important information from your participants. People behave differently when they are writing down their feelings as opposed to expressing them to another human.

A counter-argument that is often true is that people are more likely to be truthful when they are anonymous. However, with written responses, you still miss the potentially telling nonverbal cues during a usability study session.

The Focus Group

Focus groups are informal sessions composed of many participants and usually one or two moderators. A typical focus group session takes place around a big table and lasts from one to three hours. During this time, the moderators show the participants the site being evaluated and throw out questions about the site to the group, in the hope of soliciting useful input.

When to Use the Focus Group

The focus group is another tool that works well at many points during the redesign cycle. You can use a focus group in the beginning stages of design to examine a competitor's site or even a previous version of your existing site.

Additionally, you may want to use a focus group to examine individual ideas for marketing, for inclusion of new technology, or at any point at which a potentially high-impact change is likely to be made to your site.

Methodology for the Focus Group

Although there should generally be an agenda that is mostly controlled by the focus group moderators, the unplanned discussion is often the best part of a focus group. Don't discourage input that is slightly outside the context of the question at hand; you could get some really insightful input that you would never have thought of.

On the other hand, you might get a participant or two who seeks to merely hear his or her own voice, causing the entire session to go astray. Especially if you get your participants through a recruiting agency or a temporary agency, you could find that a high degree of self-selection has taken place and that your participants may not have much to offer—except an argumentative, self-promoting attitude!

In this case, as moderator you have to step in and steer the session back on course, sometimes squelching an offensive participant in the process. You should decide ahead of time how you will deal with exceptional cases like these; a bad surprise at session time can derail months of hard work.

Alternate Viewing Tools

As information appliances become more and more popular, the common Netscape Navigator or Microsoft Internet Explorer (IE) paradigm is beginning to lose footing. Many designers have discovered that making sites that look good when viewed by a WebTV user isn't always a common-sense or easy task. Likewise, special principles must be applied to sites that will work with PDAs and other sorts of browsing mechanisms. Finally, not every bona fide Web browser has the feature set of the most common two browsers—especially browsers that are part of an assistive technology solution for users with disabilities.

Fortunately for developers and users alike, several tools can be downloaded off the Web for free. Among these are the handy WebTV viewer, which allows you to preview your site as it would be seen by a WebTV user.

When to Use Alternate Viewing Tools

It's appropriate to use alternate viewing tools whenever you want to check your site design against a known user mode of access that is different from the standard two browsers, but you either cannot afford the needed equipment to preview your work or do not have access to the needed facilities.

Methodology for Alternate Viewing Tools

You can integrate these types of alternate access tools into almost any of the other techniques mentioned in this section. For example, you could conduct a heuristic evaluation of your site using only the WebTV browser and see how well the site fares. Or you might conduct full usability testing with a Lynx previewer (a piece of software that emulates the text-only nature of the popular text browser, Lynx).

Thinking Aloud

This technique is really subsumed by many other tools and techniques. You will also find that many participants use this technique without prompting. In fact, occasionally participants will chatter so much that you will find it a bit distracting!

The basic premise of this technique is to encourage participants to say out loud what they are thinking as they are performing usability tasks. When the technique works, you can capture moments of confusion or hesitation and notice user preconceptions and errors. Some people are uncomfortable thinking aloud, however, so be careful not to rely too heavily on this tool.

When to Use Thinking Aloud

Use this technique any time you ask a participant to carry out tasks as well as any time a participant passively views the site.

Methodology for Thinking Aloud

This technique is pretty straightforward as described. One point to mention is that it is really handy to video- and audiotape this portion of the session, since the things that participants say during the session can go unnoticed by a busy crew. Saving the session for later review may also help in a "difficult" situation.

This sort of footage is often just what you need to convince management of the client organization that a change really needs to be implemented to a site. One of my clients steadfastly refused to make a much needed improvement to its Web site because a manager's son had implemented much of the site. I was the "bad guy" for merely suggesting that the site was inferior.

The Walk-Up Kiosk

If you are offering a new concept in Web applications or Web services, you might need a way to both market your new site and to gather feedback about the site. A *walk-up kiosk* is usually an attractive booth or stand that features a computer with either Internet access or a static version of the site (not very useful if you have mainly dynamic content!) saved to disk.

Usually, the kiosk will be hosted by a human, such as at a trade show, a corporate meeting or retreat, or other semipublic functions. The kiosk can be unattended in a business—for example, in the hallway (a "virtual water cooler"). At any rate, the point is to get people to try out the site and to somehow solicit feedback from them.

When to Use the Walk-Up Kiosk

At any point when you have a substantial product to show, you can use the kiosk. For example, you might want to show off the beta version of a site for internal Web sites (intranets) to get feedback from users before it's too late to turn back. This application can often serve the function of validation before the real launch of a site.

Methodology for the Walk-Up Kiosk

As mentioned, a walk-up kiosk usually is equipped with a computer that has Internet access and an attendant to answer questions or ask questions. Kiosk sessions should take very little time (five minutes maximum) so that you can get lots of people to participate and so that busy people won't turn down the opportunity to use one. The nature of the session can vary; you might have a specific task for people to perform, such as registering for a free account, or you could just want to watch them surf for a few minutes and then discuss their experience.

Opinion Polls

Opinion polls constitute a very trendy technique, as evidenced by most popular magazines. Polls are not really very useful in terms of real science, but they are a quick and easy way for potential users to voice an opinion and see the feedback from their vote—automatically, in the case of Web-based polls.

When to Use Opinion Polls

Any time you want to get a basic feel for user opinion on a single topic, the poll is the way to go. You can have an opinion-of-the-day tool on your site to amass opinion data over time.

Methodology for Opinion Polls

Opinion polls are likely to be used if they are short, are easy to complete, and feature instant feedback. Polls that open up separate windows in the user's browser are not as effective as one-window polls because they are more of a distraction and are seen as "noise" compared with sufficiently visible polls embedded in the content of a page.

Contests

Even usability specialists can have fun! Why not feature a contest of some kind on your site to get people involved in usability? A Web site information scavenger hunt may reveal loads of usability problems while providing entertainment and cool (promotional?) prizes, such as T-shirts, coffee mugs, or mousepads.

CHAPTER SUMMARY

- There are many tips, tools, and techniques you can use to improve the usability of your site.
- Not every comprehensive usability plan implements every tool; use only the ones you think you really need.
- The tools themselves are only part of the overall plan.
- You should begin your planning with an initial session with your client to get the history of the site and find out what the client hopes to accomplish by doing a usability study.
- Be sure to be conscious of your budget and document what you think you'll need in resources—time, money, and otherwise.

HANDS-ON EXERCISES

1. Make an appointment with your client, employer, or other responsible party for an initial consultation. Be sure to bring along the information about the user base you gathered by performing the activities in Chapter 2. You should discuss the main points mentioned in the section "Part of a Well-Balanced Plan" at the beginning of this chapter. Ask any other questions you think might be pertinent.
2. Begin to formulate some rough ideas about which tools you think you want to use for your comprehensive usability plan.

DISCUSSION TOPICS

1. Which tools seem the most useful to you? Place them all in order of usefulness, with the most useful tool being number 1. Why are the top three the most useful to you?
2. Which tools, if any, can you not imagine using? Why?
3. Do you think these tools should be limited to one per session? Why or why not?
4. Which tools have you heard about that aren't listed here? Rate any other tools that you can think of on the same scale of usefulness.
5. Do you think that developers of information appliances should be required to provide free tools for emulating their product, or should they be a premium service?
6. How do you decide which alternate browsing methods are "worth" testing against? Can you test against all of them?

CHAPTER

4

HUMAN FACTORS

Computers are useless. They can only give you answers.

—Pablo Picasso

BEHIND THE SCENES

Human factors psychology is a field of psychology that is completely dedicated to the study of human beings and the way they interact with their environment. It is a study of the limitations and the advantages presented by the human body and the human mind and how the two interact with the world. As a usability specialist, you will study the way humans interact with your Web interfaces. Therefore, it is very useful to have an understanding of human factors psychology to help you understand the types of errors or other behaviors that your participants could make.

If you're the type of person who likes to skip to the end of the book to see how it ends or if you really aren't interested in possessing a depth of knowledge, you might want to skip this chapter. Many books on the topic of usability that are geared toward professionals who maintain helter-skelter schedules deliberately omit any information about human factors. The most commonly cited reason for this omission is that human factors psychology concepts, which are often abstract and theoretical, are difficult to make concrete and to create illustrative examples for. Although that may be true, we include a chapter on the topic. It is not strictly necessary for you to read this chapter; if you do, however, it will give you a much wider base of understanding of your participants and could even clear up a few of a little mysteries of life that you always wondered about!

The field of human factors psychology is very broad. There is an ocean of research in the field; this tiny chapter is barely able to skim the surface of a handful of concepts. After reading this chapter, you should have a topical understanding of human factors and should begin to see how the concept fits into the field of usability. If this chapter interests you, you will find an extensive list of books concerned with human factors psychology in the bibliography of this book. If you plan to make a career of usability, I strongly suggest that you make yourself familiar with the field of human factors.

WHAT IS HUMAN FACTORS PSYCHOLOGY?

Human factors psychology is an interdisciplinary field that is both theoretical and practical in approach. A human factors psychologist seeks to discover and apply information about human behavior, capabilities, and limitations to the design, evaluation, and implementation of products—whether systems, jobs, tools, or even environments. The goal of the field is to enhance productive, safe, and comfortable human use of technology and manufactured goods. The focus of the field of human factors is humans as the central component of human/product/environment systems. Note that this field is absolutely *not* involved with the study of human psychological problems and is therefore very unlike many other branches of psychology. Human factors psychology places a strong emphasis on the practical.

A Brief History of Human Factors Psychology

The study of human factors, which is also sometimes known as *ergonomics,*[1] got its start in the U.S. military during World War II. The military was very interested in matching the highly advanced technical capabilities of its arsenal of new weapons and systems to their human users. Studies performed during the military's research yielded a great deal of information about human performance, information presentation, control actions, workspace arrangement, and user skills. It was also made evident to designers that integrating the characteristics of the user into their designs was critical.

Although the study of human factors started in the military as a tool to enhance the ability to kill enemies, the science has since flourished and spread to many other fields, industrial and technological alike. Most notably for us, much of the foundation of Web site usability comes from human factors.

What Do Human Factors Specialists Do?

Human factors specialists conduct research and perform experiments to accomplish many goals. These goals include, but are not limited to, the following:

- Design products for improved safety and ease of use
- Design systems to accommodate specific user groups
- Improve information displays to reduce human error
- Raise productivity by improving human performance

[1]The term *ergonomics* is usually used to describe the study of human metrics and interaction with environments.

WHAT KIND OF TRAINING DO HUMAN FACTORS SPECIALISTS GET?

Human factors psychology is not concerned with the study of human emotional or mental disorders, nor is it concerned with counseling. Students of human factors learn about both systems design and evaluation research. They study basic concepts such as perception, environmental psychology, and ergonomics. Additionally, they focus on a specific area of application, such as aviation, automobile design, office environment design, and even human/computer interaction. Many people who go into this profession earn an advanced degree (a Master's level or higher).

WHERE DO HUMAN FACTORS SPECIALISTS WORK?

The following description comes from Division 21 of the American Psychologists Association (APA):[2]

> *Work settings range from classroom, to laboratory, to the industrial design team. We develop human-centered approaches to the design of instruments and controls on the flight deck, in space, in air traffic control centers, and on ships, planes, and other vehicles. We also are involved in the development of part-task and full-scale simulations to enhance communications, improve training, and evaluate crew resource management. Efforts are also directed toward identifying improved techniques to monitor and enhance human performance in operational environments and to develop countermeasures that will reduce fatigue-related performance changes in humans operating in a 24-hour society. Applied Experimental and Engineering Psychology is increasingly employed in design and evaluation of medical instrumentation and processes and forensic work involving product and workplace safety.*

---

[2]The URL for the APA site from which this quote was taken is *www.apa.org/ divisions/div21/Career_Education/career_education.html.* The APA consists of many divisions, each of which focuses on a specific area of discipline. Division 21 is the Division of Applied Experimental and Engineering Psychology.

We Are What We Sense

If it is true that a human being is nothing more than the sum of his or her experience, our senses are certainly critical in forming the person each of us becomes. Sensation and perception are two capabilities that enable human beings to interact with their environment and with other human beings and to learn about the things around them.

Of the five human senses, only two really play a role in Web site use: vision and hearing. Currently, *haptics* (the sensation of touch) plays only a minor and highly experimental role in computer use, let alone Web use. This field shows much promise in a number of areas, including remote-controlled surgery. However, I'm not sure about you, but I am not quite ready yet to have a tonsillectomy over the Internet. (See Figures 4.1 and 4.2.)

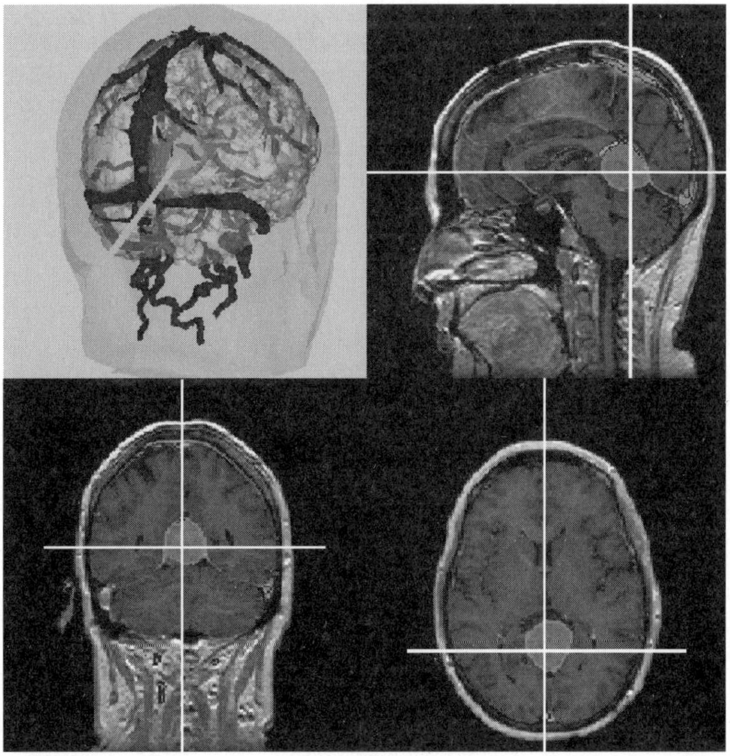

FIGURE 4.1 *An image of a human brain, used in computer-guided surgery. This photo is courtesy of the MIT Artificial Intelligence Lab; used with permission.*

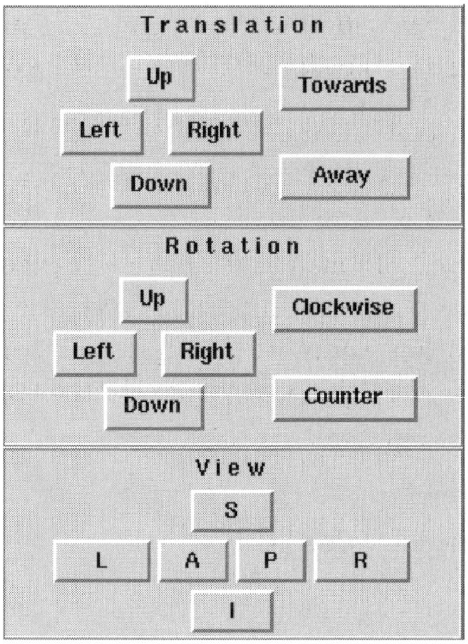
Translation
Up
Towards
Left
Right
Down
Away
Rotation
Up
Clockwise
Left
Right
Down
Counter
View
S
L
A
P
R
I

FIGURE 4.2 *The remote control console used to change views on the Internet. This console could be implemented as a Web interface at some point in the future. Such an interface would need to be analyzed thoroughly for potential usability problems.*

Likewise, the senses of taste and smell aren't very useful in the domain of computers—with the exception, of course, of the time I accidentally plugged my printer into my SCSI port on my computer. It took months to get the smell out of my office, but this probably isn't the effect you want to create with your Web site, anyway! Although it's nice to think about a taste synthesizer that would let you sample that fancy Belgian chocolate over the Web, it's not going to be a reality for quite a while, if ever.

Vision

The human race is, beyond any shadow of a doubt, a visually oriented one. The cave paintings at Lasceux are some of our earliest records of humanity's desire to express and to understand the world in a visual fashion. Even today, human beings are easily swayed by graphical content in magazines, on television, and, well, on the Web! During the current generation of Web site design, much emphasis has been put on graphic embellishments, ranging from still pictures to multimedia clips.

When we are designing Web pages that make heavy use of graphical elements—in fact, any time we try to convey our message through the use of color or images—we need to keep in mind many principles of human vision. The use of color can convey very powerful messages or, if used incorrectly, can confound or hide your message. To understand how this works, we first need to understand how the human eye works and how light information is transformed into a visual understanding of the world around us.

The Physics of Vision

Most people know that in order to see something, it must be well lit. Without an adequate light source, objects blend into a sea of grays and muted tones. The basic unit of light is called a *photon*. Photons tend to act as both particles and waves—a fact that still bothers many great physicists!

For a human being to be able to see an object, light must emanate from some source, strike the object, and bounce off the object and into the human eye. In this process, the pure white light that strikes the object becomes modified. The object absorbs some parts of the light; other parts are reflected into our eyes.

Once the light reaches our eyes, it is focused through the part of our eye called the *lens*. The lens focuses the light onto the part of our eye that handles reception: the *retina*. See Figure 4.3.

The Retina

The retina is rich with receptors, called *rods* and *cones*. Each type of receptors has a specialized job of detecting certain types of light. Without both rods and cones, human vision deteriorates substantially in some way. One of these types of receptors, the cone, is not very sensitive to dim light but is the receptor that gives us the ability to see color.

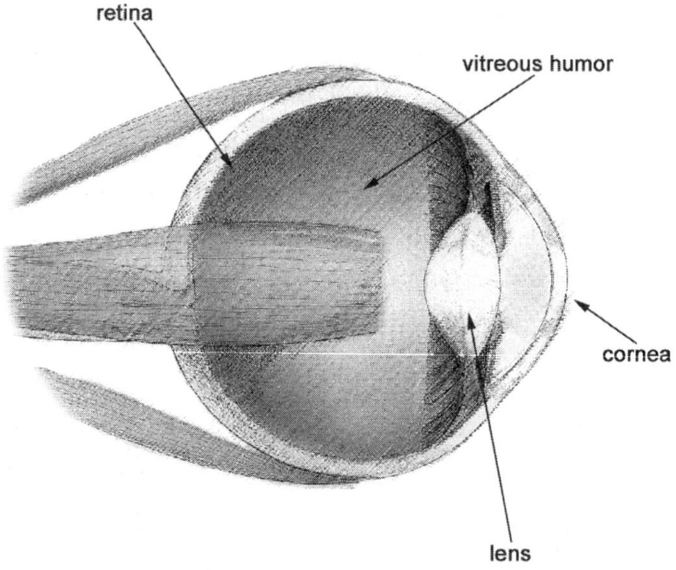
retina
vitreous humor
cornea
lens

FIGURE 4.3 *A cross-section of the human eyeball.*

Additionally, cones come in three different "flavors": red, green, and blue. Cones are given their "flavor" through the addition of a pigment that allows them to distinguish among the three colors. Therefore, humans can really only see three colors, which we call the *primary colors* of light.

As mentioned, cones don't work well under dim light conditions, which is why low light reduces our vision to muted grays. That's when the other type of receptor, called the rod, kicks in. Rods are not very sharp receptors; they can't detect color at all. However, they are very sensitive to light, even very dim light. Human night vision relies heavily on the functioning of the rods in the eye.

Here is an experiment to try: On a clear evening, go outside and try to spot a very, very dim star in the sky.[3] You'll notice that some stars are

[3]Incidentally, this might be a great time to become addicted to astronomy! If you find yourself going out to stargaze even after this experiment is done, I can highly recommend that you pick up a copy *of Star Ware: The Amateur Astronomer's Ultimate Guide to Choosing, Buying, and Using Telescopes and Accessories,* second edition, by Philip S. Harrington.

visible to you only if you look at them out of the corner of your eye. If you try to stare directly at them, they disappear. Why?

Here's the reason: The main focal point of your retina, called the *fovea*, is very rich in cones, but it lacks rods altogether. Whatever you're looking directly at is focused on the fovea. Therefore, the very dim stars in the sky are invisible when you look directly at them. Your peripheral field of vision is rich in rods, so it is a lot easier to detect faint light with this part of your visual field. (See Figure 4.4.)

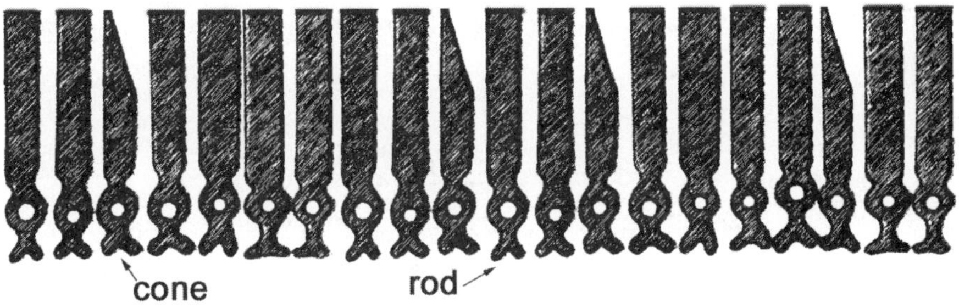
cone
rod

FIGURE 4.4 *The rods and cones, which are the two types of photoreceptors in the human eye.*

Color Blindness and Color Deficiency

Color vision is relatively rare in animals, but color vision isn't strictly necessary for an organism to survive. If a creature is a carnivore, it is probably much more dependent on the ability to smell prey and see motion well. On the other hand, if a creature is an herbivore, it might be more important to have color vision. If a tiny blueberry is good, yummy, and safe, but a slightly more purplish berry is deadly poisonous, it pays for an animal to be able to discern color.

It is important to note that a significant number of human beings have some form of color deficiency; that is, a lack of the ability to discriminate between colors. The term *color blindness* is often used erroneously when people really mean *color deficiency*. Color deficiency is caused when one or more of the three pigments that give the cone receptors the ability to see color is malformed or absent in an individual.

There are four types of color deficiency. People who have the first and most common type of color deficiency are called *anomalous trichromats.* People with this condition can see red, green, and blue, but either the red curve is shifted toward the green range of the spectrum or the green curve is shifted toward the red. However, although the curve is shifted to one direction, the eye is less sensitive to that color. When the color is very faint (lightly saturated), that color tends to disappear for these individuals. Anomalous trichromats with deficiency in the green color range account for over half the people with color vision deficiencies; depending on whom you ask, about 5 percent of all males have this condition.

People with the second type of color deficiency are known as *dichromats.* In dichromats, either the red cones contain the pigment intended for the green cones, or the green cones contain the pigment intended for the red cones. Either way, the result is complete loss of sensitivity to a portion of the visible spectrum. Nonetheless, the cones are still sensitive to light and are still technically functional. The cones are simply erroneous in their reporting of the colors that they see.

People in the third group, *cone monochromats*, are rare—about one in a million. Cone monochromats are able to see only one color.

Finally, the rarest form of color deficiency—true color blindness, called *achromatopsia*—results when an individual has no cones and therefore is incapable of sensing any color information at all. Although true color blindness is fairly rare, a significant portion of the population has at least some mild form of color deficiency.

Although defective color vision may be acquired as a result of another eye disorder, the vast majority of color deficiency cases are hereditary. Even though the condition is extant from birth, a person with color deficiency may not be aware of the handicap until early adulthood. Males are much more likely to have color deficiency (at least 5 percent of the entire male population of the world—some say as high as 9 percent). Females can be carriers of color blindness, but males are more commonly affected.

Testing for color deficiency or color blindness is usually done by an optometrist, who will likely use the Ishihara test, which is a series of colored circles made up of variously colored dots. The dots inside a circle are all of the same average value (brightness), and inside each circle is a number. The number is visible to the viewer only if the viewer can distinguish red-green and blue-yellow.

What this information should tell you as a usability specialist is that using color as the sole vehicle for communication is a very, very bad idea. Here's an example of just how bad an idea it is: My uncle Larry has red-green color deficiency, but he did not realize it until one day when, in electronics school, he got a couple wires crossed and blew up a project that he was working on. In this case, the color of the wires conveyed very important information—information that he was unable to decode due to his color deficiency.

True Blue

As we grow older, our eyes become less sensitive to the color blue. This fact is due to a type of deterioration in the human eye. The implication is that the older we are, the more difficult it becomes to distinguish one shade of blue from another.

Additionally, it becomes increasingly difficult to read small blue text, to the point of the text becoming totally illegible. This means that choosing a shade of blue for your Web site text color is a very bad idea, even if you think it looks cool. Unfortunately, it also means that the standard color for hypertext links—blue—is probably the worst possible choice. Therefore, it is very important that you do not override user preferences for text and hyperlink colors. Doing so may render your site unusable by people who have this condition.

You might find it interesting that humans in general are not very sensitive to the color blue. Both the JPEG and MPEG encoding standards are capable of leveraging this fact to their benefit. Using perceptual encodings, you can vastly reduce the amount of blue information in an image without degrading the image quality.

My Aching Head!

It never ceases to amaze me how many Web designers think it's a good idea to use bright blue and bright red juxtaposed on a Web page. I can only imagine that their line of thought is that since both blue and red are primary colors, and since they are both very strong, it must make a bold visual statement to place them side by side.

Well, it certainly makes a bold impression, but not a good one! Looking at bright blue and red together causes a very well-known headache-inducing condition called *chromostereopsis*. This condition results in the observer perceiving a noxious 3D effect, in which one color seems to float above the other.

This phenomenon is caused by the fact that red and blue, which read opposite ends of the visible spectrum, do not align quite evenly on the retina. The reason is that any time light enters a lens, short wavelengths are refracted slightly more than long wavelengths, creating a positional disparity on the retina. When the red-and-blue image is viewed by two eyes together, a stereoscopic disparity is observed.

I first became aware of this optic anomaly after getting a really cheap pair of prescription lenses from one of the nationwide chains. A common substance used in eyeglass lenses, polycarbonate, has a very high refraction index. This means that it does not reconverge the entire wavelength of light neatly, so it allows a high degree of spreading. The result was that I saw red and blue halos around everything that I looked at. Talk about a headache!

Red and blue (violet, to be exact) are the two most distant colors in the visible spectrum. Therefore, this effect is the most noticeable between these two colors. However, the same effect can be observed between any two colors that are far apart on the visible spectrum. Some people have been able to put this optical effect to good use to create cheap visual effects; but in general, it's a very bad idea to use it.

A Final Word on Color

Color is not universal. Color is highly subjective. No two people see color exactly the same way; some people can't see the colors you labor over at all. Therefore, you should use color only to communicate nonessential information; make sure that your design stands on its own, without any color. View your site in grayscale mode, and if you can't use the site like that, you have a bad design. Keep in mind that several types of color deficiency can make it difficult or impossible for people to distinguish between the colors that you might have chosen to represent different types of information.

OPTICAL ILLUSIONS

A great deal of the credit for human vision goes not to the eyes but rather to the visual cortex, which is the part of the brain that handles visual component processing. Whenever you're watching a football game on television, looking at a great work of art, or reading a book, your visual cortex is hard at work. Without your visual cortex, your eyes could do little more than transmit raw nerve impulses that would never be translated into the beautiful images you see every day.

Because your brain does a great deal of translation of the raw signals that your eyes send to it, many processes that take place in the brain assist vision in many different ways. Some of these processes are easily fooled; the result is that your eyes can play tricks on you! In actuality, your eyes aren't doing the tricking, it's your brain. Let's look at some common optical illusions to illustrate the point.

Look closely at Figure 4.5. Notice that if you stare directly at the center of the picture, out of the corner of your eye you can see tiny gray patches at the junction of any four squares. When you look directly at

FIGURE 4.5 *The Hermann Grid. Note the dark spots that you can see at points where four corners of the dark squares come together.*

these patches, they disappear. Could it be that this is the same principle at work as our disappearing midnight star?

In fact, it is not the same phenomenon. This illusion outlines a principle of human vision that is sometimes referred to as *closure*. The fact that the four very bold, dark objects appear near one another has a special meaning to our primitive visual brain: It translates the incoming information by assuming that the four squares must actually be the same object. This particular illusion is called the *Hermann square*, named after its discoverer.

Those tiny gray squares that you see are all in your mind; your eyes are not *seeing* them. This is the brain's way of trying to fill in a gap to make sense of incoming information. Much of what you see in day-to-day life is "filled out" by your brain in a very similar fashion.

This sort of optical illusion was studied in great depth by a group of German psychologists called the *Gestaltists*. Founded by Max Wertheimer (1880–1943), Gestalt psychology emerged as a theoretical school in Germany early in the 20th century. Gestalt psychology was based on the idea that the whole is greater than the sum of its parts (*Gestalt* is German for form or *shape*).

An example of this principle is provided by the *phi phenomenon*, first described by Wertheimer in 1912. The phi phenomenon is the illusion of movement created by presenting visual stimuli in rapid succession. For example, movies and TV consist of separate, still pictures shown rapidly, one after the other. Although we see smooth motion, in reality the "moving" objects merely take a slightly different position in successive frames.

When users scan the Web for information, they are unknowingly using many of the brain's capabilities to "fill in" information. The same processes allow users to filter out unwanted information—"noise." One example of this type of process hard at work is the case of unseen graphical links. One of my client companies was baffled that none of its Web site patrons could find certain locations on the site. The links to the confounding pages were in plain sight, "above the fold" of the home page. So why were users missing them?

My client had made the grave error of using animated graphic buttons for the critical links. The site designers had naively believed that the flashing and motion of the graphics would draw users' attention to them. In fact, the users never even looked at the graphics, because they were immediately perceived as "noise"—because they looked like advertisements!

After so much exposure to irritating banner ads and other blinking Web annoyances, the average user has learned to simply filter out and ignore content that looks this way. To prove the point, we revised the site such that the original moving links were replaced by text-only links. The site's success rate went up to nearly 100 percent. Without understanding the way human perception has built-in defense mechanisms against such visual assaults, we would have had a much more difficult time figuring out what was going on.

HEARING

At the moment, sound plays a much less critical role on the Web than does vision. Most sounds on Web sites either are embedded in other types of multimedia files such as video or are of the annoying MIDI file variety. (Have you ever loaded a Web page that had one of these embedded disasters in your cubicle at work? Suddenly cheesy computer-generated music is blaring from your speakers, and your coworkers begin "prairie-dogging" to see where the ruckus is coming from.)

Sound can play a helpful role in interface design, although research has shown that too much noise becomes a pain rather than an asset. Subtle sounds that indicate the finishing of a computational or disk-access task can put our mind at ease that the task has completed successfully. Generally speaking, however, this sort of helpful sound isn't an option on the Web right now due to bandwidth and network latency issues, so we won't devote space to it in this edition of the book.

SENSATION AND PERCEPTION

The Cocktail Party Effect

If you have ever been in a roomful of noisy conversation, clattering dishes, crying babies, and other extraneous sounds while trying to carry on a conversation with a friend, you have witnessed the *cocktail party effect* first-hand. Humans have the uncanny ability to single out the one thread of information they are interested in from a sea of noise and commotion. However, expecting your Web site user to rely on an innate ability to wade through your "noisy" Web pages is the wrong approach!

Ultimately, your users rely on this capability to some extent. The greater the degree to which you can enhance your users' ability to filter unwanted information, the more usable your site. There are many ways you can help users out of the noise quagmire; here are some highlights:

* If a piece of information can be taken off a Web page without impacting the user's ability to use the page successfully, throw it out. It's excess baggage.
* Use the inverted-pyramid style of writing: Put the most important points in the first few sentences of the text. Relegate less important information to the end of the text. This way, users get the gist of the information they need quickly.
* Use text heading levels to break up concepts across the page.
* Use tables for information that can be visually presented; read *Information Architects* by Richard Saul Wurman and *Explanations : Images and Quantities, Evidence and Narrative* by Edward Tufte for an introduction to presenting visual data.

Sensory Adaptation

You probably have a noisy clock somewhere in your house, or maybe your office features air conditioning units that hiss loudly and seemingly without end. Whatever the case, as a human, you have a type of built-in salvation: *sensory adaptation,* also known as *desensitization*. Any stimulus, when presented for a long enough time, will eventually lose its novelty to the human sensory system and fade into the background of consciousness, at which point you will either become oblivious to it or throw a chair out the window.

This self-defense mechanism is designed to allow humans to be able to function in an otherwise overstimulating environment. However, if you have done a poor job of designing your site, this very defense mechanism will work against you.

WHEN YOU OVERUSE ATTENTION-GETTING TEXTUAL TECHNIQUES, SUCH AS CAPITAL LETTERS OR LOTS OF BOLD OR ITALICS, YOU STAND A PRETTY GOOD CHANCE OF LOSING YOUR USERS' ATTENTION. THIS IS BECAUSE ALL THOSE ATTENTION-GETTING TECHNIQUES WORK ONLY IN SMALL QUANTITIES. WHEN SPREAD LIBERALLY THROUGHOUT YOUR MATERIAL, THEY WEAR YOUR USERS DOWN. WHAT WAS ONCE QUITE USEFUL FOR GRABBING A USER'S ATTENTION BECOMES A GREAT IRRITATION AND WILL BE FILTERED OUT BY THE USER. SEE? YOU'RE EVEN HAVING A HARD TIME READING THIS PARAGRAPH BECAUSE IT IS SO OVERDONE. IMAGINE SUBJECTING YOUR USER TO PAGE AFTER PAGE OF GRATUITOUS ANIMATED GIFS, EVEN IF THEY ARE CUTE LITTLE PICTURES OF MAILBOXES AND OTHER GOODIES.

Sorry to put you through that. By the way, don't ever underline anything on the Web unless it is a hyperlink or I will personally drive to your house and peel all the paint off your walls with a plasma gun. And please—never, ever never use the blink tag.

One common manifestation of sensory adaptation is that users tend to not look at anything on a Web page that moves, because experience has shown them that if it moves, it's an ad. Another sensory-adaptation dilemma can occur when you try to "make the Web more like television" and add too many elements that move, blink, change, scroll . . . you get the idea. Pages full of such elements usually bore the user. Use "attention grabbers" to very selectively do just that—briefly grab attention. Don't beat users' attention into the ground or you'll lose users.

HUMAN MEMORY AND THE WEB

Although memory is not a human sense, it clearly plays a vital role in the usability of your site. Optimizing how easy it is for users to remember how to use your site and reducing their memory load are two keys to good usability. In the usability classic text, *The Design of Everyday Things,* the author, Donald A. Norman, explains that knowledge (information) that is crucial to a user's ability to interact with and use a system can reside in one of two places:

- The world (usually meaning on the interface or system itself)
- The head (inside the user's memory)

A usable design (whether of a site or a product) puts much of the information needed for using it inside the design itself. A simple example is the keyboard. Imagine how much harder a keyboard would be to use if the letters weren't painted on the keys! Most of us wouldn't be able to type at all. Similarly, a usable Web site design facilitates the user's ability to remember how to use the interface, to the point that it can be done with little or no conscious effort. Many people are able to use Amazon.com's interface from memory because its interface facilitates spatial memory of important functions. Just imagine what would happen to Amazon's sales if it decided to suddenly revamp the look and feel of its site, discarding all the contextual cues on which users have come to rely!

Memory

I had a really great anecdote to open this section, but I forgot what it was. At any rate, memory is a vital concept to understand with regard to usability. For the purposes of this book, we use a model of human memory that most researchers in the field have retired as obsolete. However, this model proves useful in illustrating a few points, and it works within our context.

Our model of human memory contains three main components:

- Sensory memory
- Short-term memory
- Long-term memory

Let's look at each in detail.

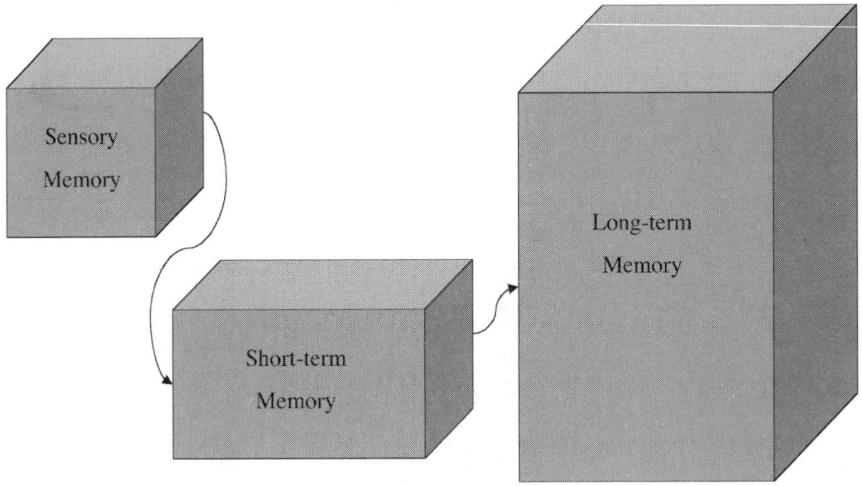
Sensory
Memory
Short-term
Memory
Long-term
Memory

FIGURE 4-6 *A model of human memory. Data enters through the sensory memory, where it may pass on to short-term memory if the stimulus is interesting or important enough. From there, rehearsal and other functions permit the data to take up residence in the long-term memory.*

Sensory Memory

This type of memory is by far the most primordial of the three. Whenever a human receives some sort of stimulus via the eyes, the ears, or one of the other senses, that sensation can, and often does, persist for some duration after the removal of the stimulus.

How many of you have ever seen the optical illusion where you stare at a picture of the U.S. flag in inverse colors (black, green, and yellow) for a minute, then stare at a wall? You then see the flag in its normal colors, red, white, and blue. Why?

This optical illusion occurs because the neuroelectrical state of your receptors remains in a nonzero-level state for some time. It takes a while for the receptors to go back to their original state, and during the interim, you have some residual information "hanging around." In the flag illusion, your neurons for vision are in an excited state while you are staring at the reversed flag. When you take the stimulus away, the neurons have a backlash effect; they go in the other direction, yielding the proper colors. (Yellow is the opponent color of blue; green is the opponent color of red; black is the opponent color of white.)

Have you ever had the experience of sitting next to a friend who asks you a question that you do not understand, and you begin to ask him or her to repeat the question, only to find that you suddenly understand what was said, even without a repeat? This effect, arguably, is sensory memory at work. The brain uses the after-impression of the sensation of hearing to process the information, even after the original sensation is gone.

Research on visual sensory memory has demonstrated that subjects who are shown an array of alphabetic characters for a short period of time (50 milliseconds) were able to recall much of the array immediately after being shown it. As the interval between the removal of the stimulus and the recall increased, the amount of recall declined.

This kind of short, visual sensory memory has been called *iconic memory;* it is believed that the part of the neural system responsible for this residual memory is the retina—specifically, the rods and cones.

It is widely believed that humans have individualized styles of interaction and ways of recognizing information in the world. One of the hot debates in Web usability has been whether people respond better to text hyperlinks or icon hyperlinks. According to Jared Spool, text is the hands-down winner.[4] I have also found this to be true through hundreds

[4]See Spool, 1997.

of usability trials. Even when users are presented with both text and an icon side by side, they filter out the icon and gain the needed information from the text.

There is a potential explanation for this phenomenon. Although it is believed that iconic representation is quicker for humans to process than textual input, when an interface is new to a user, the user is much more likely not to recognize the icon and to need the text equivalent to understand what the icon means.

If you live in the United States and you see a large red octagonal sign while you are driving, you know you're supposed to stop. How may of you actually read the word *Stop* printed on the sign in order to know what to do? This is a case of a well-known icon that was designed to be instantaneously recognized and interpreted without the additional overhead of verbal processing.

The implication for design is that using standard icons is critical to facilitating user recognition and speed of navigation. If you decide to get "clever" and design creative, artful icons that would win an award for your site, they probably won't work. I once tested a site for which the designer, a recent graduate of a well-known art school, had created an entire mythology of symbolic expression for his client. One could have written a book about the intricacies of this design. Unfortunately, the only person who understood the meaning of the icons—without reading the 10 pages of explanation—was the designer.

Improper use of iconic information can also result in failure of your site. When I had just gotten out of high school, I worked at a musical instrument retail shop where we sold karaoke machines, which we also called "singing machines" to reduce our customers' confusion about the nature of the product. We had a giant sign made up to announce the arrival of the product, which we put in the front window.

One day, to our complete amazement, a very bewildered woman walked into our store and asked if we sold sewing machines. We stared at her blankly for a moment and informed her that we did not. We shrugged it off as inexplicable, and went back to work.

A week later I realized why the woman had asked us the question. As I pulled into the parking lot to go to work, I saw our sign in the window. It read: "Singers! We Have Singing Machines!"

The word *Singers* was painted in the same color and font that the trademarked Singer sewing machine logo uses. We had inadvertently attracted the woman's attention because we had misused iconic information.

Representation of Knowledge

Humans use a vast array of techniques to assist in recalling—and forgetting—information. One technique is called *chunking*. This term was coined by G. A. Miller (Miller, 1956). Chunking is the act of reducing large amounts of information to several smaller chunks of information. You have almost without a doubt heard of the rule of 7 plus or minus 2; it comes from Miller's research. In the event that you are unfamiliar with the term, it refers to the fact that human short-term memory seems best suited to contain at most seven (plus or minus two) pieces of unrelated information at one time. Many aspiring usability specialists have taken the rule to heart, to the point that it has become dogma. I warn against this approach, however; what is the definition of "one" piece of information, anyway? The effect of chunking is that many bits of information can be taken as a whole by the memory system, so the concept of a "piece" of information is a bit abstract.

Nonetheless, the concept of chunking is invaluable. Take, for example, the following string of numbers:

```
6175551212
```

This is initially seen as a string of 10 unrelated digits. However, because I know that (617) is the area code for parts of Boston, and because I know that 555 is the prefix code for fictional telephone numbers, I can reduce this cluster of digits into three more meaningful chunks:

```
617 555 1212
```

It turns out that these three items are much easier to remember than the unrelated string of digits.

For another example, take this string of characters:

```
PHDIBMMITISPMIS
```

This looks like a bunch of gibberish and would be really hard to recall. However, when we break it up into chunks like this:

```
PHD IBM MIT ISP MIS
```

We have five chunks of information that are somewhat easier to remember. Another feature of memory, called *semantic cues*, is working behind the scenes here. The fact is that three-letter acronyms, or TLAs, make more sense to us than longer strings of characters and are easier to remember because they fit into niches in our existing memory structure. Looking at our example, we know that IBM is a major computer company. We know that a Ph.D. is a lofty degree to hold, and that MIT might be a good place to get a Ph.D. And so on. (See Figure 4.7.)

Fun with Droodles

Semantic cues are critical to the recall of visual information. In the 1950s and 1960s, now-famous experiments with fun drawings called *droodles* led to the strong evidence for this position. A droodle is a nonsensical drawing, the meaning of which cannot be readily guessed. Typically, participants who were asked to look at a large number of droodles were unable to remember how they looked later in the session, when they were asked to recall them from memory.

However, the experimental group also got a bonus: a description of the nonsensical drawing, which tied it together for the participant into a scene that "made sense." Refer to Figure 4.8 and see if you can determine what this droodle is.

Forgetting

Forgetting information is a feature, not a bug, believe it or not. Humans are meant to forget, because if you failed to forget things, your memory would be so clogged with data that you would be unable to function.

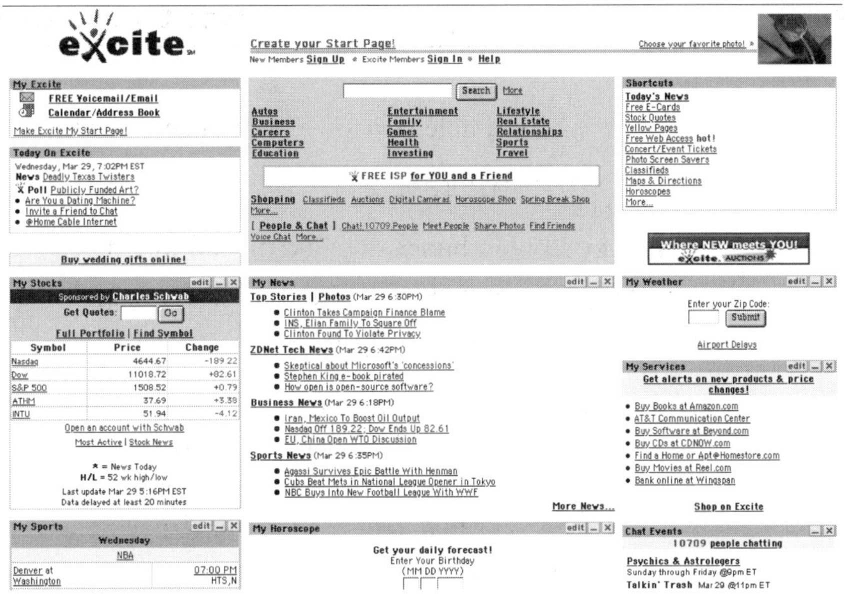
excite
Create your Start Page!
New Members Sign Up • Excite Members Sign In • Help
Choose your favorite photo! »
My Excite
FREE Voicemail/Email
Calendar/Address Book
Make Excite My Start Page!
Today On Excite
Wednesday, Mar 29, 7:02PM EST
News Deadly Texas Twisters
Poll Publicly Funded Art?
Are You a Dating Machine?
Invite a Friend to Chat
@Home Cable Internet
Buy wedding gifts online!
Search More
Autos
Business
Careers
Computers
Education
Entertainment
Family
Games
Health
Investing
Lifestyle
Real Estate
Relationships
Sports
Travel
FREE ISP for YOU and a Friend
Shopping Classifieds Auctions Digital Cameras Horoscope Shop Spring Break Shop More...
[People & Chat] Chat! 10709 People Meet People Share Photos Find Friends Voice Chat More...
Shortcuts
Today's News
Free E-Cards
Stock Quotes
Yellow Pages
Free Web Access hot!
Concert/Event Tickets
Photo Screen Savers
Classifieds
Maps & Directions
Horoscopes
More...
Where NEW meets YOU!
excite. AUCTIONS
My Stocks
Sponsored by Charles Schwab
Get Quotes: Go
Full Portfolio | Find Symbol
Symbol Price Change
Nasdaq 4644.67 -189.22
Dow 11018.72 +82.61
S&P 500 1508.52 +0.79
ATHM 37.69 +3.38
INTU 51.94 -4.12
Open an account with Schwab
Most Active | Stock News
* = News Today
H/L = 52 wk high/low
Last update Mar 29 5:16PM EST
Data delayed at least 20 minutes
My News
Top Stories | Photos (Mar 29 6:30PM)
Clinton Takes Campaign Finance Blame
INS, Elian Family To Square Off
Clinton Found To Violate Privacy
ZDNet Tech News (Mar 29 6:42PM)
Skeptical about Microsoft's 'concessions'
Stephen King e-book pirated
How open is open-source software?
Business News (Mar 29 6:18PM)
Iran, Mexico To Boost Oil Output
Nasdaq Off 189.22; Dow Ends Up 82.61
EU, China Open WTO Discussion
Sports News (Mar 29 6:35PM)
Agassi Survives Epic Battle With Henman
Cubs Beat Mets in National League Opener in Tokyo
NBC Buys Into New Football League With WWF
More News...
My Weather
Enter your Zip Code:
Submit
Airport Delays
My Services
Get alerts on new products & price changes!
Buy Books at Amazon.com
AT&T Communication Center
Buy Software at Beyond.com
Buy CDs at CDNOW.com
Find a Home or Apt@Homestore.com
Buy Movies at Reel.com
Bank online at Wingspan
Shop on Excite
My Sports
Wednesday
NBA
Denver at Washington 07:00 PM HTS,N
My Horoscope
Get your daily forecast!
Enter Your Birthday
(MM DD YYYY)
Chat Events
10709 people chatting
Psychics & Astrologers
Sunday through Friday @9pm ET
Talkin' Trash Mar 29 @11pm ET

FIGURE 4.7 *The Excite site has used a form of chunking to help make its information easier to digest. Note how headings set apart groups of information categories, and the strong visual grid of the page makes it easier for the eye to filter through the sea of information. ©2000 Excite.*

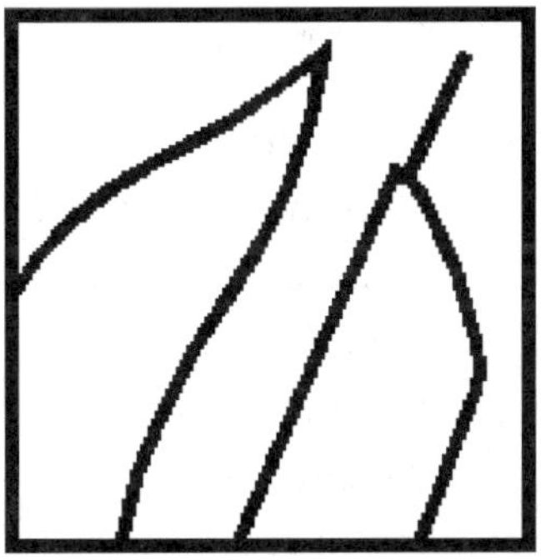

FIGURE 4.8 *A droodle is a nonsensical sketch, the meaning of which is usually impossible to guess until the viewer is told an interpretation for the sketch. The implication is that things that have a semantic framework are easier to remember than things without a semantic framework. The group that got the explanation was vastly more capable of recalling the image and was generally able to draw it from memory once they had an explanation for it. The meaning of this phenomenon is that icons that are used for navigation are effective only insofar as they make sense to the observer. For this reason, attempts to "make art," when what is really needed is an understandable icon, usually fail, although these attempts might win a design award.*[5]

[5]This is a curse in usability fields. To say that something "should win an award" is usually taken to mean that it is unusable. See Norman, 1989.

It is widely held that humans don't really totally lose memories; the memories just become impossible or very difficult to recall. This is due to the fact that memory for an event or object is strengthened through use. Have you ever heard the old cliché, "If you don't use it, you'll lose it"? It's true. Memories that are "rehearsed" or recalled many times over have stronger neural pathways in the brain than do "unrehearsed" memories. Therefore, forgetting isn't so much a function of losing memories; it's a function of being less able to dredge memories up from their deeply nested hiding places.

A couple things can prevent a human from remembering a bit of important information. One is *interference*, in which another memory that is stronger than the one the human is trying to recall interferes with it. For example, you might be trying to recall where you left your keys, and all memory points you to the top of the refrigerator. You have a vivid memory of this scene. You look and look, but you find no keys on top of the fridge. You are experiencing interference, because a previous memory is overshadowing the one you are really trying to recall.

Another barrier to memory is *decay*. Decay is also known as the *Power Law of Forgetting* (Wixted and Ebbesen, 1991). It has been shown that memories decay over time in a logarithmic fashion. This means that memories are forgotten quite rapidly at first, but that the rate of forgetting decreases sharply after a short while and then levels out.

Mental Models

The concept of a *mental model* is a predominant one in human factors psychology. A distinguishing feature of humans is their ability to turn complex stimuli in the world into a thought model that they can understand, interact with, and use to assimilate new bits of information that they experience.

The concept of mental models emerged from the human/computer interaction field as a mental metaphor for describing the conceptions that humans develop for internally describing the location, function, and structure of objects and phenomena in computer systems. The facility with which users apply and exploit the functionality of computer systems depends, mental model theorists argue, on their conceptual models for describing the components and interactions of those systems. Are mental models merely conceptual? Mental models have been distinguished from other types of models that are also used to aid the development of user interfaces.

Another term for mental model is *schema*. Schemas are "cognitive structures that represent knowledge about a concept or type of stimulus, including its attributes and the relation among those attributes."[6] A consistent theme throughout good usability practice is the notion of leveraging a user's existing schemata; that is to say, making use of the things that a person already knows or is familiar with—for example, a competitor's interface, if you are the smaller underdog; but beware of lawsuits—remember the "one-click" fiasco! Don't reinvent the wheel just to be proprietary or clever.

It is largely believed that humans form a mental model of anything that they use. For example, when a locksmith uses lockpicks to open a lock, it is important that she have a strong mental model based on subtle sensory input from the picks and from the sounds coming from the tumblers. By envisioning how all of the insides of the lock might look, the locksmith can better guide the tools to open the lock.

My upstairs neighbor once explained to me how he utilizes the mental model to enable himself to perform his job. He is a programmer, and the kind of software he writes is understood by only two people on Earth and a handful of beings from a race of intelligent space-dolphins. When he arrives at work, he spends quite a while reconstructing an elaborate model of his programs in his head. He can visualize all the parts, and this enables him to work with the code.

Gordon H. Bower and Daniel G. Morrow have said of mental models, "We build mental models that represent significant aspects of our physical and social world, and we manipulate elements of those models when

---

[6]Fiske and Taylor, 1991, p. 98.

we think, plan, and try to explain events of that world. The ability to construct and manipulate valid models of reality provides humans with our distinctive adaptive advantage; it must be considered one of the crowning achievements of the human intellect."[7]

When humans interact with software, it is believed that they form a mental model of where certain functions should belong. For example, where would the option to export a file to a different format be likely to be found in a traditional Windows interface? The answer: probably under the File menu. I know this because in my head I have a model of a "typical" Windows application. Whenever I have to use a new, previously unseen application, I am likely to draw on my mental model to find things I need (see Figure 4.9).

Curiously enough, Jared Spool has asserted that users of Web sites do not form mental models of the sites. Based on his data, I am not convinced that this is true, although I am not sure that he is incorrect. I tend to find that participants with whom I work do, in fact, have at least a weak mental model of the Web site that they are using. I think that this concept of "mental model-less" Web use was possibly true when the Web was young; Web sites were ineffective, with no good use of hierarchical systems of navigation.

But as Web sites have matured, they have begun to homogenize a bit, with most of the better sites following many de facto standards. This standardization facilitates the development of a universal Web site mental model. For example, most commercial sites have a products section that includes a catalog of all the sponsoring company's available goods and services. As simple as this concept may seem, it wasn't always the case.

My point is that the mental model or schema is one of the most powerful built-in human tools you have at your disposal. The techniques for leveraging the user's existing schema include many of the points we have already discussed, including consistency and standards.

---

[7]"This Week in Science," Gordon H. Bower and Daniel G. Morrow, *Science,* Volume 247, January 5, 1990, p. 7.

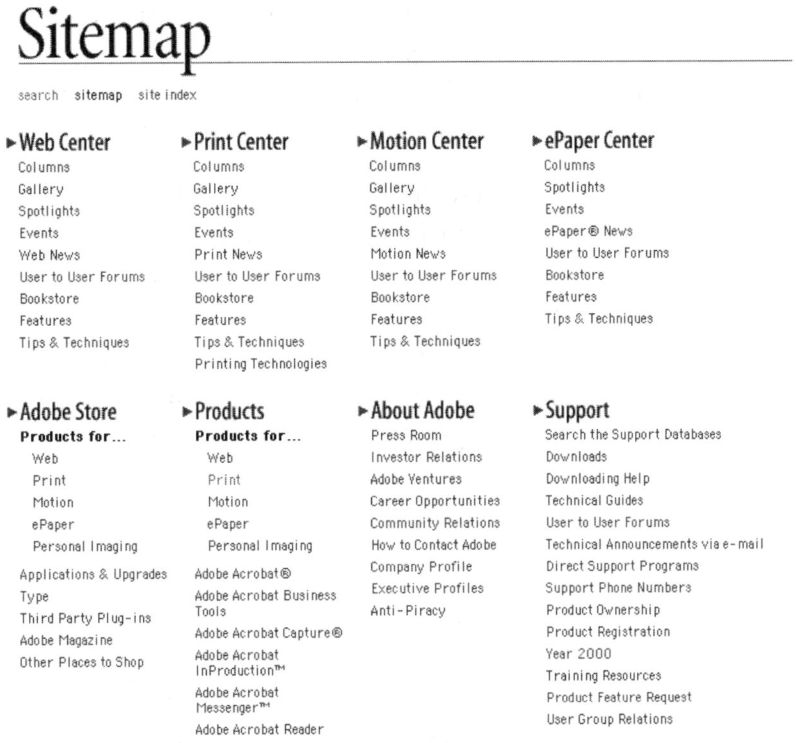
Sitemap
search sitemap site index
Web Center
Columns
Gallery
Spotlights
Events
Web News
User to User Forums
Bookstore
Features
Tips & Techniques
Print Center
Columns
Gallery
Spotlights
Events
Print News
User to User Forums
Bookstore
Features
Tips & Techniques
Printing Technologies
Motion Center
Columns
Gallery
Spotlights
Events
Motion News
User to User Forums
Bookstore
Features
Tips & Techniques
ePaper Center
Columns
Spotlights
Events
ePaper® News
User to User Forums
Bookstore
Features
Tips & Techniques
Adobe Store
Products for...
Web
Print
Motion
ePaper
Personal Imaging
Applications & Upgrades
Type
Third Party Plug-ins
Adobe Magazine
Other Places to Shop
Products
Products for...
Web
Print
Motion
ePaper
Personal Imaging
Adobe Acrobat®
Adobe Acrobat Business Tools
Adobe Acrobat Capture®
Adobe Acrobat InProduction™
Adobe Acrobat Messenger™
Adobe Acrobat Reader
About Adobe
Press Room
Investor Relations
Adobe Ventures
Career Opportunities
Community Relations
How to Contact Adobe
Company Profile
Executive Profiles
Anti-Piracy
Support
Search the Support Databases
Downloads
Downloading Help
Technical Guides
User to User Forums
Technical Announcements via e-mail
Direct Support Programs
Support Phone Numbers
Product Ownership
Product Registration
Year 2000
Training Resources
Product Feature Request
User Group Relations

FIGURE 4.9 *A nicely organized site map that provides the user with help in forming a mental model © 2000 Adobe Systems, Inc.*

TIPS FOR TEXT-HEAVY WEB PAGES

Executive summary: Don't create them. Period.

The design mistake of virtually every first-generation Web site is that the designers tried to simply reformat their existing print material for the Web. The end result is many, many pages with tons of text. You should simply avoid lengthy text on the Web altogether. The physiological act of reading an on-screen document and the act of reading a paper document are wholly different. Reading on-screen documents is painful. Here are a handful of the reasons this is true:

- **The resolution.** Computer screens can display only about 70 or 80 dots per inch (dpi), which at best forms grainy text. Even low-resolution printers (300dpi) produce an output that is much more tolerable to the human eye.
- **Human posture.** In order to read from a screen, you are forced to view material from a more or less fixed physical position. Although laptop computers and wireless networks have helped alleviate this dilemma somewhat, the desktop computer and CRT-style monitor are still the most common combination. Conversely, when reading a paper document, you are free to sit, stand, slouch, or adopt almost any posture that suits you.
- **Glare.** Since monitor screens are made of glass, they naturally exhibit some degree of reflectivity of ambient light sources. This means that the text may be hard to read if the natural room lighting is sufficient to be comfortable when you are not viewing the monitor screen. Paper is rarely reflective, so the viewer does not need to overcome this obstacle.
- **Monitor flicker.** Even though you see a more or less solid image when you look at your computer monitor, you are actually looking at a screen that is drawn one pixel-thin line at a time. If your monitor has a refresh rate of 60 Hertz, that means that the screen gets redrawn 60 times a second. This is fast enough to "fool" the brain into seeing a solid image, but in reality, the brain must constantly correct for the flicker and expend brainpower just to allow you to look at a monitor. Setting the refresh rate higher can help the situation a little, but the fact remains that paper doesn't flicker at all.

Alternatives for Text-Heavy Sections

However, if you must include lengthy amounts of text on your site, all is not lost. The trick is to simply make it as easy as possible for your users to print the document for offline reading. One alternative, in my opinion the superior solution, is to create a print-ready version of the text as an Adobe Portable Document Format (PDF) file. PDF files can be viewed on any platform that has a port for the free Adobe Acrobat

Reader. PDF documents you create will look the same no matter where they are viewed. This is a plus for portability (hence the name!). The reader is available for free download from the Adobe Web site *(www.adobe.com).*

The main disadvantage to the PDF approach is that it requires the user to have yet another piece of software, even if it is free. Fortunately, the Acrobat Reader is found in so many places that the severity of this problem is not great.

The second solution is to create a version of the page with print-friendly HTML. This means several things: First, the text must fit horizontally on a single page. If your text is wide enough to overlap onto a second page horizontally (it's okay for the text to go onto subsequent sheets vertically), it isn't print friendly. Second, you must make sure that the page doesn't have a dark background and light or even white text, because this combination will not print.

Implications for Design

Today, humans are immersed in a constant torrent of information, much of which is perceived as noise. With so much new information reaching each person, it is critical that designers reduce the load on users' short-term memories. Although one of the goals of UCD is to increase learning retention for user tasks, it is unwise to offload so much rote memorization onto the user.

For example, the UNIX program called Emacs features one of the richest feature sets of any program. It is a programming environment, a text editor, and an e-mail client, and it features hundreds of other goodies that few people completely master. The command syntax for the program is executed via keyboard commands. For example, the command to save a file is the key sequence Ctrl+x Ctrl+s (Control and the letter *x* pressed at the same time, followed by Control and the letter *s* pressed at the same time). The command to "visit" a file (in other words, to open it) is Ctrl+x Ctrl+f. There are hundreds of such commands, and the user can completely redefine key commands as well as create new ones.

Although the Emacs program is a great favorite among the slide-rule savvy, in my opinion it is not a friendly program for the everyday, average user.[8] The problem with Emacs is that there are far too many key sequences for the average, harried individual to remember.

The way to solve the problem, in part, is to reduce the load placed on the user's memory. If the options were available in an organized, nonobtrusive fashion, the user would be able to locate needed features. Note that executing a command by locating it in a menu system and choosing it will always be slower than knowing a shortcut, usually a keyboard command. However, a system should support both types of access: menu-driven options for novice and intermediate users and shortcuts (called *accelerators*) for expert and power users.

ACCELERATORS ON THE WEB

Unfortunately, Web applications have not quite reached the state of utility of native programs constructed in C, C++, variants of BASIC, and so forth. One of the features that Web applications lack is the ability to intercept and utilize keyboard shortcuts. For example, it is impossible to create keystroke-actuated accelerators in Web applications except for the ones supported by the browser itself. Additionally, few portable solutions exist for generating menu systems for Web applications.

The solutions that do exist are Dynamic HTML (DHTML) and Java, both of which afford some functionality like that of native applications. The problem is that standards for DHTML are not really standards, with much browser-dependent variation, and Java is not always a viable option because of the sluggishness of the Java Virtual Machine (JVM) on many systems. However, it is likely that some combination of these

---

[8]Disclaimer: I am playing devil's advocate here. I use Emacs every day and find it very useful and more productive than any other combination of tools I have used before. But I am a propeller-head. In defense of Emacs, the designers have modeled the command syntax in such a way that the keyboard commands make sense. However, the user must make a large up-front investment, which is usually enough to drive away the average (American) potential user. And by the way, the official name is GNU/emacs, named after the organization that created it. Visit *www.gnu.org* to learn more.

technologies will allow designs to implement such features in the very near future.

It would be nice to be able to invoke a Web site's search engine by simply pressing Ctrl+F anywhere within the site. Unfortunately, this keystroke combination brings up the browser's Find feature, which can only scan the text of the currently loaded page.

If Web site designers used a standard interface for search engines, Web authors could embed in every page a metatag that points to the site's search engine. Browser vendors could then allow users to set their preferences, so that for example, pressing Ctrl+F would follow the metatag and open up the search engine page for the site, potentially in a new window (which would need to be a user preference option).

CHAPTER SUMMARY

- The field of human factors psychology forms much of the basis of usability testing, and the field has its roots in military research.
- Some people have discounted the field of human factors as useless for the purposes of short-turnaround Web usability. This outlook is myopic and misinformed.
- Understanding how people think and interact with their environment can only help usability specialists interpret participant behavior and understand the limitations and advantages of being human.
- A significant percentage of Earth's population has some form of color deficiency. The implication is that color should be used on your Web site in only a supplemental, not a critical, fashion.
- Successful interface design relies on the principle of reducing the memory load of the user.
- Another key to good design is to take advantage of existing constructs in the user's experience.

HANDS-ON EXERCISES

1. Learn more about human factors. A good place to start is by reading *Human Factors for Technical Communicators* by Marlana Coe.
2. Take a course on human factors at your local college or university.
3. Take a test for color deficiency. Have you ever taken one?
4. Familiarize yourself with whatever method you have to use to set your monitor display to grayscale.
5. Look at five commercial Web sites at random and try to see whether and how they implement information chunking.

DISCUSSION TOPICS

1. What do you think about the magic "7 plus or minus 2" formula with regard to Web sites?
2. What accelerators do you use, if any, in traditional software applications? What are some accelerators for the Web? They can exist today, or they might be ones you make up.
3. Why do we really have to worry about human factors? Shouldn't we take a Darwinian approach to Web site use? Explain.
4. Do you think that the current limitation of reading electronic documents can be solved? If so, how? If not, why not?

CHAPTER

5

DESIGN GUIDELINES

Decision maker, n.:
The person in your office who was unable to form a task force before the music stopped.

JUST THE FACTS

Part of the fun of a book such as this one is to see the "design secrets" that will make your site better than the next. The rest of this book is more reactive in nature, telling you how to analyze a site that you've already designed. This chapter tells you how to be proactive with a new design. Although design isn't the main topic of this book, good design is part of good usability. In this chapter, you will find a list of many of the most common tips for increasing your site's usability (and in some cases, accessibility). These are "common-sense" tips that, unfortunately, people are still ignoring.

However, I should point out that this list is not the solution to all your Web usability problems. Going through your site and making sure it complies with every single tip is still not license for you to avoid doing any other usability work! Tips are just that: tips. A successful site is the result of a seasoned team of people making decisions based on their collective experience. A cookbook-style approach to web site usability is about as reasonable as a cookbook-style approach to brain surgery.

This list is by no means exhaustive, but it should provide you with a starting point for developing your own set of design guidelines. Where I have been able to find sites that exemplify the principles I discuss here, I have included screen shots. As per the disclaimer at the front of this book, please note that my inclusion of individual sites is neither an endorsement nor an attempt to libel. All of these sites are available for public inspection.

Don't Create Orphaned Pages

Pages to which a user can link and then become "stranded" (only able to navigate elsewhere by clicking the Back button) are a definite no-no. Sometimes these pages are called "tar pits" because you can get in, but you can't get back out! Make sure that every page on your site at least has a way to go back to the very top of the site as well as a way to go up one level to the parent page.

Name Categories in Terms of User Tasks and Goals

Whenever you create links or topic headings, make sure that you create the names in terms of user actions, not in terms of what is going on behind the scenes on the site. For example, instead of including the instructional link "Process session," use the phrase "Go to checkout," since your user is more likely to be recognize the meaning of that label. This tip goes back to the design heuristic, "Use the user's natural language." (See Figures 5.1 and 5.2.)

PETsMART.COM
My PETsMART • Help
Select → Dogs Cats Birds Fish Reptiles Small Animals
Search: Select a pet type go! More Search Options
Shopping
Dogs
Cats
Birds
Fish
Reptiles
Small Animals
Answers
Dogs
Cats
Birds
Fish
Reptiles
Small Animals
Community
Dogs
Cats
Birds
Fish
Reptiles
Small Animals
Free Buzz! w/ any $20 purchase Click Here.
Register Now for PETsMART.com!
Special Treats
Shop with the Big Dogs
Free Pound Puppy ®
Affiliate Partners
Got a website? Make $$$
Build Your Pet a Web Page! Sign up to start...
Regular Home Delivery You Sit, We Fetch™ Get regular delivery of the items you use most.
PETsMART Stores
PETsMART Q4 1999 Quarterly Earnings
Store Locator Find the PETsMART store nearest you
PETsMART, Inc. Corporate Information
Petsmart Charities PETsMART Charities has
Special! for new customers
Buy one
Get one free
on pet food
Buy any pet food item and get the second identical item for FREE!
Click here to begin shopping with this promotion.
Today
In Answers
A Day in the Life of a Cancer Therapy Beagle
At Cedars-Sinai Comprehensive Cancer Center in Los Angeles, Dani, the therapy dog, is on the job. Having survived cancer himself, he's the perfect dog to reassure children going through the same ordeal. more...
Flea and Tick Season is Fast Approaching
Check out our Flea and Tick Map to find out what months are the peskiest in your state.
NEW Use our pet food calculators for your Dog or Cat.
Frequently Asked Questions about Birds
Choosing Your Fish Aquarium
Dog Speak: How to Understand Your Dog and Help Him Understand You
Pick of the Litter
20% off!! the natural store
Click here for details!
Endangered Species Bed-Big Bear
Let your pet "take a nap on the wild side" in this unique bed. Sold only at PETsMART! $89.99
Snuggle Safe
Heat the Snuggle Safe in the microwave then slip it into your pet's bed for up to 12 hours of comforting warmth. $23.99

FIGURE 5.1 *Here's an example of a site that frames the content in terms of the user's language. What do you normally want to do when you go to a pet supply site? Probably buy pet supplies, so the designers framed the navigation in terms of action—the things that the user wants to do. ©2000 PetSmart.*

FedEx Express
Global Home
Welcome to fedex.com
FedEx Regions
U.S.
Canada
North America
Latin America
Asia/Pacific
Caribbean
Europe
Middle East
Africa
Track A Package
Enter Up To 25 Airbill Numbers:
(Enter one Airbill Number per line.)
How To
Track It
Please complete the field above and click the Track It button to track your package.
Other FedEx Services
Choose your country
Go
© 1995-2000. Federal Express Corporation.
This site is protected by copyright and trademark laws under U.S. and international law.
Review our privacy policy. All rights reserved.

FIGURE 5.2 *Since FedEx obviously hopes to reduce expenses and provide a valuable service for customers, the package-delivery company is wise to put the number-one requested user activity—tracking a shipment right on its home page. ©2000 Federal Express.*

Keep Elements Consistent

A foolish consistency is the hobgoblin of little minds, but on the Web, there probably aren't too many foolish consistencies. There are, however, plenty of foolish inconsistencies!

Make sure that every page in your site has some commonality that helps the user identify the site that he or she is on. You should also use consistent navigation styles throughout the site. Shifting from a left-side-of-the-page navigation style on the home page to a strange hyperlinked-pictures-in-the-middle-of-the-page paradigm two pages into the site will be confusing and aesthetically displeasing.

This guideline can be hard to follow if you are trying to coordinate content within an umbrella site with other parts of your company. It's easy to become inconsistent, so you must compensate by agreeing on a standard with the other departments. (See Figures 5.3, 5.4, 5.5.)

YOUR ACCOUNT | HELP | SELL ITEMS
WELCOME
BOOKS
MUSIC
DVD & VIDEO
ELECTRONICS & SOFTWARE
TOYS & VIDEO GAMES
HOME IMPROVEMENT
AUCTIONS
zSHOPS
HOW TO ORDER
GIFT IDEAS
DEALS OF THE DAY
COMMUNITY
E-CARDS
SEARCH
All Products
GO!
Search of the Day: Cranium
Amazon.com Auctions: First-Edition Books, Used CDs, Rare Videos, Electronics Deals, Comics
Monday, January 31, 2000
amazon.com
Hello! New to Amazon.com? Find out how to order.
Already a customer? Sign in.
BROWSE
• Books
• Music
• DVD & Video
• Electronics
• Software
• Toys
• Video Games
• Home Improvement
• Auctions
• sothebys.amazon.com
• zShops
• Gift Ideas
• Free e-Cards
All-Products Search
Great Moments on Film
zShops
DVD & Video
Electronics & Software
Relive the Saga
Pre-order Star Wars: Episode I, The Phantom Menace on widescreen or standard VHS.
Amazon.com 100 Hot Books
Updated Hourly
1. The Brethren by John Grisham
2. Harry Potter and the Chamber of Secrets (Book 2) by J. K. Rowling
3. Harry Potter and the Prisoner of Azkaban (Book 3) by J. K. Rowling, Mary Grandpre (Illustrator)
More Hot Books
Today in DVD & Video
Thanks for the Memories
It's movie awards season, and we're becoming positively obsessed with all things celluloid. If you're equally addicted, pan over to our weekly list of DVD new releases to find out instantly when gems like Cinema Paradiso go on sale. Next, wander through zShops and check out mysterious and exotic (and well-priced!) film memorabilia. And since everybody wants to direct, let our expert reviews set you up with the best camcorder. Action!
More from Our Stores:
• Ten Movie Masterpieces
• Camcorder Accessories
• Multimedia & Video Editing Software
• Classic Movie Soundtracks

FIGURE 5.3 *Here's the Amazon.com home page, which you probably instantly recognize by now. ©2000 Amazon.com.*

amazon.com.
YOUR ACCOUNT | HELP | SELL ITEMS
WELCOME BOOKS MUSIC DVD & VIDEO ELECTRONICS & SOFTWARE TOYS & VIDEO GAMES HOME IMPROVEMENT AUCTIONS zSHOPS
BOOK SEARCH BROWSE SUBJECTS BESTSELLERS FEATURED IN THE MEDIA AWARD WINNERS COMPUTERS & INTERNET CHILDREN'S BOOKS BUSINESS & INVESTING
Monday, January 31, 2000
SEARCH
BROWSE
WELCOME TO
Amazon.com Books
What We're Reading
Mind Games
Half-Price Calendars
Amazon.com 100 Hot Books
Updated Hourly
Recent "What We're Reading" Picks:
More Recent Picks
Interviews, Articles, and More
Future Shock
More Hot Books
10 Under $10
In Bestsellers
Coming Soon

FIGURE 5.4 *Here's another page from the Amazon.com site, only in a different section. Note that the designers have maintained consistency throughout, meaning that users do not have to arbitrarily relearn a new interface every few steps. ©2000 Amazon.com.*

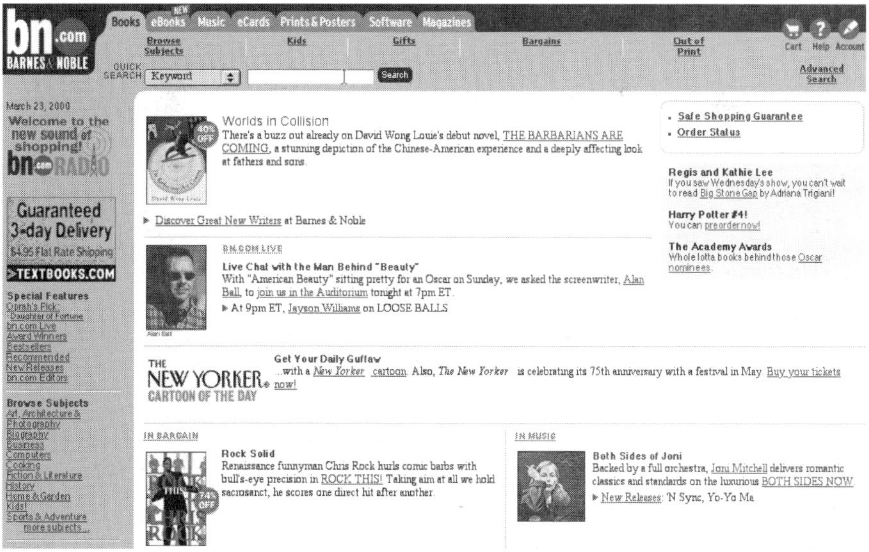
bn.com
BARNES & NOBLE
Books eBooks Music eCards Prints & Posters Software Magazines
QUICK SEARCH
Search
March 23, 2000
Welcome to the new sound of shopping!
Guaranteed 3-day Delivery
TEXTBOOKS.COM
Worlds in Collision
Safe Shopping Guarantee
Order Status
Discover Great New Writers at Barnes & Noble
THE NEW YORKER CARTOON OF THE DAY
Get Your Daily Guffaw
Rock Solid
Both Sides of Joni

FIGURE 5.5 *Companies have begun to follow the strong standards of other companies in order to leverage the user's existing schemata. Can you imagine how screwy the world would be if every automobile company had to create a new, totally different steering mechanism for its cars just because someone at a rival company had patented the steering wheel? ©2000 Barnes and Noble.*

Test Your Work in Many Browsers and Conditions

Remember the story from Chapter 2 about my students who wouldn't preview their work in any browser other than the one they had to use? It led to a lot of wasted time and energy. I'll say it one more time: It is absolutely, positively critical that you preview your work in several browsers, on several platforms, at several resolutions, with several different screen sizes. In fact, it pays to have a lab set up in your company with a variety of computers for the sole purpose of testing your designs.

Test your site under multiple download conditions. If your site is dreadfully slow over a modem connection, you'll need to revise it. (See Figure 5.6.)

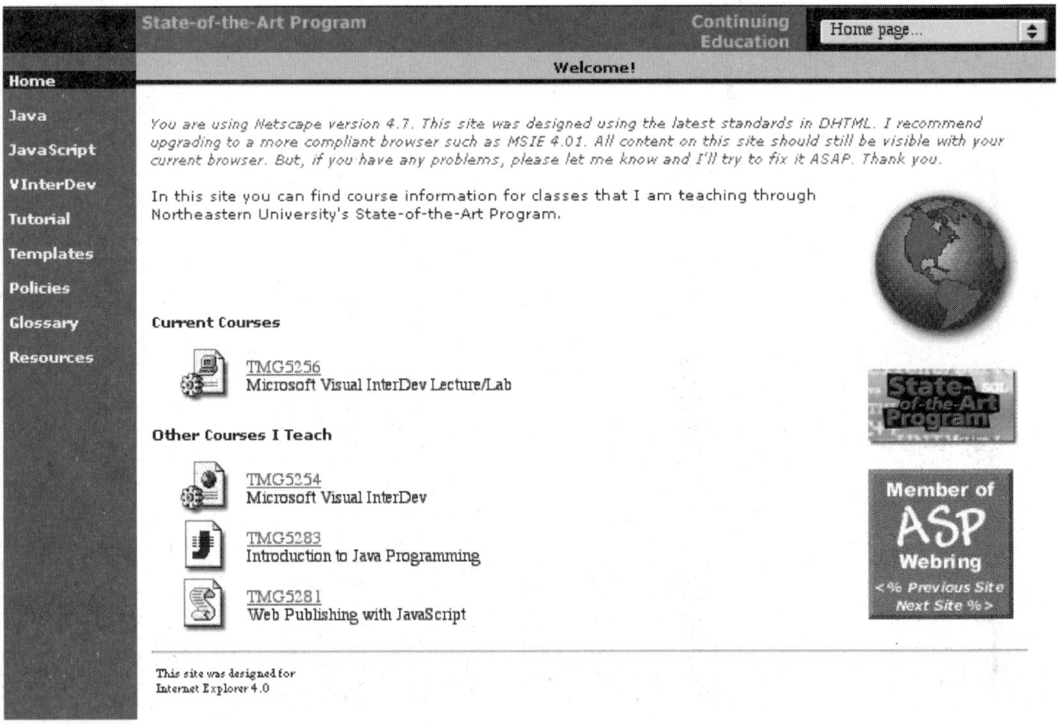
State-of-the-Art Program
Continuing Education
Home page...
Welcome!
Home
Java
JavaScript
VInterDev
Tutorial
Templates
Policies
Glossary
Resources
You are using Netscape version 4.7. This site was designed using the latest standards in DHTML. I recommend upgrading to a more compliant browser such as MSIE 4.01. All content on this site should still be visible with your current browser. But, if you have any problems, please let me know and I'll try to fix it ASAP. Thank you.
In this site you can find course information for classes that I am teaching through Northeastern University's State-of-the-Art Program.
Current Courses
TMG5256
Microsoft Visual InterDev Lecture/Lab
Other Courses I Teach
TMG5254
Microsoft Visual InterDev
TMG5283
Introduction to Java Programming
TMG5281
Web Publishing with JavaScript
This site was designed for Internet Explorer 4.0
State-of-the-Art Program
Member of
ASP
Webring
<% Previous Site
Next Site %>

FIGURE 5.6 *With apologies to a fellow instructor! If your site needs stiff disclaimers like the one on this site, you need to rethink your design. Remember, do not design like Procrustes, stretching the user to fit the site. ©2000 Northeastern University.*

Keep Important Information "Above the Fold"

Web site users observe information by the screenful; because for one reason or another many people don't scroll, you have to make sure that you keep the most important information on the top part of your Web page.

Specifically, you need to make sure that all the vital information is available when viewed on a 15-inch screen at a resolution of 640 by 480 pixels. (This figure will change over time, as bigger monitors become commonplace.) And yes, you still need to be concerned with bit depth of images, because many people don't have 24-bit video—or, if they do, they don't know that they can change their settings from 8 bit to 24 bit. (See Figures 5.7 and 5.8.)

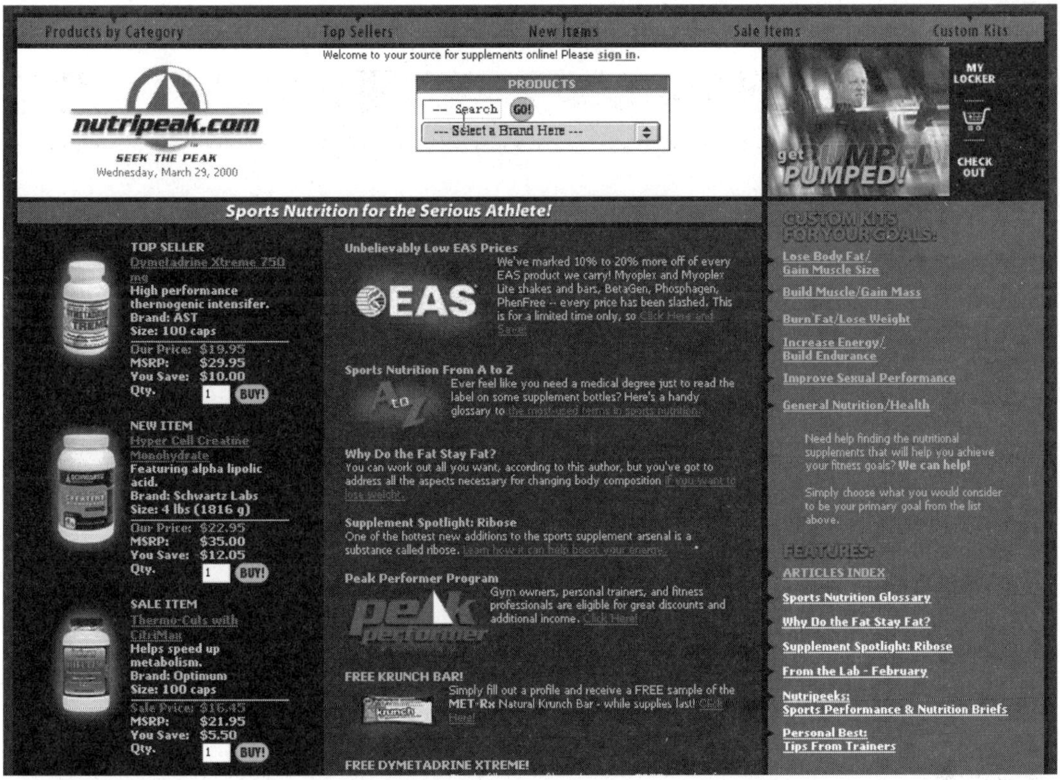
Products by Category
Top Sellers
New Items
Sale Items
Custom Kits
Welcome to your source for supplements online! Please sign in.
nutripeak.com
SEEK THE PEAK
Wednesday, March 29, 2000
PRODUCTS
-- Search
GO!
--- Select a Brand Here ---
MY LOCKER
CHECK OUT
get PUMPED!
Sports Nutrition for the Serious Athlete!
TOP SELLER
High performance thermogenic intensifer.
Brand: AST
Size: 100 caps
Our Price: $19.95
MSRP: $29.95
You Save: $10.00
Qty.
BUY!
NEW ITEM
Hyper Cell Creatine Monohydrate
Featuring alpha lipolic acid.
Brand: Schwartz Labs
Size: 4 lbs (1816 g)
Our Price: $22.95
MSRP: $35.00
You Save: $12.05
SALE ITEM
Helps speed up metabolism.
Brand: Optimum
Size: 100 caps
Sale Price: $16.45
MSRP: $21.95
You Save: $5.50
Unbelievably Low EAS Prices
EAS
Sports Nutrition From A to Z
Why Do the Fat Stay Fat?
Supplement Spotlight: Ribose
Peak Performer Program
FREE KRUNCH BAR!
FREE DYMETADRINE XTREME!
CUSTOM KITS FOR YOUR GOALS:
Lose Body Fat/ Gain Muscle Size
Build Muscle/Gain Mass
Burn Fat/Lose Weight
Increase Energy/ Build Endurance
Improve Sexual Performance
General Nutrition/Health
FEATURES:
ARTICLES INDEX
Sports Nutrition Glossary
Why Do the Fat Stay Fat?
Supplement Spotlight: Ribose
From the Lab - February
Nutripeeks: Sports Performance & Nutrition Briefs
Personal Best: Tips From Trainers

FIGURE 5.7 *In this screen shot, you can see that the designers have put many of the most-needed features "above the fold." However, their navigational system is spread out to the bottom of the page, putting several possibly critical elements below the fold. ©2000 Nutripeak.*

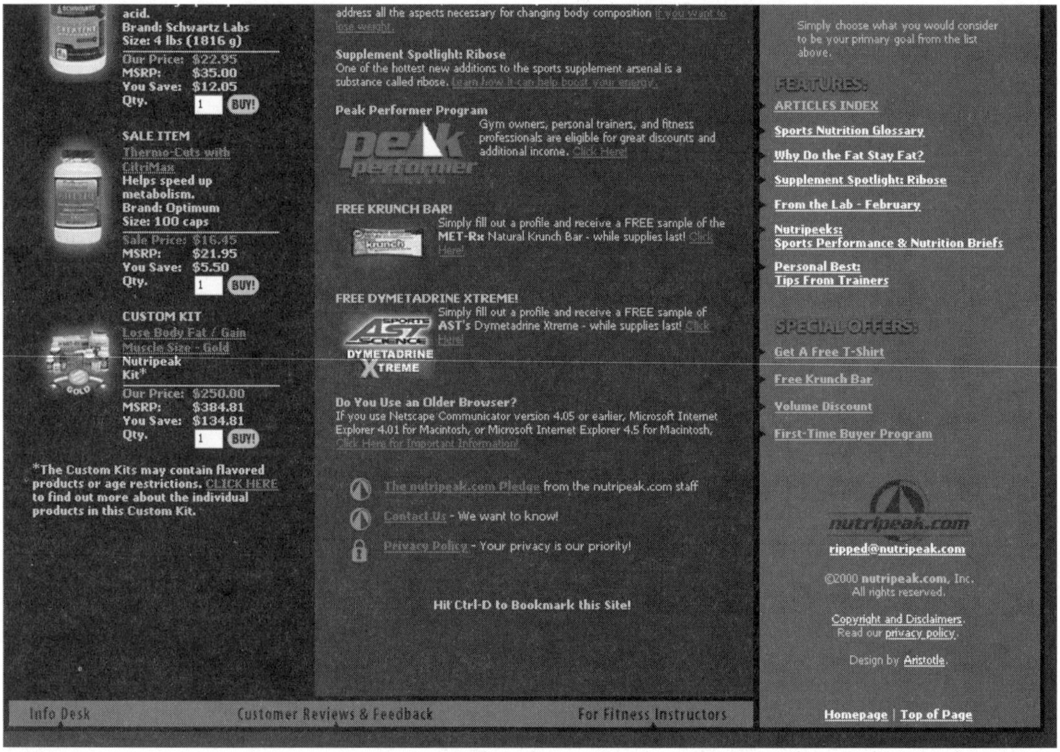
acid.
Brand: Schwartz Labs
Size: 4 lbs (1816 g)
Our Price: $22.95
MSRP: $35.00
You Save: $12.05
Qty.
BUY!
SALE ITEM
Thermo-Cuts with CitriMax
Helps speed up metabolism.
Brand: Optimum
Size: 100 caps
Sale Price: $16.45
MSRP: $21.95
You Save: $5.50
CUSTOM KIT
Lose Body Fat / Gain Muscle Size - Gold
Nutripeak Kit*
Our Price: $250.00
MSRP: $384.81
You Save: $134.81
*The Custom Kits may contain flavored products or age restrictions. CLICK HERE to find out more about the individual products in this Custom Kit.
Supplement Spotlight: Ribose
Peak Performer Program
Gym owners, personal trainers, and fitness professionals are eligible for great discounts and additional income. Click Here!
FREE KRUNCH BAR!
Simply fill out a profile and receive a FREE sample of the MET-Rx Natural Krunch Bar - while supplies last! Click Here!
FREE DYMETADRINE XTREME!
Simply fill out a profile and receive a FREE sample of AST's Dymetadrine Xtreme - while supplies last! Click Here!
Do You Use an Older Browser?
If you use Netscape Communicator version 4.05 or earlier, Microsoft Internet Explorer 4.01 for Macintosh, or Microsoft Internet Explorer 4.5 for Macintosh, Click Here for Important Information!
The nutripeak.com Pledge from the nutripeak.com staff
Contact Us - We want to know!
Privacy Policy - Your privacy is our priority!
Hit Ctrl-D to Bookmark this Site!
Simply choose what you would consider to be your primary goal from the list above.
FEATURES:
ARTICLES INDEX
Sports Nutrition Glossary
Why Do the Fat Stay Fat?
Supplement Spotlight: Ribose
From the Lab - February
Nutripeeks: Sports Performance & Nutrition Briefs
Personal Best: Tips From Trainers
SPECIAL OFFERS:
Get A Free T-Shirt
Free Krunch Bar
Volume Discount
First-Time Buyer Program
nutripeak.com
ripped@nutripeak.com
©2000 nutripeak.com, Inc. All rights reserved.
Copyright and Disclaimers. Read our privacy policy.
Design by Aristotle.
Info Desk
Customer Reviews & Feedback
For Fitness Instructors
Homepage | Top of Page

FIGURE 5.8 *Here's the part that was below the fold on the site shown in Figure 5.7. ©2000 Nutripeak.*

Don't Make Users Scroll Horizontally

Arguably, scrolling vertically is acceptable, but if you rely heavily on scrolling, don't expect users to see information that is below the fold. However, scrolling horizontally is absolutely out. Never make a page that is too wide to fit on a screen running at a width of 640 pixels (and don't forget to account for browser "real estate" and the possibility that a user might not maximize the browser window).

WebTV users are constrained even further; they can only view pages that are a maximum of 544 by 372 pixels. Pages that are wider than 544 pixels are scaled down, and this usually results in a nasty look.

Think Globally

It is, after all, the *World* Wide Web, not the North American (excluding Canada) Web. This means making sure that your content is available to your users who don't speak the language you speak. I mention this elsewhere in the book, but it bears mentioning again: machine translators are simply not appropriate for enterprise Web sites. They are fun and can help you fumble through an otherwise hopelessly unintelligible Web site, but they are not "smart" enough yet for you to dispense with human translators (see Figure 5.9).

Furthermore, be sure not to mistakenly use icons of the flags of countries to represent languages. There is not a one-to-one mapping of languages and flags; one nation might support three or four languages

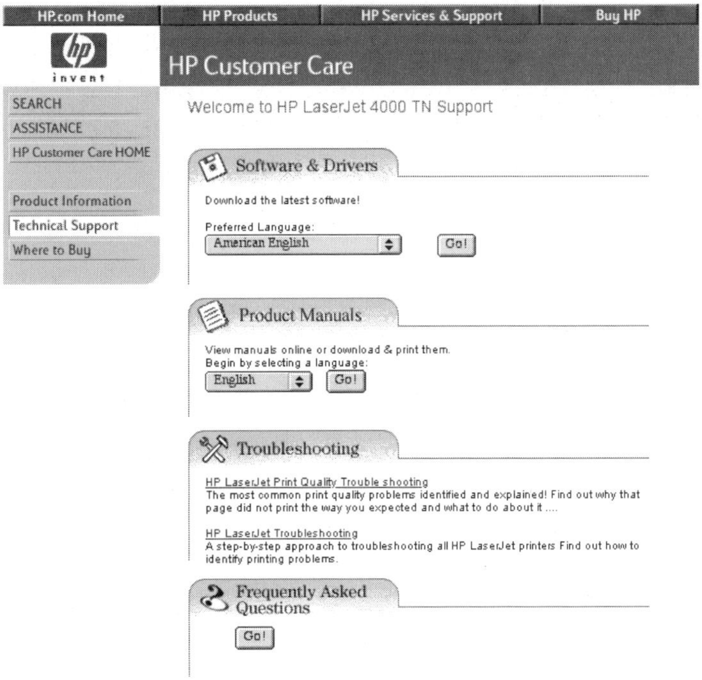
HP.com Home
HP Products
HP Services & Support
Buy HP
invent
HP Customer Care
SEARCH
ASSISTANCE
HP Customer Care HOME
Product Information
Technical Support
Where to Buy
Welcome to HP LaserJet 4000 TN Support
Software & Drivers
Download the latest software!
Preferred Language:
American English
Go!
Product Manuals
View manuals online or download & print them.
Begin by selecting a language:
English
Go!
Troubleshooting
HP LaserJet Print Quality Trouble shooting
The most common print quality problems identified and explained! Find out why that page did not print the way you expected and what to do about it ....
HP LaserJet Troubleshooting
A step-by-step approach to troubleshooting all HP LaserJet printers Find out how to identify printing problems.
Frequently Asked Questions
Go!

FIGURE 5.9 *The Hewlett-Packard Web site used to have a frustrating feature. If you did a search for drivers for a LaserJet printer, for example, every version of that driver, in every available language, was returned as a hit. I don't normally speak German, so I am almost never going to care to see the German software descriptions. Now at least HP allows you to select your language. ©2000 Hewlett-Packard Co.*

and even more dialects. You can actually auto-detect the vast majority of your users' language preferences. Every time a user requests a document from your Web server, you can access an environment variable via CGI that has the user's language preference encoded (at least, whatever language to which the user's browser default is set).

Warn Users About File Sizes

If you link to a file, such as an Adobe PDF file, a video clip, or any other type of file that is larger than a Web page (say, over 45 kilobytes), you should include the file size in the link text itself or somehow convey the file size of the thing to which you are linking. This gives the user the option of choosing not to click on the link if they don't want to wait for a huge file to download. It is also a nice touch to include projected download time at some known speed, such as 28.8K or even 56K.

GETTING AROUND

Use Top and Left of Screen for Navigation

In the attempt to be too clever, many Web page designers try to put navigation features in novel places. Don't! If you do, you are reducing the usability of your site. Through use, the left-hand side of the screen has become by far the most common place that users anticipate finding navigation information. Along the top of the page is also suitable for navigation items.

One particularly bad design I saw recently was one in which the designer had put critical navigation features on the right-hand side of the page and made the links animated GIF images. No one saw the crucial navigation items because the participants thought they were advertisements (remember: animation + right side of the page = noise).

Avoid Confusingly Redundant Navigation

It's a good idea to include some form of redundant navigation on your pages. For example, if you use an image map at the top of the page for your site's primary navigation, including a text-only set of links at the bottom of the page is helpful.

On the other hand, having two sets of navigation items on the page in the same visual field can be confusing. In screen shots Figure 5.10 and 5.11, notice that there are at least three main navigation sections to the page. How are these three sections different? What does it mean to the user that they are separated like that? Which is the right one to use?

Menu
Nutrition Guide
Store Locator
TACO BELL
TACO BELL MENU
|Gorditas | Tacos | Burritos | Specialties | Chalupas | Nachos & Sides | Breakfast |
Nutritional Info
TOSTADA - Flat corn tortilla topped with beans, red sauce, lettuce and cheddar cheese
MEXICAN PIZZA - Seasoned beef and beans between two crisp flour tortillas topped with pizza sauce, melted jack and cheddar cheese, tomatoes and green onions.
BIG BEEF MEXIMELT - Soft flour tortilla filled with seasoned beef, Pico de Gallo, and melted cheddar & pepper jack cheeses.
TACO SALAD - Crispy flour tortilla shell filled with beans, lettuce, seasoned beef, cheddar cheese, sour cream, tomatoes and green onions with a side of salsa dressing.
CHEESE QUESADILLA - Soft flour tortilla filled with melted cheddar and pepper jack cheeses and green sauce. Also available with grilled chicken
Copyright 1999, Taco Bell Corp. All rights reserved.
Legal Notices

FIGURE 5.10 *In this screen shot, you can see that the navigation system is somewhat chaotic; there is nothing consistent about it all through the site. Note too that the "clever" use of names for its seemingly top-level information areas leaves a bit too much to the imagination. Erm, exactly what is a "grindable?" ©2000 Taco Bell.*

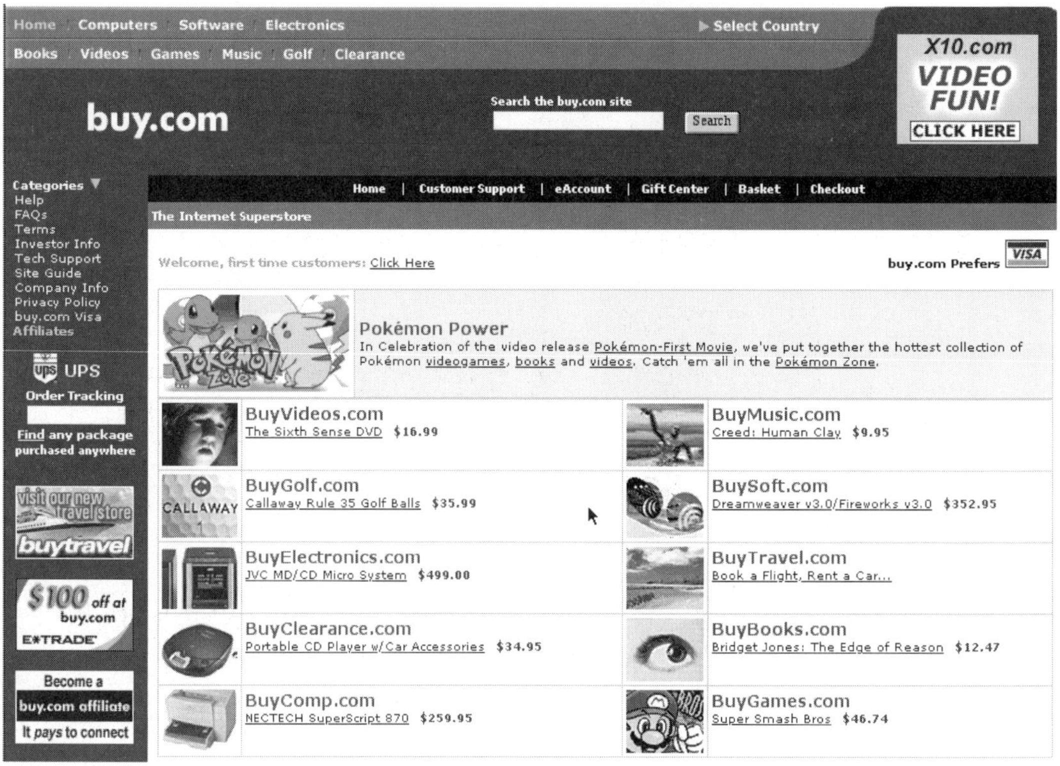
Home Computers Software Electronics
Select Country
Books Videos Games Music Golf Clearance
X10.com
VIDEO FUN!
CLICK HERE
buy.com
Search the buy.com site
Search
Categories
Help
FAQs
Terms
Investor Info
Tech Support
Site Guide
Company Info
Privacy Policy
buy.com Visa
Affiliates
Home | Customer Support | eAccount | Gift Center | Basket | Checkout
The Internet Superstore
Welcome, first time customers: Click Here
buy.com Prefers VISA
Pokémon Power
In Celebration of the video release Pokémon-First Movie, we've put together the hottest collection of Pokémon videogames, books and videos. Catch 'em all in the Pokémon Zone.
UPS
Order Tracking
Find any package purchased anywhere
BuyVideos.com
The Sixth Sense DVD $16.99
BuyMusic.com
Creed: Human Clay $9.95
BuyGolf.com
Callaway Rule 35 Golf Balls $35.99
BuySoft.com
Dreamweaver v3.0/Fireworks v3.0 $352.95
visit our new travel store
buytravel
BuyElectronics.com
JVC MD/CD Micro System $499.00
BuyTravel.com
Book a Flight, Rent a Car...
$100 off at buy.com
E*TRADE
BuyClearance.com
Portable CD Player w/Car Accessories $34.95
BuyBooks.com
Bridget Jones: The Edge of Reason $12.47
Become a buy.com affiliate
It pays to connect
BuyComp.com
NECTECH SuperScript 870 $259.95
BuyGames.com
Super Smash Bros $46.74

FIGURE 5.11 *Here's an example of a site that has a potentially confusing multitier navigation system. For instance, what's the difference between the two "Home" links? © 2000 Buy.com.*

Provide Supplemental Navigation

Part of what makes up a person is individual preferences. People learn in different ways; similarly, people have different habits for navigating your Web site. You should provide the basic three modes of navigation: *links on each page, a site map, and a search engine.* (See Figures 5.12 and 5.13.)

Make Links Self-Explanatory

Be careful how you word hyperlinked text. Try to make it as descriptive of the destination as possible. Don't leave your user guessing as to the purpose of a link or where it will lead.

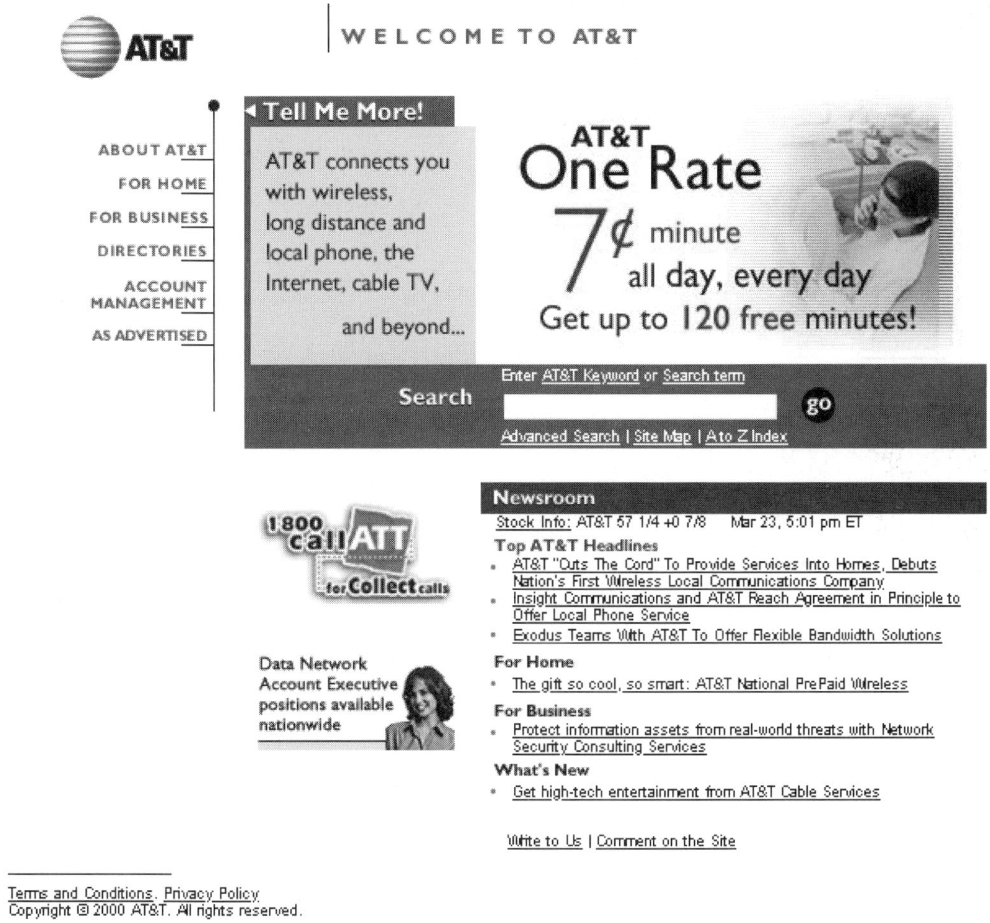
WELCOME TO AT&T
ABOUT AT&T
FOR HOME
FOR BUSINESS
DIRECTORIES
ACCOUNT MANAGEMENT
AS ADVERTISED
Tell Me More!
AT&T connects you with wireless, long distance and local phone, the Internet, cable TV, and beyond...
AT&T One Rate
7¢ minute all day, every day
Get up to 120 free minutes!
Search
Enter AT&T Keyword or Search term
go
Advanced Search | Site Map | A to Z Index
1800 call ATT for Collect calls
Data Network Account Executive positions available nationwide
Newsroom
Stock Info: AT&T 57 1/4 +0 7/8 Mar 23, 5:01 pm ET
Top AT&T Headlines
AT&T "Cuts The Cord" To Provide Services Into Homes, Debuts Nation's First Wireless Local Communications Company
Insight Communications and AT&T Reach Agreement in Principle to Offer Local Phone Service
Exodus Teams With AT&T To Offer Flexible Bandwidth Solutions
For Home
The gift so cool, so smart: AT&T National PrePaid Wireless
For Business
Protect information assets from real-world threats with Network Security Consulting Services
What's New
Get high-tech entertainment from AT&T Cable Services
Write to Us | Comment on the Site
Terms and Conditions. Privacy Policy
Copyright © 2000 AT&T. All rights reserved.

FIGURE 5.12 *Note that although this Web page has some usability problems, the designers have at least enabled the user to use four types of navigation: a site map, standard navigation, an alphabetical index, and a search engine. Unfortunately, the site map and alpha index are accessible only from the home page. ©2000 AT&T.*

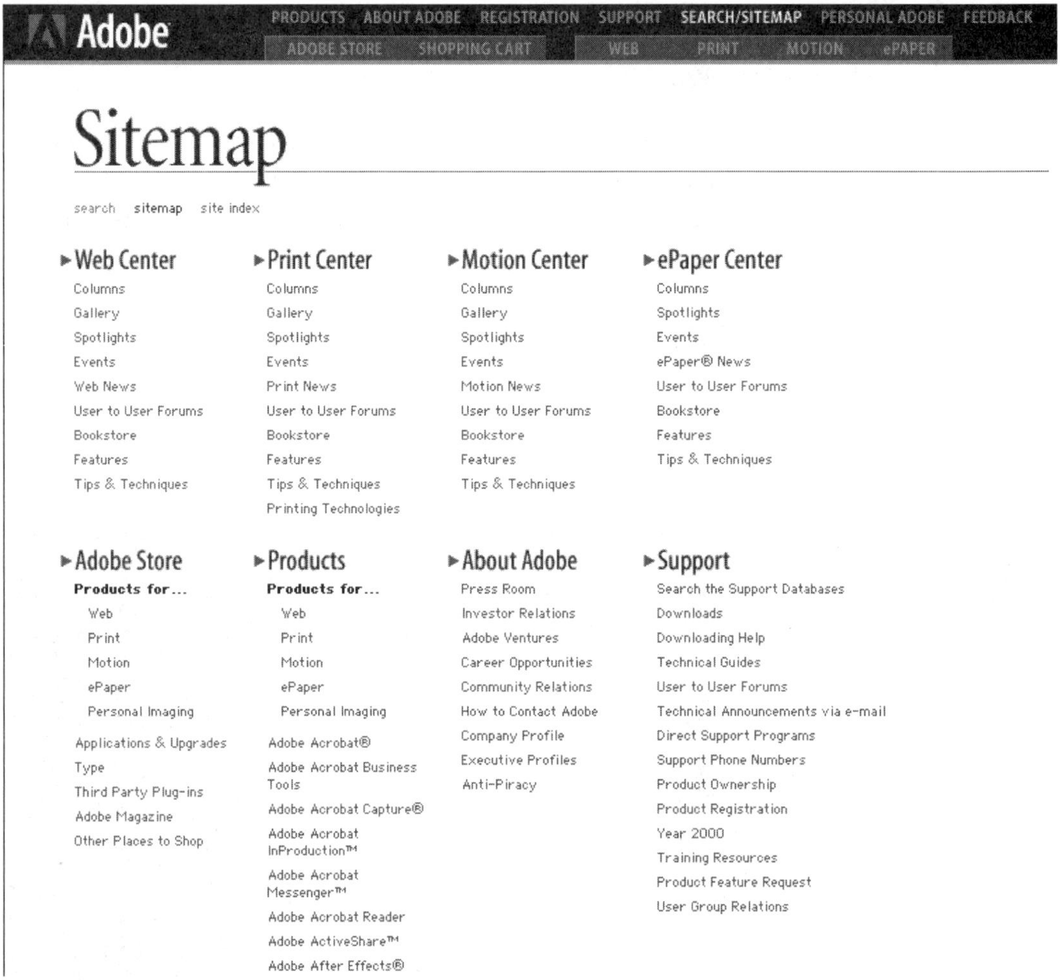
Adobe
PRODUCTS
ABOUT ADOBE
REGISTRATION
SUPPORT
SEARCH/SITEMAP
PERSONAL ADOBE
FEEDBACK
ADOBE STORE
SHOPPING CART
WEB
PRINT
MOTION
ePAPER
Sitemap
search sitemap site index
Web Center
Columns
Gallery
Spotlights
Events
Web News
User to User Forums
Bookstore
Features
Tips & Techniques
Print Center
Columns
Gallery
Spotlights
Events
Print News
User to User Forums
Bookstore
Features
Tips & Techniques
Printing Technologies
Motion Center
Columns
Gallery
Spotlights
Events
Motion News
User to User Forums
Bookstore
Features
Tips & Techniques
ePaper Center
Columns
Spotlights
Events
ePaper® News
User to User Forums
Bookstore
Features
Tips & Techniques
Adobe Store
Products for...
Web
Print
Motion
ePaper
Personal Imaging
Applications & Upgrades
Type
Third Party Plug-ins
Adobe Magazine
Other Places to Shop
Products
Products for...
Web
Print
Motion
ePaper
Personal Imaging
Adobe Acrobat®
Adobe Acrobat Business Tools
Adobe Acrobat Capture®
Adobe Acrobat InProduction™
Adobe Acrobat Messenger™
Adobe Acrobat Reader
Adobe ActiveShare™
Adobe After Effects®
About Adobe
Press Room
Investor Relations
Adobe Ventures
Career Opportunities
Community Relations
How to Contact Adobe
Company Profile
Executive Profiles
Anti-Piracy
Support
Search the Support Databases
Downloads
Downloading Help
Technical Guides
User to User Forums
Technical Announcements via e-mail
Direct Support Programs
Support Phone Numbers
Product Ownership
Product Registration
Year 2000
Training Resources
Product Feature Request
User Group Relations

FIGURE 5.13 *Here's another example of a supplemental method of navigation: the site map. ©2000 Adobe Systems.*

Don't Bury Links

Early Web authors insisted that hyperlinks should be part of the normal flow of text. Unfortunately, in practice, this doesn't work. Avoid burying links in the body of a paragraph. The number of users who still click only when they see the words "Click here" is frighteningly large.

OTHER NICETIES

Consider WebTV

All WebTV-based systems in North America and Japan (both use the NTSC television standard) display Web pages in a fixed 544 by 372 pixel screen space. This means that if you want your pages to be usable by people using this device, you'll need to observe this rule for real estate. For more information on WebTV design, visit *developer.webtv.net/design/designguide/Default.htm.* (See Figure 5.14.)

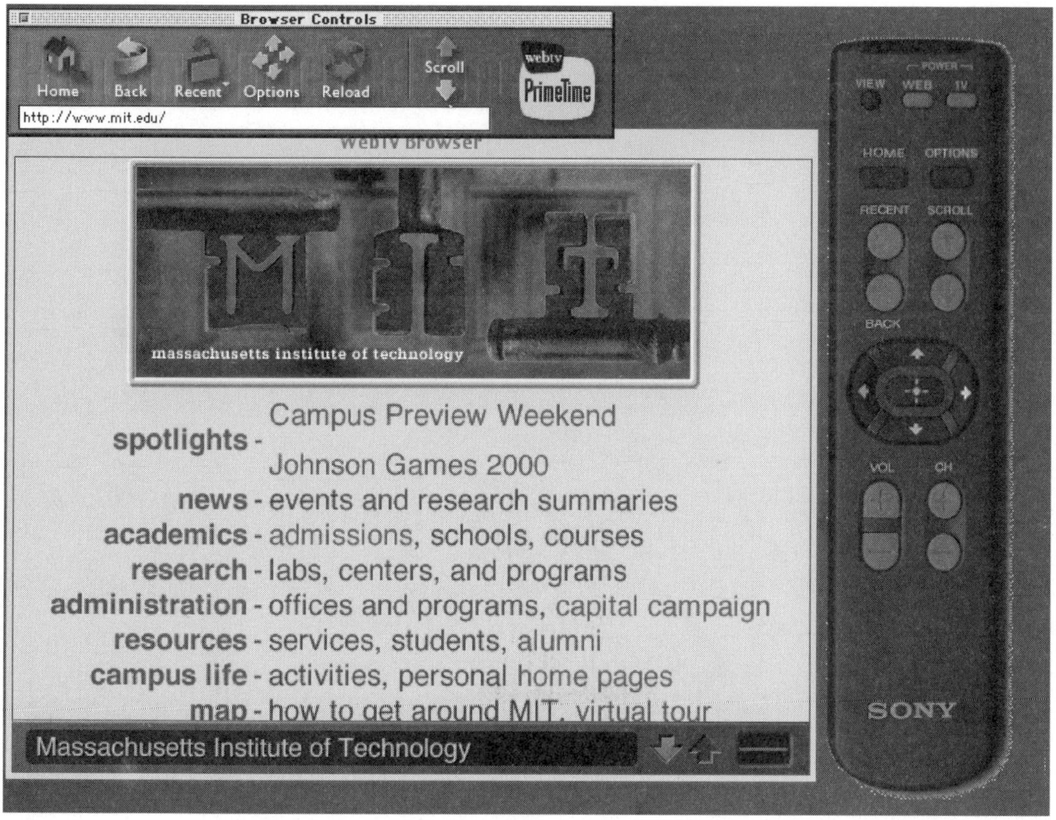
Browser Controls
Home
Back
Recent
Options
Reload
Scroll
webtv
PrimeTime
http://www.mit.edu/
massachusetts institute of technology
Campus Preview Weekend
spotlights -
Johnson Games 2000
news - events and research summaries
academics - admissions, schools, courses
research - labs, centers, and programs
administration - offices and programs, capital campaign
resources - services, students, alumni
campus life - activities, personal home pages
Massachusetts Institute of Technology
HOME
OPTIONS
RECENT
SCROLL
BACK
VOL
CH
SONY

FIGURE 5.14 *The WebTV emulator is just the beginning of the type of tool that developers will likely need to use in the near future as Web appliances become more common.*

Provide a "You Are Here" Feature

Sometimes this feature is called a "trail of bread crumbs" because it is a visual way of letting the user know where he or she is on the site. Some people use the "bread crumbs" as a navigational tool; others simply like to look at it to know where they are on the site. (See Figure 5.15.)

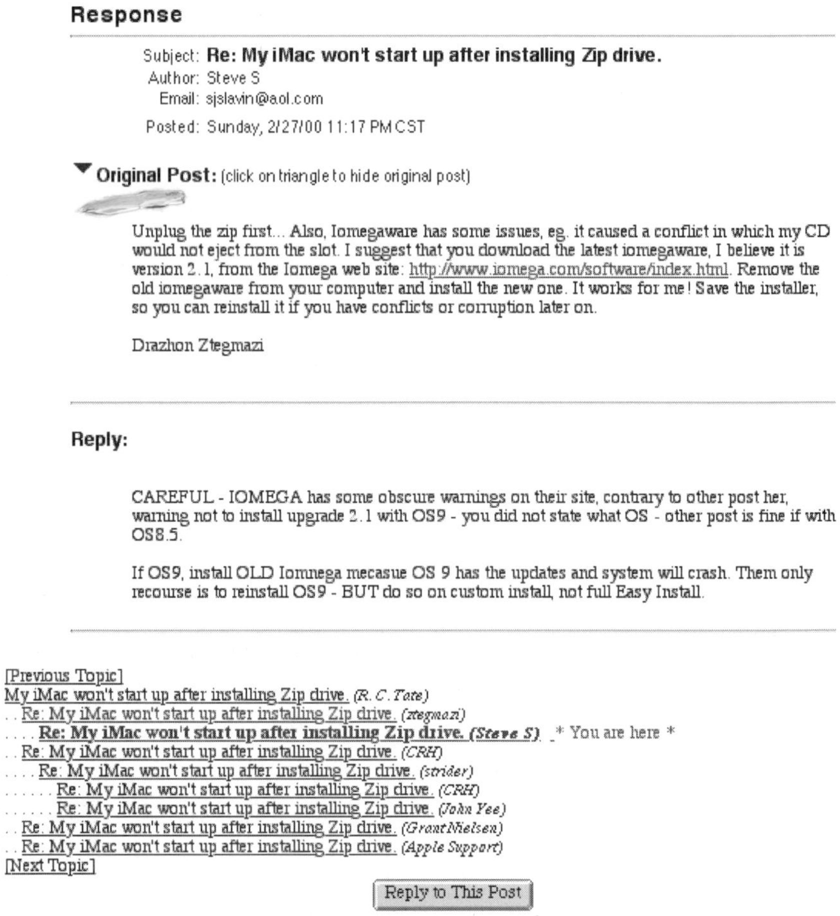
Response
Subject: Re: My iMac won't start up after installing Zip drive.
Author: Steve S
Email: sjslavin@aol.com
Posted: Sunday, 2/27/00 11:17 PM CST
Original Post: (click on triangle to hide original post)
Unplug the zip first... Also, Iomegaware has some issues, eg. it caused a conflict in which my CD would not eject from the slot. I suggest that you download the latest iomegaware, I believe it is version 2.1, from the Iomega web site: http://www.iomega.com/software/index.html. Remove the old iomegaware from your computer and install the new one. It works for me! Save the installer, so you can reinstall it if you have conflicts or corruption later on.
Drazhon Ztegmazi
Reply:
CAREFUL - IOMEGA has some obscure warnings on their site, contrary to other post her, warning not to install upgrade 2.1 with OS9 - you did not state what OS - other post is fine if with OS8.5.
If OS9, install OLD Iomnega mecasue OS 9 has the updates and system will crash. Them only recourse is to reinstall OS9 - BUT do so on custom install, not full Easy Install.
[Previous Topic]
My iMac won't start up after installing Zip drive. (R. C. Tate)
.. Re: My iMac won't start up after installing Zip drive. (ztegmazi)
.... Re: My iMac won't start up after installing Zip drive. (Steve S) * You are here *
.. Re: My iMac won't start up after installing Zip drive. (CRH)
.... Re: My iMac won't start up after installing Zip drive. (strider)
...... Re: My iMac won't start up after installing Zip drive. (CRH)
...... Re: My iMac won't start up after installing Zip drive. (John Yee)
.. Re: My iMac won't start up after installing Zip drive. (Grant Nielsen)
.. Re: My iMac won't start up after installing Zip drive. (Apple Support)
[Next Topic]
Reply to This Post

FIGURE 5.15 *Note that in this screen shot and the one in Figure 5.16, the site authors have provided a sort of orientation system to let users know their whereabouts on the site. This one does so through a listing at the bottom of the page. ©2000 Iomega*

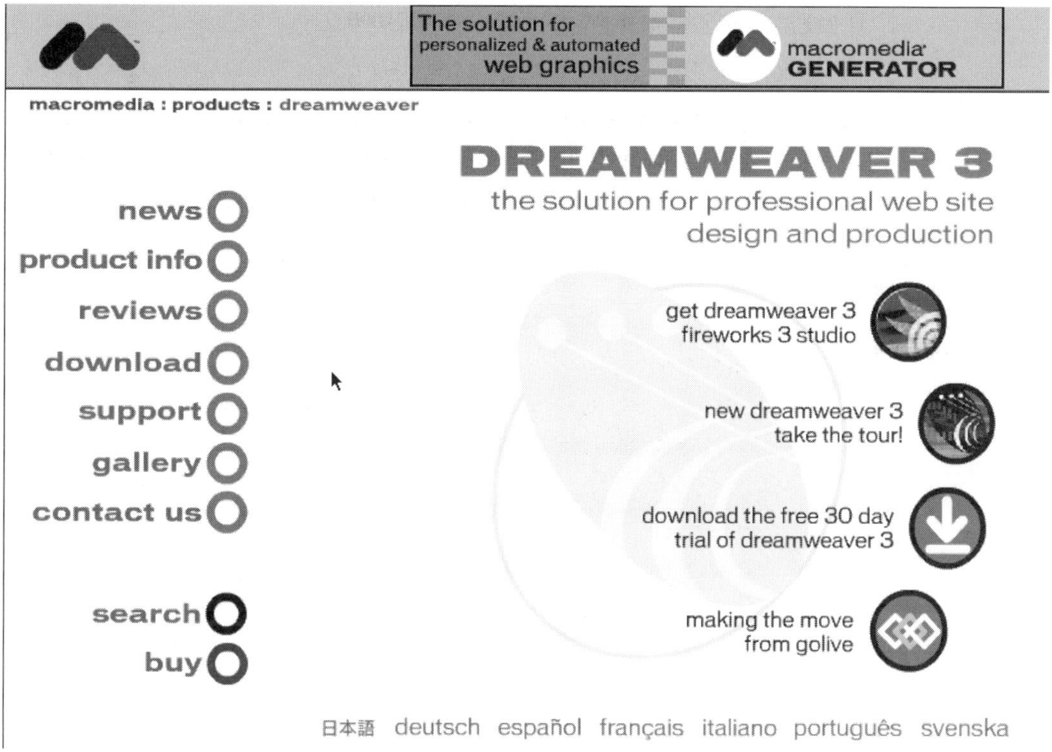
The solution for
personalized & automated
web graphics
macromedia
GENERATOR
macromedia : products : dreamweaver
DREAMWEAVER 3
the solution for professional web site
design and production
news
product info
reviews
download
support
gallery
contact us
search
buy
get dreamweaver 3
fireworks 3 studio
new dreamweaver 3
take the tour!
download the free 30 day
trial of dreamweaver 3
making the move
from golive
日本語 deutsch español français italiano português svenska

FIGURE 5.16 *This site helps orient the user via the icons at left. ©2000 Macromedia.*

Use Four or Fewer Colors for Table Legends

If you plan to create a data table that utilizes color as a means of differentiating types of data, you should limit yourself to four colors total, with six as an absolute outside number. When you use tons of colors for table information, you not only make it harder for users with a color deficiency to use your site, but you also make your table more confusing for people with "perfect" color vision.

In reality, the more colors you use, the less distinction you can actually make between colors that might be confused with one another. It's far more distinctive to use color sparingly, to highlight only one or two key points or ideas, or to make clear the commonality among items in categories.

Don't Be Too Clever

You might think that it's cute to take a nautical theme and apply it to your boating Web site. But calling common parts of the site, such as the site map, user help, and ordering information, "Sextant," "Landlubbers Only," and "Treasure Chest" will result in confused, even if slightly amused, users. Stick with names that the user knows and uses regularly; save the clever ideas for greeting cards. (See Figures 5.17 and 5.18.)

I'm here!
Love your Car
Joy Ride
Facts & Figures
Thanks!
Feedback
Help
I'm here!

FIGURE 5.17 *The person who designed this site probably had a lot of fun using Kai's Power Tools. The navigational items are subdued, activating in a mysterious fashion only when the mouse rolls over an item. ©2000 Volkswagen.*

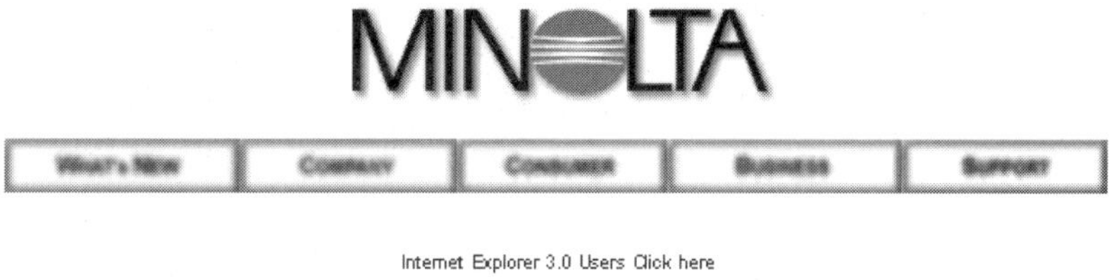
MINOLTA
Internet Explorer 3.0 Users Click here

FIGURE 5.18 *This is another example of a theme that has been taken too far. The trick is that when the user rolls his or her mouse over the fuzzy test, it "snaps" into focus. However, if you have disabled JavaScript or if you just don't have it at all, you're stuck with rubbing your eyes two or three times when you try to navigate this site. ©2000 Minolta.*

Provide Alternative Content

Make sure that you include a text-only version of your site, accessible from every page, for users who cannot use graphics for one reason or another (users without sight, users of devices such as PDAs that aren't able to display graphics, and so on).

Another strong argument for using good text content for your site is that indexing and search engines can't index your site if it's made of only images! (See Figure 5.19.)

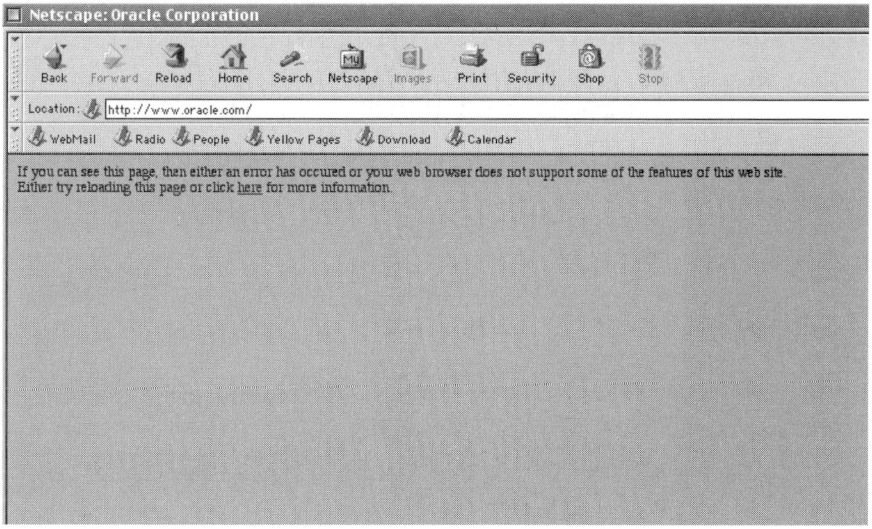
Netscape: Oracle Corporation
Back
Forward
Reload
Home
Search
Netscape
Images
Print
Security
Shop
Stop
Location: http://www.oracle.com/
WebMail
Radio
People
Yellow Pages
Download
Calendar
If you can see this page, then either an error has occured or your web browser does not support some of the features of this web site.
Either try reloading this page or click here for more information.

FIGURE 5-19 *This page comes from Oracle. You lose, game over. ©2000 Oracle.*

Use ALT Attributes in Image Tags

When you do use images, observe this simple rule to make your site more accessible to everyone: use ALT attributes in your image tags so that people who can't see the graphics can at least access the description of the items.

By the way, one tip for ALT attribute content: Always put a period at the end of your ALT descriptions. That way people who use speech synthesizer readers don't have to hear a long run-on sentence.

Repeat Images Where Possible

To help reduce download time, try to reuse images as much as possible. Once an image has been downloaded to a user's hard drive, it remains in the browser cache for a while. You can enhance your ability to reuse images by dissecting large images into smaller ones, such as navigational images. That way, if you change one small part of the main navigational system to let the user know his or her current location, you can just update that small part of the image and reuse the rest.

Several tools can help you do this, such as Macromedia Fireworks and Adobe Photoshop. (This feature used to be in the Adobe product ImageReady, but it has now been absorbed—kind of—by Photoshop.)

Use Cross-Linking

Ever spend an hour looking for your flashlight after your roommate, spouse, parent, significant other, or pet komodo dragon rearranged your room to be "better organized"? Hoo boy. Not everyone looks for items in the same place, and a big problem with finding things on the Web is that designers pretend to be the authorities on where items should be categorized. When you're designing your site, take my advice: do some card sorting with real users; they will show you where the things should really go. If items consistently end up in more than one pile, cross-link them. (See Figure 5.20.)

administration
about mit
academics
research
resources
groups
news
These are MIT's administrative offices listed by name. If you are looking for a particular service but do not know the organizational unit that provides it, please try the resources listings, or search for an office or program in the directory.
Academic Resource Center
Academic Services (formerly Registrar, UAA)
Adaptive Technology
Admissions Office
Alumni Association
Archives
Arts, Office of the
Athletics Office
Audio Visual Service
Audit Division
Benefits Office
Biosafety Office
Bursar's Office
Campus Activities Complex
Campus Police
Career Services
Central Machine Shop
Cogeneration Facility
Communications Office (PRS)
Computer Connection
Controller's Accounting Office (CAO)
Conference Services
Copy Technology Centers
Corporate Relations, Office of
Corporation, the MIT
Counseling and Support Services
Credit Union
Dean for Graduate Education
Dean of Students and Undergraduate Education (ODSUE)
Disabilities Services Office
Division of Comparative Medicine
Document Services
Endicott House
Engineering Systems Division (ESD)
International Scholars Office
International Students Office
Learning Center
Lemelson-MIT Prize: Invention Dimension
Libraries
Mail Services
Medical Department
Minority Education
MIT Cable Television
MIT Card
MIT Museum
MIT Press
Music and Theater Arts
News Office
Ombuds Office
Parking
Personnel Office see Human Resources)
Physical Plant (see Facilities)
Planning Office
Policies and Procedures
Procurement Office
Property Office
Public Service Center
Publishing Services Bureau
Radiation Protection Office
Reengineering Project
Registrar's Office (see Academic Services)
Residential Life and Student Life Programs
Resource Development
Safety Office
Space Accounting (Previously OFMS)
Special Community Services
Sponsored Programs, Office of (OSP)
Student Employment Office

FIGURE 5.20 *One of MIT's Web pages that has what could be an unmanageable amount of information; fortunately, the designer simply alphabetized the items instead of trying to constrain them to some arbitrary form that makes sense to only a few people. Note how several items are cross-referenced to facilitate discovery. ©2000 Massachusetts Institute of Technology.*

Avoid Animation Altogether

One of the biggest eyesores of the current generation of Web sites is the ubiquitous animated GIF. As more designers use animation for bothersome banner ads and other extraneous information, fewer users are responding to them.

If you do need to use animation for your site, try to use it sparingly. It is possible to use animation to convey useful information. (See Figure 5.21.)

ZDNet | Reviews | Shopping | Business | Help | News | Investing | GameSpot | Tech Life | Downloads | Developer
ZDNet COMPUTER SHOPPER.com
MicroWAREHOUSE
Click Here for HOT Products from Microwarehouse...
ZDNet > computershopper.com
SPOTLIGHT
THE MALL
TECH WATCH
Search:
All Categories
GO
Welcome
need help?
Products
Desktops Digital Cameras Graphics Cards Handhelds Memory Monitors Motherboards Notebooks Printers Upgrades Scanners Software Storage... Complete List
Brands
Canon Compaq CyberMax Dell Epson Gateway HP Toshiba Viewsonic... Complete List
Specialty Shopping
College Shopping ZDNet Auctions Technology Bookstore Outlet Store Consumer Electronics AMD Athlon Showcase
Shopping Services
Buyer's Alert delivers the latest shopping news to your in-box.
Enter E-Mail
Sign Up
Subscribe to Computer Shopper Magazine
Find great savings with ZDNet e-centives
Computer Shopper Magazine
Dell Home Computing
Shopping Tips
Product Reviews
Smart Shopper
College Guide
Safe Shopping Tips
How To Buy Guides
Computer Cures Forum
Compaq Presario
5700T
The ultimate gaming machine
WEEKLY SPECIALS
Sponsored by
Desktops
GO
LIVE AUCTIONS!
Powered by:
ONSALE
Gateway
Connect with us.
DELL
GIGABUYS
SOFTWARE and ACCESSORIES
eCOST.com
CLICK HERE!
Or Pay More
FREE SHIPPING
The computer store inside your computer.
egghead.com
go!
CYBER WAREHOUSE
emachines etower 333
$299.99
Cyrix MII 333-2.1GB-32MB
ViewSonic
INTEL® PROCESSORS
Desktops
Notebooks
Need More Help?
intel. WebOutfitter
Pentium III processors
BUY IT NOW FROM:
MIDWEST MICRO PC Solutions
TOSHIBA
FUJITSU BUY PC DIRECT
Gateway Connect with us.
MicronPC.com

FIGURE 5.21 *Obviously this book cannot show you the animation on this Web page, but this page has a lot of it. It's still going to take a while for designers to grasp the fact that making the Web more like TV is not necessarily a good thing; even if it were a good thing, using excess animation isn't the best solution. ©2000 Computer Shopper.*

Don't Use Images That Look Like Ads

Critical navigation elements of a site should look like just what they are—navigation elements. This may sound simple enough, but so many sites violate this principle, it's positively frightening! In the screen shot in Figure 5.22 and 5.23, notice the "Call me now" icon on the left side of the screen. This is actually a very important link, but because it uses ambiguous labeling and because it looks like a button, it is very possible that people won't understand how to use it. It looks like an ad, and many users avoid clicking on ads.

Authoria
WHAT IF YOUR HR DEPARTMENT NEVER CLOSED?
PRODUCTS
CUSTOMER PROFILES
PARTNERS
EVENTS
NEWS
COMPANY
CAREERS
CONTACT US
Looking for Answers?
What is a knowledgebase?
How can I deploy an effective call center?
Why Authoria?
CALL ME NOW
"Before Authoria HR, our HR service center earned less than 40% employee satisfaction rating.
After implementing the product, satisfaction soared to 92%."*
What Authoria Can Do For You
Authoria Announces New Product Authoria Outsourcer
Select Customers...
Sprint
Hot News
Authoria and Towers Perrin Partner to Provide Companies with Web-based HR Solutions
Waltham, Mass and New York - February 22, 2000
Authoria Announces New Product - Authoria Outsourcer
Register
TOP TEN WINNER HUMAN RESOURCE EXECUTIVE 1998 HR PRODUCT
AUTHORIA 2000

FIGURE 5.22 *Thanks to the relentless hammering of animated GIFs and other clutter of the "Webiverse," users may tune out items that look like ads, such as the "Call me now" image on this site. ©2000 Authoria.*

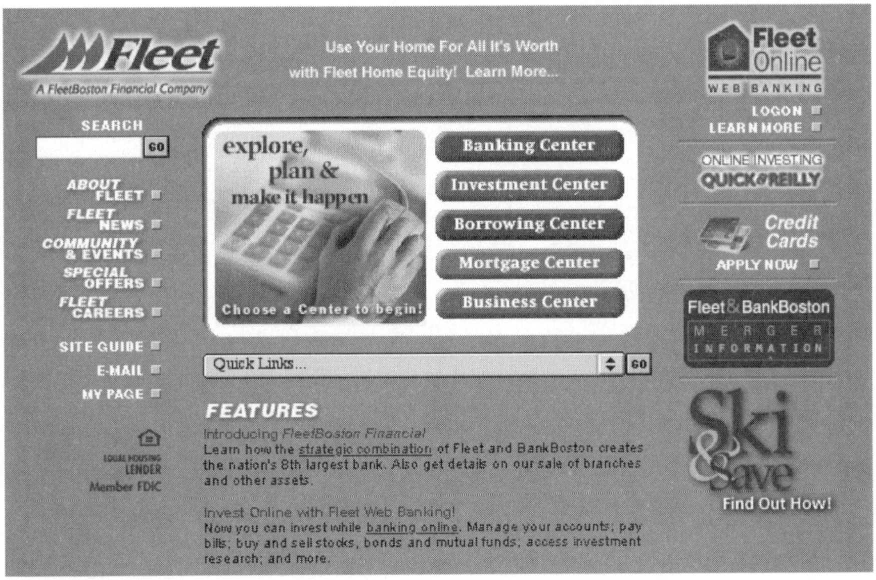

Fleet
A FleetBoston Financial Company
Use Your Home For All It's Worth with Fleet Home Equity! Learn More...
Fleet Online
WEB BANKING
LOGON
LEARN MORE
SEARCH
GO
ABOUT FLEET
FLEET NEWS
COMMUNITY & EVENTS
SPECIAL OFFERS
FLEET CAREERS
SITE GUIDE
E-MAIL
MY PAGE
explore, plan & make it happen
Choose a Center to begin!
Banking Center
Investment Center
Borrowing Center
Mortgage Center
Business Center
Quick Links...
ONLINE INVESTING
QUICK & REILLY
Credit Cards
APPLY NOW
Fleet & BankBoston MERGER INFORMATION
FEATURES
Introducing FleetBoston Financial
Learn how the strategic combination of Fleet and BankBoston creates the nation's 8th largest bank. Also get details on our sale of branches and other assets.
Invest Online with Fleet Web Banking!
Now you can invest while banking online. Manage your accounts; pay bills; buy and sell stocks, bonds and mutual funds; access investment research; and more.
EQUAL HOUSING LENDER
Member FDIC
Ski & Save
Find Out How!

FIGURE 5.23 *Once again, look at all the navigational items that ought to be "real" navigational items. In several studies users failed to see these types of icons outright at least 70 percent of the time. ©2000 Fleet Bank.*

Don't Include Broken Links

It's easy to automate the process of checking links on your site to update links to sites that become defunct. There are Perl scripts or commercial products that do this. Yet the Web is full of broken links; even Fortune 500 sites have broken links.

Monitor User Search Words

If users tend to search for the same words or concepts on your site frequently, it's probably a sign that you need to improve the visibility of that information.

Make a Sitewide Search Feature Available on Every Page

Search tools are necessary on all but the tiniest Web sites. Although you should never plan on the search engine being the primary navigation method for your site, it's a good idea to make the engine available from every page.

It can be very confusing if you have two search engines on your site that perform two different tasks.

Don't Include a Web Search Engine on Your Site

It is perfectly okay to include a search engine on your site, as long as the search engine searches only your site, not the entire Web. Users know where to go to find a whole-Web search engine; it is confusing and frustrating to use a site's search engine that searches the whole Web when all you want to find is whether an item exists on that site.

Be Careful with Metaphors

Although the use of metaphor in design can be quite effective in enabling users to understand the site better, the improper use of metaphor is far more destructive than constructive. Some common mistakes in metaphor use include the following:

- Too many metaphors cause confusion because of too many signals.
- Clashing or mixed metaphors are not only stylistically bad, they are confusing to users.
- Metaphors that do not make sense to the user are worthless. Just because a metaphor about memory segmentation faults makes sense to you, that might not be true of your users. Not everyone is a programmer, and your metaphor could sound like nonsense to nonprogrammers. Even worse, the metaphor might sound like something entirely different from what you intend!
- Don't paint yourself into a corner. If you choose to use a metaphor, you can't decide to use it only when it's convenient or when it pleases you, or there will be a break in continuity. You can force yourself into contrived situations when you choose a weak metaphor.

Perform Usability Tests on Competitors' Sites

"Knowing thy user" also means knowing thy competition! Doing a usability assessment of your competitors' sites can arm you with an advantage.

Don't Overuse Emphasis

Remember the horrible capitalized paragraph from Chapter 4? Reserve emphasis items, such as bold text, italics, or other attention-getting techniques, for really important, sparse usage. Doing so will help ensure that when you do need to use emphasis, your users will not have attained sensory adaptation levels.

Use "Bleeding-Edge" Technology Sparingly

Just because the latest version of the new Zap technology has hit the shelves, there's no inherent, compelling reason you should use it. In fact, you should lag behind just a little to make sure that any bugs in the new technology get sorted out before you plunge your site design into it. (See Figures 5.24–5.26.)

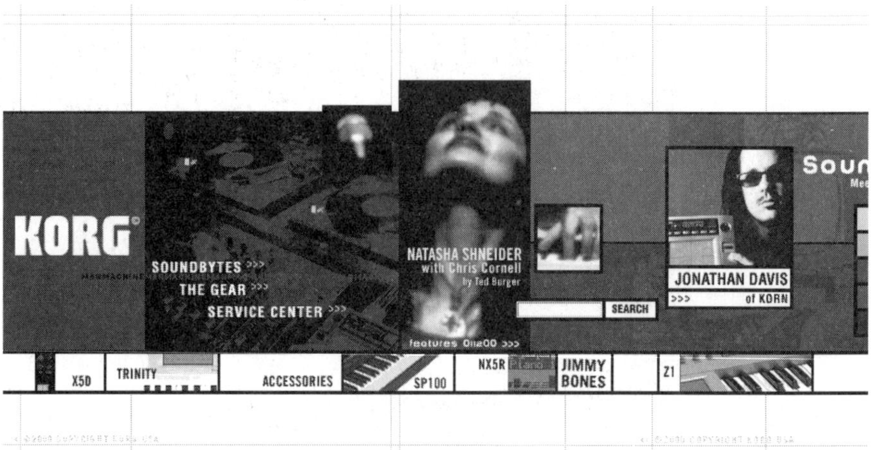
KORG
SOUNDBYTES >>>
THE GEAR >>>
SERVICE CENTER >>>
NATASHA SHNEIDER
with Chris Cornell
SEARCH
JONATHAN DAVIS
>>> of KORN
X5D
TRINITY
ACCESSORIES
SP100
NX5R
JIMMY BONES
Z1

FIGURE 5.24 *This site should certainly win a design award. It uses a lot of DHTML features to make the site move, shake, and shimmy. Here's how it ended up looking in my browser. ©2000 Korg.*

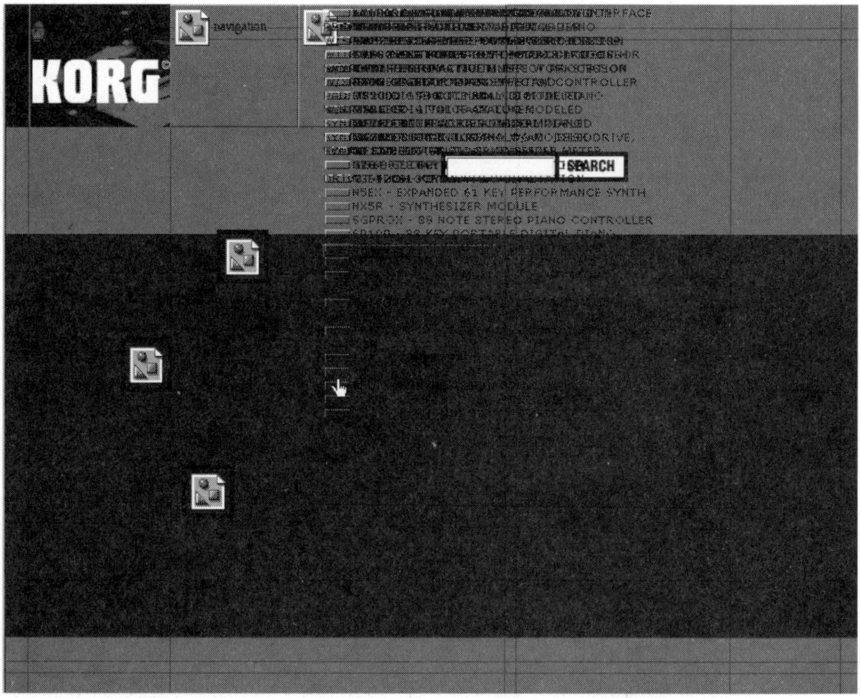
KORG
SEARCH

FIGURE 5.25 *Make sure that you thoroughly test new technologies before you commit to them. It pays to have a site that is slightly less buzzword compliant but robust. ©2000 Korg.*

PHILIPS
Search
Contact Us
Global Home
Let's make things better
Welcome to Philips USA Consumer Electronics
Philips USA home
innovative!
Philips 13" NuVision TV
A Sense of Style
See Demo!
Shelf System with CDR
Write your own mix.
Philips sponsors new sports arena
Catch a
this April!
Register now for a chance to win a Philips Personal TV Receiver with TiVo Service
"The best new consumer electronics product in 20 years" - ETown
SITE MAP
HELP
PRIVACY PROMISE
TM & COPYRIGHT

FIGURE 5.26 *This site also uses DHTML to provide a menu-driven system. This is all fine and good, but make sure that if a user cannot access the DHTML features of the site, he or she can still navigate to at least a page containing the top-level items. In addition, this site contains a major "don't": tiny blue text, virtually impossible to read, on top of a blue background. That's a formula for inaccessibility for a lot of people. ©2000 Philips.*

Use Easy-to-Understand URLs

Unfortunately, all the good domain names have already been taken (as of the writing of this book, the only domain names left are *www.powercabbage.com* and *www.death-by-oatmeal.com.*[1] So it might be hard to get domain names that are easy to remember without lots of advertising.

Nonetheless, one thing that you can control is the naming convention that you use inside your site for pages and directories. Making directory

[1] Just kidding. Those are taken, too.

names that map to the contained concepts can help people find their way around. For example, it's convenient to be able to go to *www.apple.com/macos* to see the latest information on the Macintosh operating system.

Please note that you should never rely on such a convention as a primary means of navigating a Web site. You still have to provide clear and helpful navigation for your site, regardless of your directory naming convention.

Text vs. Icon Navigation

Which is better, text-based navigation or icon-based navigation (see Figure 5.27). They both are good, depending on the situation. Text is the hands-down winner when a user is unfamiliar with a site, but icons

Welcome to Travelocity.com!
Travelocity.com
A Sabre Company
Exclusive Offer
Spring Fares from $59
Find/Book a Flight
Find/Rent a Car
Find/Reserve a Hotel
Vacations & Cruises
Special Deals
Destination Guide
Travel Tools
Reservations
Todays Deals
Information/Guides
Fare Watcher
Find the best fare for your roundtrip flight now!
Go!
Vacation Finder Express
Any Destination
Any Month
Any Price
Partners
BRITISH AIRWAYS
Special Offers
keep the clutter away! win a Visor™
FREE OKLAHOMA GETAWAY
Last Minute Ski Deals! click now!
Travel Tips
Travel News
Featured Vacations
Featured Destinations
Road Warrior
VISA
The World's Best Way To Pay

FIGURE 5.27 *Look at this screen shot and try to find the link for reserving a hotel. Once you find it, think about how you located it. Did the icon help you? Or did the text? Could you have located the link if one of the two had been missing? Under what conditions do icons work best? When does text work best? © 2000. Sabre Inc.*

have a much quicker recognition rate when the user knows what they mean. Therefore, you should provide a parallel mechanism that supports both: text for novice users of your site and icons for power users.

Breadth vs. Depth

Popular belief has it that it is better to create a "wide" Web site (one that has many links on each page, minimizing the number of clicks that a user has to make before arriving at the desired information) than a "narrow" one (fewer links per page but more clicks to get to information). My experience has tended to corroborate this notion.

Note that if you do use the "wide" approach to site design, you need to also employ lots of other techniques to make your pages manageable by the user. Chunking information and using spatial cues effectively can help in this regard.

Plan Default Fonts

Wouldn't it be nice if you could use any font in the world to create your Web pages? Wouldn't it be nice if everyone who then viewed your site would see it the same way? Unfortunately, this scenario isn't a reality yet.

Instead, always make sure that your pages look right using the system default fonts for each operating system, and use CSS to ensure that if one font isn't available, another suitable one can substitute.

Make Printer-Friendly Pages

If you have to use lots of text, especially if you must break the text up over a series of pages, make sure that a printable version of the document (either a PDF file or just one giant HTML file) is also available on the site (see Figure 5.28).

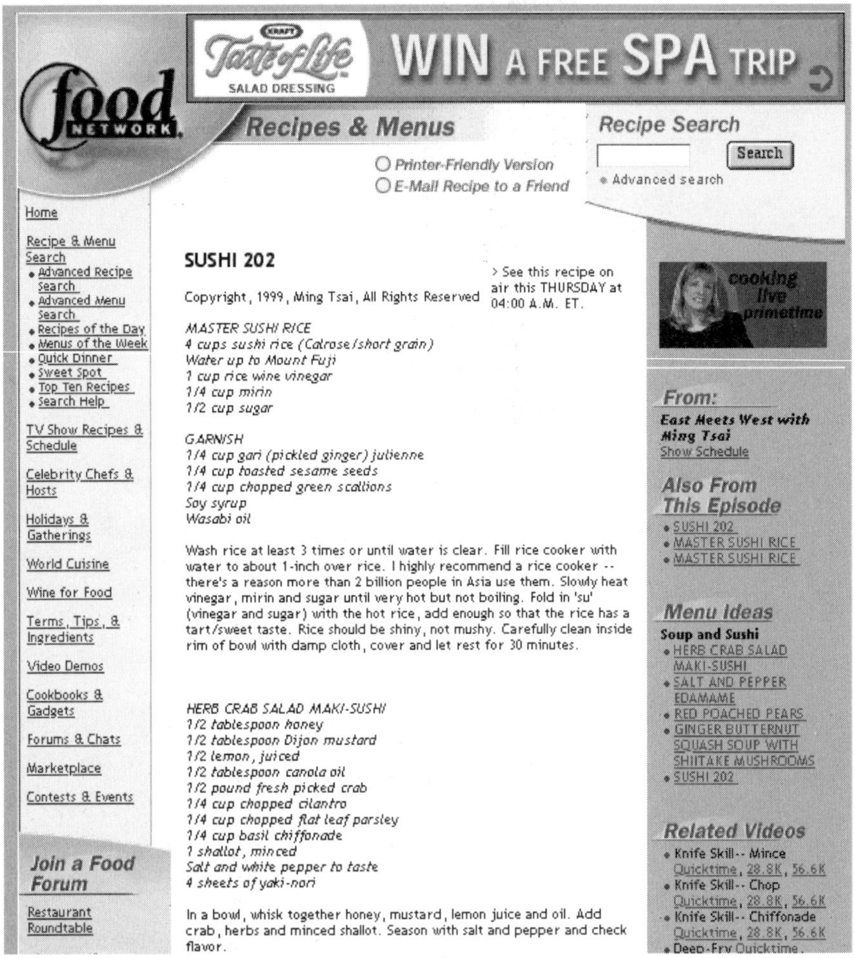
food NETWORK
Taste of Life SALAD DRESSING
WIN A FREE SPA TRIP
Recipes & Menus
Recipe Search
Search
Advanced search
Printer-Friendly Version
E-Mail Recipe to a Friend
Home
Recipe & Menu Search
Advanced Recipe Search
Advanced Menu Search
Recipes of the Day
Menus of the Week
Quick Dinner
Sweet Spot
Top Ten Recipes
Search Help
TV Show Recipes & Schedule
Celebrity Chefs & Hosts
Holidays & Gatherings
World Cuisine
Wine for Food
Terms, Tips, & Ingredients
Video Demos
Cookbooks & Gadgets
Forums & Chats
Marketplace
Contests & Events
Join a Food Forum
Restaurant Roundtable
SUSHI 202
Copyright, 1999, Ming Tsai, All Rights Reserved
> See this recipe on air this THURSDAY at 04:00 A.M. ET.
MASTER SUSHI RICE
4 cups sushi rice (Calrose/short grain)
Water up to Mount Fuji
1 cup rice wine vinegar
1/4 cup mirin
1/2 cup sugar
GARNISH
1/4 cup gari (pickled ginger) julienne
1/4 cup toasted sesame seeds
1/4 cup chopped green scallions
Soy syrup
Wasabi oil
Wash rice at least 3 times or until water is clear. Fill rice cooker with water to about 1-inch over rice. I highly recommend a rice cooker -- there's a reason more than 2 billion people in Asia use them. Slowly heat vinegar, mirin and sugar until very hot but not boiling. Fold in 'su' (vinegar and sugar) with the hot rice, add enough so that the rice has a tart/sweet taste. Rice should be shiny, not mushy. Carefully clean inside rim of bowl with damp cloth, cover and let rest for 30 minutes.
HERB CRAB SALAD MAKI-SUSHI
1/2 tablespoon honey
1/2 tablespoon Dijon mustard
1/2 lemon, juiced
1/2 tablespoon canola oil
1/2 pound fresh picked crab
1/4 cup chopped cilantro
1/4 cup chopped flat leaf parsley
1/4 cup basil chiffonade
1 shallot, minced
Salt and white pepper to taste
4 sheets of yaki-nori
In a bowl, whisk together honey, mustard, lemon juice and oil. Add crab, herbs and minced shallot. Season with salt and pepper and check flavor.
cooking live primetime
From:
East Meets West with Ming Tsai
Show Schedule
Also From This Episode
SUSHI 202
MASTER SUSHI RICE
MASTER SUSHI RICE
Menu Ideas
Soup and Sushi
HERB CRAB SALAD MAKI-SUSHI
SALT AND PEPPER EDAMAME
RED POACHED PEARS
GINGER BUTTERNUT SQUASH SOUP WITH SHIITAKE MUSHROOMS
SUSHI 202
Related Videos
Knife Skill -- Mince
Quicktime, 28.8K, 56.6K
Knife Skill -- Chop
Quicktime, 28.8K, 56.6K
Knife Skill -- Chiffonade
Quicktime, 28.8K, 56.6K

FIGURE 5-28 *After flipping channels and catching a show on how to make sushi, I had to check out the recipe on the Web. Fortunately, someone has a clue at this web site and has linked to a "printer-friendly" version of the recipe. ©2000 The Food Network.*

Optimize Images

Although the topic of optimizing images is outside the scope of this book (see any of Lynda Weinman's books at *www.lynda.com*), it remains an important point. Reducing image bloat is critical to maintaining a lean, mean Web site. If you haven't actively optimized the images on your site, you really should. You'll be amazed at the space savings. (See Figures 5.29 and 5.30.)

webhighway.jpg @ 100% (RGB)
100%
Doc: 386K/386K

FIGURE 5.29 *Note the behemoth image on the home page of Torrent Systems. (See the design tip, "Parsimony Always," at the end of the chapter.) By the way, that's a picture of the "Web Highway." At any rate, it started off as a JPEG, weighing in at a whopping 386K.*

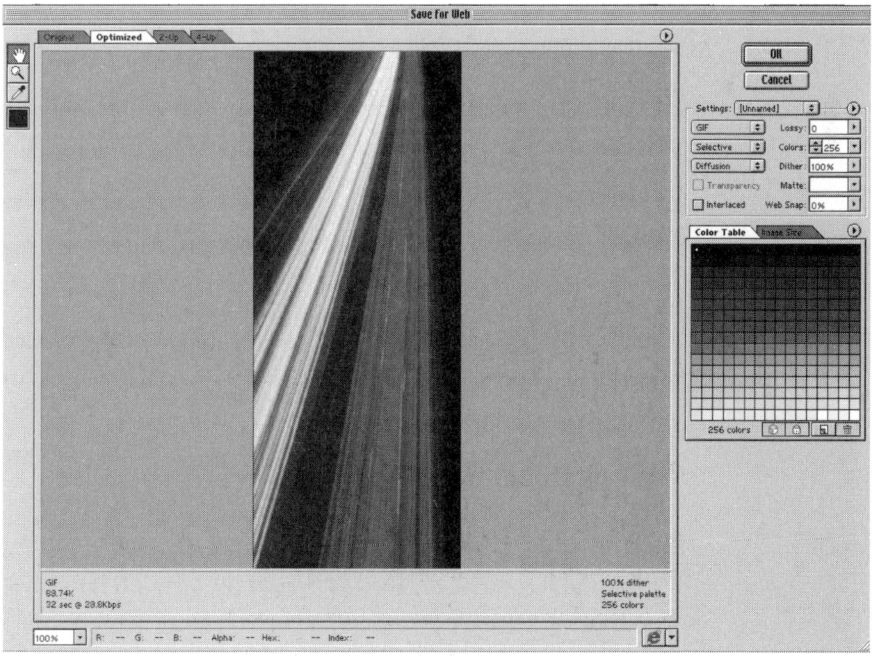
Save for Web
Original
Optimized
2-Up
4-Up
OK
Cancel
Settings: [Unnamed]
GIF
Lossy: 0
Selective
Colors: 256
Diffusion
Dither: 100%
Transparency
Matte:
Interlaced
Web Snap: 0%
Color Table
Image Size
256 colors
GIF
68.74K
32 sec @ 28.8Kbps
100% dither
Selective palette
256 colors
100%
R: -- G: -- B: -- Alpha: -- Hex: -- Index: --

FIGURE 5.30 *I was able to open it in Photoshop 5.5 and select the "Save for Web…" option, which nicely optimized the image to a much tidier 80K.*

Use CSS Instead of Image Text

You can eliminate a good many unnecessary graphic files by using CSS to control fonts on your site. Sure, you may not be able to use that fancy calligraphic script that you like so much, but you'll save a lot of time for the user by including regular text and applying a style to it instead. See the HTML/CSS package on the accompanying CD-ROM.

Provide Contact Information on Every Page

Always include at least a link to a contact information page on your site, if not the information itself. Often, people who come to your site just want to know how to call you or otherwise contact you.

It's understandable that some companies want to keep users at arm's length in the interest of reducing their operating costs. After all, it costs a lot more to fulfill a customer order over the phone than it does to simply have the user order via the Web site. The same goes for technical support issues; if the user can find the information on the site, the company doesn't have to pay the long-distance charge on the call, nor does it have to pay someone to take the call.

This works great if your Web page can quickly and efficiently solve the vast majority of problems a user might have. Until your site can do that, however, you need to provide contact information.

Have Great FAQs

The whole idea of a frequently asked question (FAQ) section is to include questions people ask you often, with answers, on your site, so that people don't have to keep contacting you to find answers. Unfortunately, many sites feature FAQs that never develop beyond a handful of questions that the MIS people thought of when the site was put together. Keep your FAQs updated; your users will provide a constant stream of new material for them (see Figure 5.31).

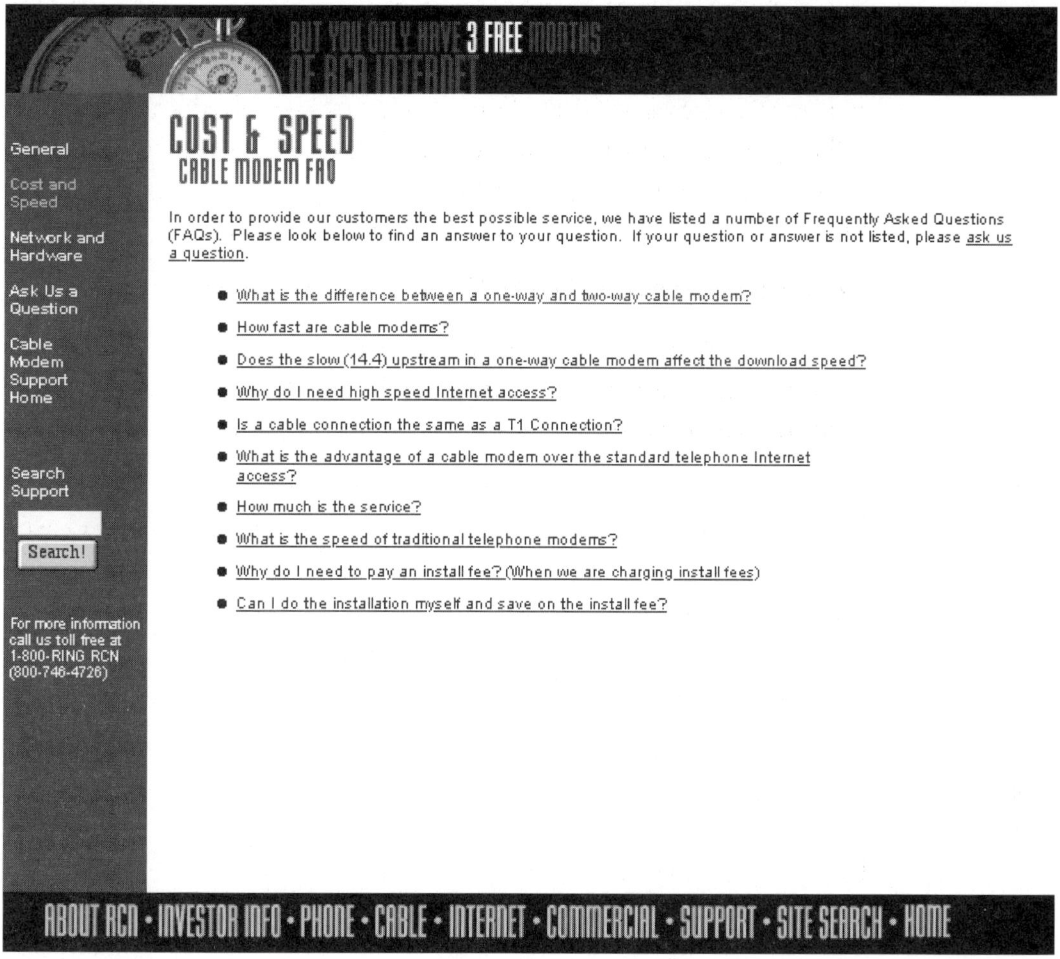
BUT YOU ONLY HAVE 3 FREE MONTHS OF RCN INTERNET
General
Cost and Speed
Network and Hardware
Ask Us a Question
Cable Modem Support Home
Search Support
Search!
For more information call us toll free at 1-800-RING RCN (800-746-4726)
COST & SPEED
CABLE MODEM FAQ
In order to provide our customers the best possible service, we have listed a number of Frequently Asked Questions (FAQs). Please look below to find an answer to your question. If your question or answer is not listed, please ask us a question.
What is the difference between a one-way and two-way cable modem?
How fast are cable modems?
Does the slow (14.4) upstream in a one-way cable modem affect the download speed?
Why do I need high speed Internet access?
Is a cable connection the same as a T1 Connection?
What is the advantage of a cable modem over the standard telephone Internet access?
How much is the service?
What is the speed of traditional telephone modems?
Why do I need to pay an install fee? (When we are charging install fees)
Can I do the installation myself and save on the install fee?
ABOUT RCN • INVESTOR INFO • PHONE • CABLE • INTERNET • COMMERCIAL • SUPPORT • SITE SEARCH • HOME

FIGURE 5.31 *When I looked up "one way" and "two-way cable modem" in the site's FAQ section, it was there, but the important question for me was, "Which one am I going to get when I order service?" No one knew the answer. ©2000 RCN.*

Design for Nonlinear Use

Never assume that your users will always enter your site through your home page or that they will move through the material in any kind of a predictable fashion. People use the Web in a very nonlinear fashion; they don't read a Web site like a novel. Therefore, if you provide critical navigation information only on the home page, you are ensuring that your site will be unusable by people who find their way to your site via a search engine. This also obviates the need for ineffective "entry tunnel" pages (see Figure 5.32).

The Future
in
FUTURES
Viewed best in 800X600
Enter
mercurian
Powered by THING-Z.COM
Send mail to our webmaster with questions or comments about this web site.
Copyright© 1999 Mercurian Ltd.

FIGURE 5.32 *Were any design tips broken here? This page is an entry tunnel. The site has been designed for 800 by 600 viewing; again, try not to put these kinds of constraints on the users. ©2000 Mercurian.*

Don't Throw People Off Your Site

If you need to link to Web pages that are not part of your site, make sure that you provide the user with cues to let them know that they are leaving your site; don't just cast them out without a warning.

Furthermore, if you expect someone to leave your site and then come back, you had better provide a mechanism to do that! For example, if you use an Adobe PDF file on your site, you can require users to download the free reader before they view your site. Make sure that you provide a mechanism to let them get back to your site when they are done—and don't just "magically" transport them there; that's very disorienting for users.

Avoid Highly Saturated Colors

Highly saturated colors are good at catching the eye because they are so bright, but this quality also makes them tiring to look at for long periods of time. Using a splash of bright red (R:255,G:0,B:0) might be okay, but making your background color bright red isn't a good idea!

Many great sites use less saturated colors (pastel colors, for example). These colors are a lot easier to look at for long periods of time.

Don't Go Font Happy

Just because you learned how to use CSS font attributes doesn't mean that you should use every available font in your Web site. In reality, more fonts usually make for elementary-looking sites. The fewer fonts, the better. A good policy is to pick one font for headings and another for body text (although both fonts should probably be **sans serif**). Make sure that you provide alternate fonts via CSS in case the ones you specify aren't on the user's system. Finally, make sure that your site works even in the total absence of custom fonts; the defaults should work fine, too.

Don't Override Users' Text Color Preferences

You might like to color coordinate your site by making your link colors match some other part of the site. However, this can confuse users; people have come to understand that blue means hyperlink (an unfortunate choice for a text color since small blue things become progressively harder to see as humans age). If you provide custom colors for these things, don't use the CSS "important" directive to override your user's preferences.

Avoid Frames

Browsers have gotten a bit better with regard to handling frames, but frames still confuse people and can be a difficult to navigate. If you can avoid using frames, do so. There are, of course, legitimate reasons to use frames, so don't shun them entirely.

Avoid Opening New Windows

In general, the opening of a new browser window baffles users, especially if it happens so fast that they don't notice it until suddenly they're plunged into an alternative universe. This can be a real barrier to usability because the new window doesn't contain the history of the previous window (see Figure 5.33).

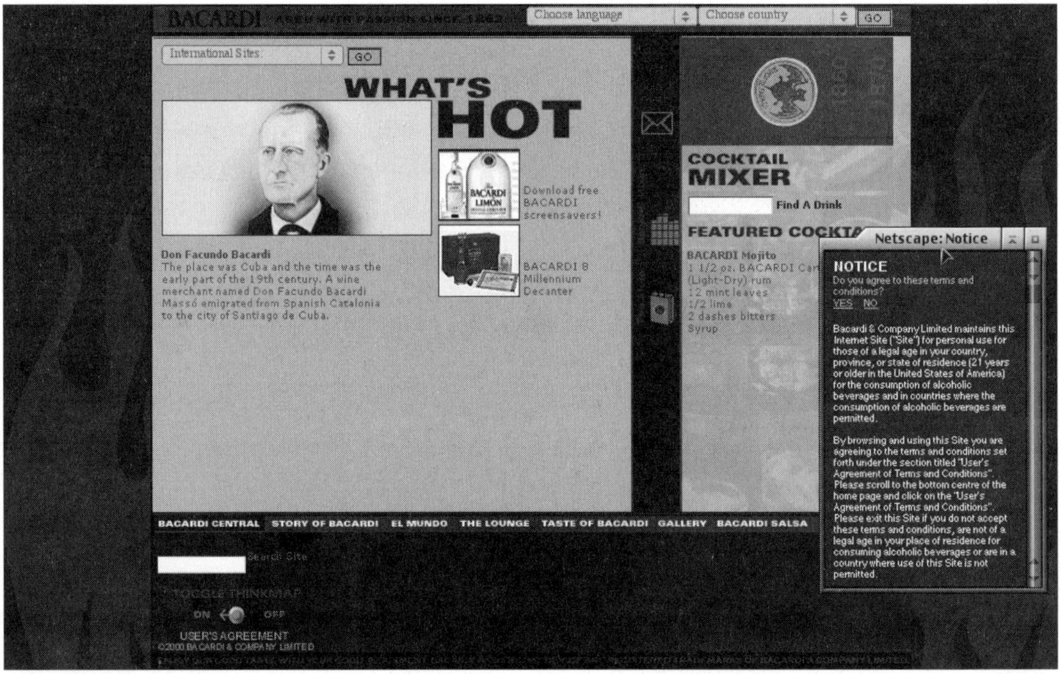
BACARDI
Choose language
Choose country
GO
International Sites:
GO
WHAT'S HOT
Download free BACARDI screensavers!
BACARDI 8 Millennium Decanter
Don Facundo Bacardi
The place was Cuba and the time was the early part of the 19th century. A wine merchant named Don Facundo Bacardi Massó emigrated from Spanish Catalonia to the city of Santiago de Cuba.
COCKTAIL MIXER
Find A Drink
BACARDI Mojito
(Light-Dry) rum
12 mint leaves
1/2 lime
2 dashes bitters
Syrup
Netscape: Notice
NOTICE
Do you agree to these terms and conditions?
YES NO
Bacardi & Company Limited maintains this Internet Site ("Site") for personal use for those of a legal age in your country, province, or state of residence (21 years or older in the United States of America) for the consumption of alcoholic beverages and in countries where the consumption of alcoholic beverages are permitted.
By browsing and using this Site you are agreeing to the terms and conditions set forth under the section titled "User's Agreement of Terms and Conditions". Please scroll to the bottom centre of the home page and click on the "User's Agreement of Terms and Conditions". Please exit this Site if you do not accept these terms and conditions, are not of a legal age in your place of residence for consuming alcoholic beverages or are in a country where use of this Site is not permitted.
BACARDI CENTRAL STORY OF BACARDI EL MUNDO THE LOUNGE TASTE OF BACARDI GALLERY BACARDI SALSA
USER'S AGREEMENT

FIGURE 5.33 *Note the pop-up window; these little miracles of JavaScript can be irritating. ©2000 Bacardi.*

Use Context-Independent Titles for Pages

Ever see a Web page title like this one?

```
<title>Our Home Page</title>
```

That's an example of a really bad title because it has absolutely no value out of context. *Whose* Web page? If a search engine indexes the site, this useless title is probably going to show up in the search results. Furthermore, bookmark titles take the page title as the default label. Make sure your titles can stand on their own.

Provide Feedback

As mentioned before, always provide feedback to let the user know what is happening as he or she moves around your sites. Studies have shown that if the user cannot detect that a page or page element has updated within about 1 second, he or she will feel that the system is lagging.[2]

Be Smart with Screen Shots

How likely would you be to click on one of the screen shots in this book? Not very likely, because you can plainly tell that they aren't real interfaces. Not so when you have a screen shot featured as part of a Web site! I have watched users click repeatedly on screen-shot images on sites because the images look as "real" as any other part of the screen.

The solution? Modify the screen shot slightly so that it is obviously not a real interface. One trick is to use a ghosted bit of text over the screen shot ("Screen shot" or something like that). Another technique is to use add noise to the image in Photoshop.

Listen to User Feedback

Always provide a way for users to send you criticism and comments, and be sure to pay attention to what they say! Remember, in some cases a

---

[2] Visit *www.useit.com/papers/responsetime.html* for more information.

low-tech solution is okay. You don't need to spend lots of money to develop a complex complaint registration system; just make sure that users can find an e-mail address to which they can send information and from which they will get a personal response in a timely fashion.

E-mail autoresponders are often used for this type of e-mail address to let users know immediately that their mail was received. However, most people realize that this is just an automated response, which may degrade the perceived value of any such reply. A personal response will gain you the most respect from your users.

Parsimony, Always

Parsimony is the state in which a creation cannot have anything taken away from it or added to it without disrupting its meaning. You should strive for this state in your designs. If there is no benefit to adding something to a Web page, don't add it. Every image, every piece of text, and every animation must compete for your users' limited attention. In addition, images equate to wait time for the user.

CHAPTER SUMMARY

- Although reading "quickie" tips and tricks is fun, simple cookbook-style usability should never replace real user testing.
- A combination of tips, techniques, tools, and testing makes the most usable type of Web site.
- The nature of design tips will change dramatically with time, because the technologies used to implement Web sites will change rapidly.
- Many good design tips are based in the act of creating from the user's perspective—seeing the material as the user sees it.

HANDS-ON EXERCISES

1. Do an informal review of your Web site. How many of the tips in this chapter were observed in the creation of your site? How many were blatantly not observed?

2. Download the WebTV viewer from the WebTV site and view your site with it. Take notes about anything that seems broken or odd. How can you repair the problems?
3. Calculate the download size of pages in your site. You can do this in a couple of ways: by hand (painful if you have anything other than a tiny site) or by using a commercial or shareware application.

DISCUSSION TOPICS

1. What tips do you know about that are not listed in this chapter?
2. Are there tips presented here that you disagree with? Why?
3. Would a Web site be perfect if it implemented all the tips in this chapter? Why or why not?

CHAPTER 6

Heuristic Evaluation

Any sufficiently advanced bug is indistinguishable from a feature.

—*Rich Kulawiec*

What Is a Heuristic?

One dictionary definition of the word *heuristic* is as follows:

> *Heuristic,* n.: *Involving or serving as an aid to learning, discovery, or problem solving by experimental and especially trial-and-error methods* (heuristic techniques; a heuristic assumption); *also, of or relating to exploratory problem-solving techniques that utilize self-educating techniques (as in the evaluation of feedback) to improve* performance (a heuristic computer program).[1]

If that definition still sounds a little opaque to you, think of it a different way: A heuristic is a rule of thumb. Heuristic evaluation, then, is the act of estimating the state of usability of a Web site by applying well-known rules of thumb to the site and deriving a score for the site based on how closely it fulfills the requirements of these rules.

[1]This definition was found on *www.m-w.com.*

Normally, the way a heuristic evaluation works is that two to five "expert evaluators" examine a site, taking special note of the way the site adheres to or violates the heuristic list items. To avoid peer bias, each evaluator does this work in isolation (not in the same room at the same time as the other evaluators, that is).[2] Each evaluator comes up with a list of usability problems that he or she finds; in almost every case, the usability problem exists because one or more of the heuristics have been violated. After the evaluation session, the evaluators share their results and begin to form recommendations for change.[3]

The main selling point of heuristic evaluation is that it can be done quickly, often be done on a tight budget. Since most companies want virtually instant turnaround on Web-based projects, this tool is a perfect fit for helter-skelter schedules. You can produce a relatively comprehensive heuristic evaluation in two to three days.

---

[2]Nor on a remote desert island, although sometimes that wouldn't be so bad!

[3]You can read more about this process at *www.useit.com/papers/heuristic/heuristic_evaluation.html.*

TEN USABILITY HEURISTICS

The pioneer of heuristic evaluation, Jakob Nielsen, developed a list of 10 heuristics in collaboration with his colleague Rolf Molich in 1990. Needless to say, this list of heuristics predates the popularity of the World Wide Web. Much of the list is still quite pertinent in the context of the Web, however; some items are a little dated. Additionally, the list lacks new heuristics that should probably be included. Much has been written on this topic. For now, we discuss the original 10 heuristics; later we'll look at some new heuristics that can be applied. The list that makes up the first portion of this chapter comes from Nielsen's article, *Ten Usability Heuristics.*[4]

Heuristic #1: Visibility of System Status

This simple principle says that the user should always know what state the Web site is in at any given moment. This rule is most applicable to transactional Web pages, such as electronic commerce forms. The user needs to know where he or she is in terms of the ordering process ("Is my order complete?" "Did I successfully cancel that order?" "Am I shopping again?").

Additionally, users need to know where they are in the Web site, especially when the main site contains many microsites. This can be especially challenging when many different groups are responsible for the upkeep of the microsites (see heuristic #4 for more on this topic). A clearly labeled system for navigation helps users know where they are.

This heuristic also concerns the all-important idea of feedback: You should always provide the user with some way of knowing what is going on. In the early days of Web transactions, many users were billed multiple times for a charge that they had only authorized once. The reason? Slow Web servers and a lack of system status visibility led users to believe that their transactions had not worked, so they clicked "Submit"

[4]You can find this article at *www.useit.com/papers/heuristic/heuristic_list.html.*

again. And again. Clearly, you must provide some sort of feedback mechanism to let users know what's happening between transactions.

Very recently I was browsing a very big computer company's site and found myself in the middle of a transaction. This multibillion-dollar company provided me with a system status indicator—a little animated GIF that flashed like a progress bar. It was cheap, it was simple, but it let me know that something was happening, and that's all I needed to feel secure that my transaction was being handled.

Heuristic #2: Match the System to the Real World

This heuristic, as designed by Nielsen and Molich, is actually two heuristics in one. Here's what their paper says about this rule:

> *The system should speak the users' language, with words, phrases and concepts familiar to the user, rather than system-oriented terms. Follow real-world conventions, making information appear in a natural and logical order.*

The two parts to this heuristic are as follows:

- Use the natural language of the user, not jargon or system terms.
- Follow real-world conventions; provide natural mappings.

The first concept is critical. I have seen hundreds of usability problems come from violating this principle. What is meant by employing the user's natural language is avoiding jargon or terms that would otherwise expose the inner workings of the system. This also means using the terms that the user would normally use to describe an action, a piece of information, and so on.

One of the most famous violations of this principle involves the Northeastern University (NEU) Online learning system. NEU had decided to put many of its courses in an electronic format for delivery via the Web. The company NEU employed was fairly new to the area of user interface design.

In the company's design for the students' view of the course material, the student could navigate from one week's lecture to the next (each week's material was called a *module* via the main course menu. This part almost made sense.

However, when the student got deep into the lesson material, the button that would bring the student back to the main course menu was marked "Exit." No one was able to return to the course menu, because Exit meant something very different to everyone who was using the system: it meant to, well, exit—to leave the system, to no longer use it.

Fortunately, the crack expert designers and engineers put a team on the case of the mislabeled button. After considerable research, they came up with a new label to solve the problem. Instead of Exit, they labeled the button "Return." (See Figure 6.1.)

Another instance of violation of this heuristic involved a client of mine, a large bank. The users of the bank's Web site were unable to find information that was lumped under a particular heading. After doing a usability study with real users, we found that the users did not understand the meaning of the name of the heading. Hence, they would not look at information under the confounding heading unless they had scoured the rest of the site first.

We later found that the name of the heading was originally something much more sensible to the users, but that it had been changed by a vice president because the word didn't sound "upscale" enough. Our job then became to convince the VP that his ego was less important than millions of dollars in business.

The moral to the story is that being too clever can often lead to stranded, confused, or angry customers. Being clever is almost never a good idea, even if you are in the business of being clever.

Likewise, you should eliminate all industry jargon from your site so that users must interface only with terms they know and use. Although this example overlaps a little with heuristic #9 below, error messages should not contain diagnostic, debugging codes used by programmers. For example, you should not print a message that says, "Error: The server encoun-

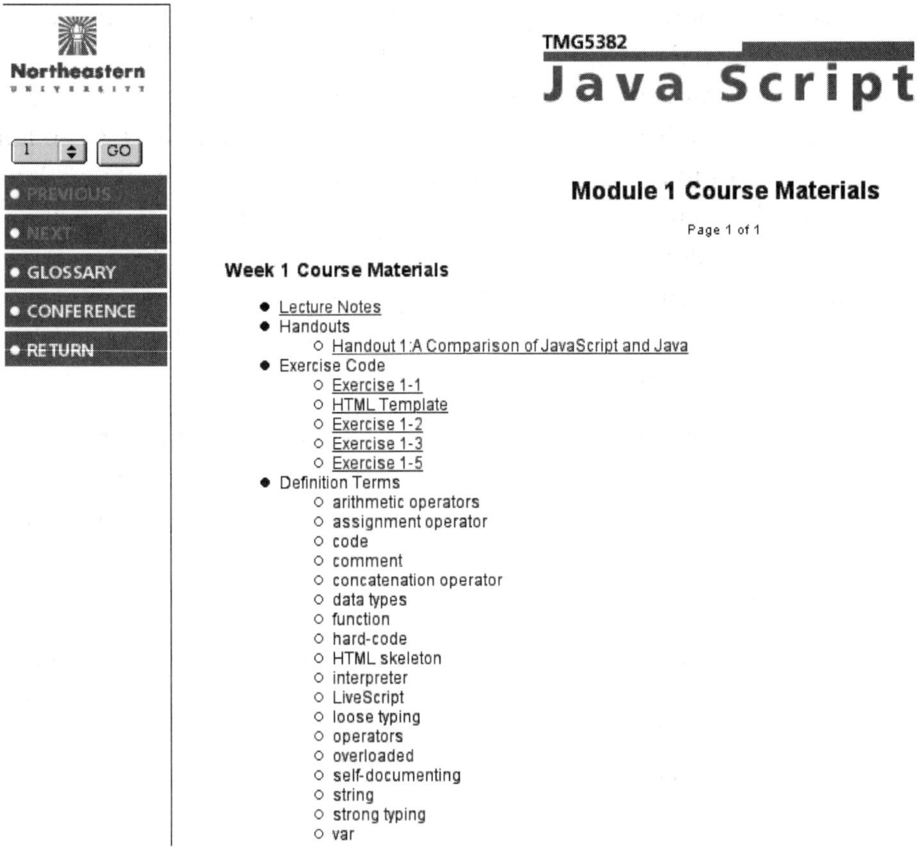
Northeastern
UNIVERSITY
GO
PREVIOUS
NEXT
GLOSSARY
CONFERENCE
RETURN
TMG5382
Java Script
Module 1 Course Materials
Page 1 of 1
Week 1 Course Materials
Lecture Notes
Handouts
Handout 1:A Comparison of JavaScript and Java
Exercise Code
Exercise 1-1
HTML Template
Exercise 1-2
Exercise 1-3
Exercise 1-5
Definition Terms
arithmetic operators
assignment operator
code
comment
concatenation operator
data types
function
hard-code
HTML skeleton
interpreter
LiveScript
loose typing
operators
overloaded
self-documenting
string
strong typing
var

FIGURE 6.1 *An example of a designer not matching a control to a user's own natural language. This is the vastly improved version of this system. © 2000 Northeastern University Online.*

tered server error 9812791. The SQL statement was malformed. Please mail the following stack trace to your system administrator."

Instead, you should provide a user-friendly version of the error message, and instead of making the user report the error, you should write robust code that can self-report these kinds of electronic mishaps![5]

---

[5]After all, there are refrigerators now that can e-mail a service technician when service is needed. The Web should be at least as useful as a refrigerator.

One other note on language: don't use machine-generated translations for your site. Although translation tools like the one found at *babelfish.altavista.com*[6] are hilarious and lots of fun to play with, in the wrong hands they can yield some questionable translations. It's also not a good idea to try to translate a page with only a dictionary if you don't speak the source and target languages. In defense of the *babelfish* site, Systran has done an excellent job of making an automated machine translator of human languages. However, until computers possess a similar type of "understanding" of language as humans use it, you may still favor a human translator over a machine.

The second part to this dual heuristic, "Match the system to the real world," refers to a concept called *natural mappings,* covered thoroughly by Donald A. Norman in his book *The Design of Everyday Things.*[7] A natural mapping is the approximation of the "real world" by a control interface.

Some examples of natural mappings include your car's steering wheel. Turning the wheel to the left causes the car to turn to the left, and so on. Another natural mapping is the console of a VCR or tape recorder. Pressing the Rewind button, which points in the backward direction,[8] causes the tape to run backward.

Once an interface such as the VCR or tape player becomes ubiquitous, it makes sense to base new interfaces on the old to help leverage the

---

[6]I have been in tears before after playing with this site. Here's what to do: Enter a sentence in English, then translate it into French. Then take the French translation, and translate it back into English. Next, take that English translation and translate it into German. Then, back to English.

[7]This is one book that you absolutely must read. It's both entertaining and informative; it's a fairly quick read, and it will forever change the way you look at everyday objects, including Web pages.

[8]It points backward to Westerners who read from left to right, that is. Note that the direction may not intrinsically make sense to people who read primarily Arabic, Hebrew, or any other language written from right to left. However, through use, even contradictory controls can be learned. But this is a bad idea generally.

user's existing schema.[9] This helps reduce the amount of retraining that needs to be done. See heuristic #4 for more detail.

Heuristic #3: User Control and Freedom

This heuristic probably evolved from too many dead-end, noncancelable dialog boxes. The basic premise of this heuristic is that you should always do the following:

- Provide clearly marked exits
- Support undo and redo transactions
- Make it harder to perform irreversible actions

What this means in the context of the Web is that for any given transaction state that a user might be in on your site (in the middle of a purchase, for example), there must be a way for the user to gracefully back out that doesn't involve crashing the browser.

Additionally, users should be able to undo and redo actions. This can be a bit tricky to support via Web programming, but it is a very worthwhile feature. An example of undo might be allowing users to take an item out of their shopping carts after they put it there ("Gee . . . do I really need that DVD of the movie *Tron*?"). You should also allow redo ("Now that I think about it, yes, I *do* need that *Tron* DVD!")

At the same time, you should use the principle of constraint to make it hard to commit irreversible actions. If the effects of any action are in some fashion irreversible, you need to go to great lengths to let the user know about it in advance.

Additionally, you should know when to use *modal dialog boxes*[10]—that is, dialog boxes that block the user's ability to do anything else until the dialog box has been acknowledged. Be warned that such widgets can be very frustrating to a novice user, since he or she may lose track of the

---

[9]A *schema*, to be brief, is a mental model of something.

[10]For an example of creating a modal dialog box in JavaScript, see *developer.netscape.com/viewsource/goodman_modal/goodman_modal.html.*

window that is blocking them, causing them to become frustrated when their attempts to click or make anything else work fail. Modal dialogs are good when your Web application presents a finite task, such as getting the user's confirmation of a potentially irreversible act[11] or the submission of a large amount of data.

All of this harks back to the fact that users of computer systems generally feel intimidated and isolated,[12] and many people fear getting trapped in programs and interfaces that cause them to "bungle" something. Providing the user with many ways to reverse actions and providing restraints to deter potentially irreversible actions gives the user a safety net. A more relaxed user is a happier user.

Heuristic #4: Consistency and Standards

Imagine that you have just purchased a new car. To open the doors on the car, you learn that you have to push in on three separate buttons while turning a knob on the door a quarter-turn counterclockwise. Once inside the car, you discover (after consulting the user manual) that the ignition is in the passenger side floorboard and that you activate it by putting the key in and turning it while pushing a knob on the gearshift.

Once you're up and running, the air conditioning and heat are controlled by separate consoles, but the fan has a single control knob. To increase the amount of heat, the heat slider must be pushed to the left, while A/C is increased by pushing its individual slider to the right. The fan knob must be turned in the opposite direction of the slider to actuate airflow.

Sound like fun? No? Well, what if you knew that this particular design allowed you to have a car that costs half the price of a comparable

---

[11]Remember, there should be no irreversible acts in the first place. However, where technological limitations force your hand, you need to give the user a chance to opt out before the action is committed.

[12]Not you, of course! You're an expert computer user.

ergonomic car? Still wouldn't buy it? Rightfully so. Such a car would not only be a disadvantage to the poor driver, it would be a menace to society because of all the accidents it would cause.

The reason that few automobile makers brazenly disregard common control system design is that it would severely work against them. The fact that the industry has settled on some consistent standards means that users (drivers) have little relearning to do when they get a new car.

Software developers have settled on some similar standards (partially because operating system developers have facilitated doing so), which enable users to quickly "find their way around" on new software.

On the other hand, some software vendors have chosen to go in the other direction entirely. Take, for example, the program Kai's Power Tools by MetaCreations. This program has an interface that looks much more like the dashboard of an alien cruise ship than a computer program! The creator of the program threw traditional standards out the window (pun intended) to make a bold, new, "fun" interface. The program is aimed at graphic designers who want to have fun while they work.

Would this approach work with tax software? Just imagine . . .

The truth of the matter is that standards allow users to survive in an otherwise churning sea of rapidly changing technology. Note that there isn't a well-known, widely adopted standard for Web page layout. The Web applications that we create are usually not based on a style guide or any kind of accepted norm. Ad hoc standards are starting to emerge as dominant organizations gain recognition. Again, think Amazon.com. Its model for shopping online has become a de facto standard without the aid of a publicly available style guide.

The notion of widespread standards for Web style and implementation has gotten the attention of at least some people. The Web Standards Project (WSP), whose site can be found at *www.webstandards.org,* is one group that is pushing for such standards. Of course, the best-known Web standards organization is the World Wide Web Consortium (W3C, whose URL still confounds me: *www.w3.org*).The W3C steers the development of most of the critical Web standards, such as HTML, Extensible Markup Language (XML), DOM, and many others. However, the W3C does not usually concern itself with higher-level issues such as interface layout, style (not CSS style sheets, but rather tasteful implementation), or any other such areas. For this reason, other external standards organizations might be necessary to accomplish the goal of standards organization in these outlying areas.

Heuristic #5: Error Prevention

No matter how well you document your Web applications, no matter how nice your search engine is, no matter how great your online help system can be, none of these items holds a candle to simply making your site easy to understand and use.

The same outfit that brought us the now-famous Exit button also produced a hefty user guide for its Web site-based content authoring tool. The tool was nonintuitive enough to merit some lengthy explanation. If you need to produce a manual so that people can use your Web site, something is really wrong!

Furthermore, it is much more desirable to simply prevent error conditions than to make lavish and information-heavy error messages. In the case of the Web, you should include automated spiders in your bag of site administration tools to ferret out broken links. As charming and warm a welcome as it is, "Error 404" would be a welcome omission from almost every user's world.

Heuristic #6: Recognition Rather Than Recall

Donald Norman's *The Design of Everyday Things* discusses an experiment involving total recall vs. recognition. A group of people was asked to draw a U.S. one-cent piece (a penny) and to include all the features they could remember. Try this task yourself! Although no one got the penny quite right, all of the participants could pick out a penny from a fistful of change. How?

Humans are rarely required to remember all the features of any object by rote memory. Almost always, the world offers cues that help the human discriminate among various stimuli. As Dr. Norman points out, critical information can exist in one of two places:

- In the head (memorized information)
- In the world (labels, "obvious" information, and so on)

Part of the success of an interface rests on how well the information needed to operate it is distributed between these two options. Via recall (knowledge in the head), users are required to "just know" something. This is a good thing in small doses, but the more information you can delegate to the interface—without compromising its coherence and simplicity—the better.

A common way to delegate information to the interface is through labels. If a user must recognize many different icon buttons to perform a task, it's best if there is a legend describing the function of those buttons, or some other alternative to rote memorization. Note that it is very easy to clutter an interface with too many labels; a type of interface parsimony is the answer.

Heuristic #7: Flexibility and Efficiency of Use

You can't please everyone all the time. It's a fact. However, you should endeavor to make your Web site customizable, if that's feasible, so that users can make things the way they feel is most efficient for them. For example, if you have a search engine on your site, you should initially expose only the most minimal set of input elements for conducting a search. You should also provide an advanced search feature for intermediate and power users as an option.

It's generally considered good design to make default interfaces as simple as the task will allow, with more powerful (and optional) features hidden but available to the knowing intermediate or expert user via accelerators. An *accelerator* is a feature available through a keyboard shortcut, key combination, or some other subtle mechanism. Accelerators are designed to facilitate repetitious or common tasks for users who are comfortable enough to use them.

Note that this heuristic can be over-applied all too easily. My great-aunt was complaining once about a dreadful thing that had happened to her while using Microsoft Word. She had been typing a letter to her friends, and, after using a dash somewhere in the body, the program began to format her document for her automatically—in a fashion that was not what she wanted! The program was too "smart" to be helpful.

I assured her that it wasn't her fault (users almost always blame themselves!) and produced a recent *Macworld* issue in which a reader had mailed in a similar complaint. The "fix" was to disable the "feature." So be careful that you don't create the Sorcerer's Apprentice Effect[13] in your "helpful" designs!

Heuristic #8: Aesthetic and Minimalist Design

This heuristic is really just saying not to throw in the kitchen sink and everything else when all it takes to get the point across is a simple word or image. Adding items to a page does not automatically make it better; they usually make it worse if the addition isn't carefully thought out.

There are many reasons for adopting this minimalist stance. First, bandwidth is a critical resource, so adding content that isn't critical will work against you. Second, the average attention span (especially in Americans) is short, so the more you have on a page, the less likely each item is to be noticed. Finally, the more information on a page, the poorer the signal-to-noise ratio.

Note that minimalist design does not mean that in order to have a truly usable site, you must have an incredibly ugly, 1994-ish looking site, although many usability specialists have sites that take this approach. The truth of the matter is that you cannot have just form or function; you need both. Truly excellent sites combine both aspects of design.

---

[13] Watch the Disney classic *Fantasia* if you don't know what I am talking about.

Moving away from less complex systems usually results in more chaos and more errors; a carefully designed and appropriately grown site can include good looks and good usability. Designs such as these don't happen overnight; they are the result of iterative redesign.

Heuristic #9: Help Users Recognize, Diagnose, and Recover from Errors

One of my pet peeves is poorly designed Web forms, especially forms that do not employ client-side validation. Many times I have filled out forms that scrolled down the screen for miles and then submitted them, only to get an error message in return—but a well-hidden error message! I have seen many Web forms that return the same screen the user filled out, plus an obscure error message hidden somewhere on the page. Sometimes, the programmer was thoughtful enough to make the error message appear in a novel color (red, usually).

If a user makes a mistake on your site—by improperly filling out a form, by entering a botched query string, or whatever—you should have an obvious method for letting the user know about it. Consider using JavaScript to do client-side form validation for browsers that are capable of it. (Always design your server-side programs to be robust against unexpected input, though.) See the Javascript Package on the CD-ROM for more information.

When reporting an error to the user, make sure that you observe heuristic #2. Use the user's natural language to report the error condition, and explain to the user how to fix the problem.

Heuristic #10: Help and Documentation

This is the last heuristic because if you have observed the other nine, you shouldn't need too much of this final one. No matter how well designed your site is, you'll still need to employ some sort of online help, even if it is just a list of FAQs that you keep updated. If the user needs documentation to use the help system, you're in big trouble.

The topic of writing great online documentation and help is outside the scope of this book, but here are some basic tips that come from the *Apple Developer's Guide*[14] to get you started:

- Your list of topic areas should be a logical outline of the guide file contents, similar to the table of contents for a book.
- Choose a method of organization that makes sense from the user's standpoint, not the system designer's. If in doubt, list topics alphabetically.
- For your main help instructions, topic names should form a complete question or statement from the user's point of view—for example, "How do I sign on?"
- The topic name should always focus only on the main goal that the user wants to achieve and not on any choices associated with that goal.
- Use a help heading that begins with "Why can't I . . ." for topics that explain why the user cannot perform a certain action (for example, "Why can't I print a file?").
- Use a help heading that begins with "How do I . . ." for topics that show the user how to accomplish a task (for example, "How do I create a custom dictionary?").

SOME ADDITIONAL HEURISTICS FOR THE WEB

It's important to understand that the preceding list of heuristics is a good starting point, but it is by no means the only such list that is valid. Additionally, as the technology used to implement Web documents evolves, the heuristics will also necessarily evolve. The list that you end up using may consist of just a subset of the ones we've examined, a combination of those and the ones I suggest in this section, or even a hybrid with your own special heuristics that come from your personal experience.

---

[14] You can find the *Guide* at *www.devworld.apple.com/techpubs/mac/AppleGuide/AppleGuide-17.html.*

Now that you have seen the original heuristics as per Jakob Nielsen, here are some newer suggestions for Web-specific evaluations. Some of these were mentioned earlier in Chapter 4.

Additional Heuristic #1: Chunking

Chunking is a cognitive tool that humans use to simplify their perception of the environment. When many pieces of similar information are presented in a spatially related fashion (i.e., close together), the perceptual system distills them into larger pieces of information called *chunks.*

In the early days of telephone research, it was discovered that human beings could keep roughly seven, plus or minus two, unrelated bits of information in their working memory at once—information, for example, such as digits. This is the reason U.S. phone numbers have seven digits.

But note that chunking has a profound effect on phone-number memorization. For example, I can't help but think of area codes as single pieces of information, since they have meaning to me. I know that (617) is the area code for most of Boston and surrounding areas; I know that 72206 is the ZIP code for the Arkansas governor's mansion. Chunking is hard at work in these examples, making those otherwise meaningless bits of information seem much more manageable and meaningful.

It is also known that assigning semantic cues to otherwise meaningless stimuli is very effective for facilitating recall. Take, for example, the experiment conducted with "droodles." Check out *www.droodles.com;* it's fun and informative.

So how do you make this information a part of your Web site? If you have a complex page that has much more than the magic 7 ± 2 items, you should consider chunking as a partial solution. Try to cluster like pieces of information near one another, and provide white space around them to make them visually distinct.

Additional Heuristic #2: Use the Inverted Pyramid Style of Writing

Journalists know a lot about this technique. The idea is that you should put the most important information in a text-heavy page or segment at the very top, leaving less important details for later in the text. This way, users have to read a minimal amount of information before they can move on. Reading on-screen text is painful (more on this in a moment), so reducing the amount of text a user has to read is a great benefit.

Although a discussion of online writing style is out of the scope of this book, here are some general suggestions for creating good inverted pyramid-style text. Always remember that you want to wrap up the most important details in the first sentence. Subsequent sentences should contain information of decreasing importance. How do you determine the importance of a piece of information? There is no exact answer, nor is there a formula to calculate importance. What you can do is refer to this well-known list of news values, which is the sort of list that journalists use to prioritize information in their articles:

- **Impact: Information has impact if it affects a large number of people.** If information will impact a significant number of your users, it is important. If the information details how a raccoon broke into the employee lunchroom and scarfed Bill's peanut-butter-and-bologna sandwich, that's not really a high-impact story (although it might qualify for the "strange" category listed below!)
- **Timeliness: Information has timeliness if it happened recently.** The meaning of "recently" varies, depending on the type of publication. For a weekly newspaper, "recently" would be anything that had happened this week. For news services such as CNN, anything older than 24 hours is certainly old news. On the Web, you should strive for a very small window of currency, at least on par with news channels. Of course, this will vary based on your business and your company; maybe nothing interesting happens at your company!

- **Prominence: Information has prominence if it involves a well-known person or organization.** When a major company becomes a client of yours, that's important. When your company makes a $10 million donation to a Children's Hospital, that's important. When Jane falls off the roof after chasing a raccoon through your office building, that's, erm, not as important.
- **Proximity: Information has proximity if it involves something that happened somewhere nearby.** This is a classic journalism news value, but its utility is somewhat lost on the Web. Define "local" on the Web—Earth? So unless your user population is confined geographically (which is very possible, depending on the nature of your site), you have an open field here.
- **Conflict: Information has conflict if it involves some kind of disagreement between two or more people.** Alas, many humans, especially Americans, are drawn to conflict, hence the popularity of many confrontational "talk" shows and professional wrestling. I do not condone gratuitous violence on a Web site, but a hot debate over a topic that might be appropriate for and of interest to your users is at least moderately important.
- **Weirdness: Information has weirdness if it involves something unusual or strange.** People tend to be drawn in by information that is bizarre. Take, for example, tabloid headlines such as "Techno-Squid Eats Parliament" or "JFK Fathered My Half-Alien Elvis Baby." Some Web journals have used this principle as their primary gimmick. Things that are novel tend to grab people's attention. Be careful, though, that you don't sink into sleaze or cheap effects.
- **Currency: Information has currency if it is related to some general topic many people are already talking about.** This one is a double-entendre, since people are also generally interested in "currency"—i.e., money! There is something to be said for tossing around buzzwords, but at the same time, there is much to be said for credibility and competence.

Additional Heuristic #3: Important Information Belongs "Above the Fold"

To borrow yet another concept from journalism, the most important information on a Web page must go near the top of the page. Depending on how paranoid you want to be, you should preview your work at a resolution of 640 by 480 on a 14-inch monitor to ensure that the most important information is visible without scrolling.

If you don't believe me right now, you will after you do a few usability tests: A frightening number of users are either blissfully unaware that they can scroll vertically in a browser or they opt not to. Some people can't scroll easily in either dimension (for example, if they are using WebTV, which cannot scroll horizontally). Hence, you should make sure that the vital bits of your message go on the first screenful.

Additional Heuristic #4: Avoid Gratuitous Use of Features

Just because a cool new technological toy exists does not mean that you are obligated to incorporate it into your site. Don't use frames unless you really need to and are ready to pay the price; frames are still problematic for most users. The same can be said of Flash, Java applets, JavaScript, or anything else that you might hear is "the latest and greatest."

Recently, Northeastern University made a major revision to its web site *(www.neu.edu)* to include numerous Flash animations. In my opinion the animations don't do anything to truly make the site a better tool for its patrons. After being teleported through two "entry portals" a la David Siegal,[15] the NEU site takes you to a page that is full of Java applets, image-based navigation, and scriptlets that were generated by GoLive. So the site is 100 percent buzzword compliant. But if you are visually impaired, the game is over. There is absolutely no textual content on the "home" page for a speech synthesizer to read aloud.

[15]David Siegal is the author of the book *Creating Killer Web Sites*.

Any time you feel the temptation to use toys like these, make sure that you are truly adding value to the site, not just arbitrarily adding more fluff for the sake of keeping up with the Web-Joneses.

Additional Heuristic #5: Make Your Pages "Scannable"

Many early Web site designs drew heavily from printed products such as brochures, magazines, and other traditional media. These sites featured vast quantities of text in the same fashion that you would find in the traditional media, since most companies felt that this was the correct approach. Now that we're a few generations of site design wiser, it's pretty well known that this is absolutely the wrong approach.

It is now widely accepted that users of Web sites read those sites in a vastly different fashion than they would read a book, a newspaper, or magazine: They scan. Instead of diving into chunks of text and trying to understand it all, Web site users look quickly for keywords, hyperlinks, and other important eye-catching features in order to progress to the next important page. Heavy textual content on the Web is usually ignored completely or, in the best case, it is printed for easier reading. In many cases, if you must use large amounts of text, it's wise to consider an alternative media type, such as Adobe Portable Document Format (PDF).

Web pages that are easy for users to scan have several common characteristics. Some, although not all, of the characteristics are as follows:

- Sans serif fonts
- Short, concise self-describing hyperlinks that are set apart by white space
- Brief, easily digestible paragraphs that follow the inverted pyramid style

Sans serif fonts are held to be more readable on-screen than serif fonts, for many reasons. In traditional typography, the body of a document is normally set in a serif font because it is believed that serif fonts are generally more readable over the long haul. Sans serif fonts are typically much more prominent optically and so are often used to set headlines in printed material (see Figure 6.2).

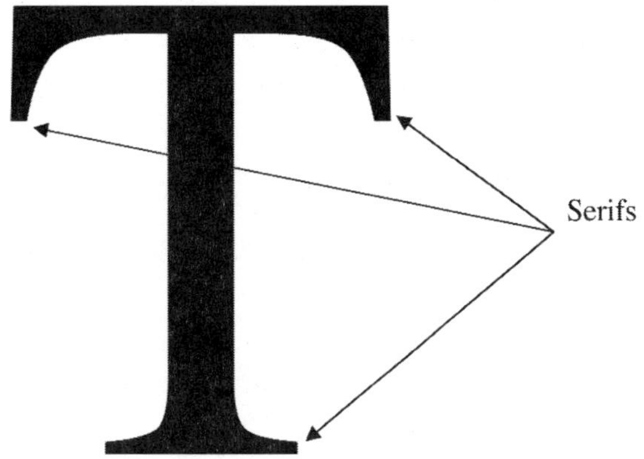
Serifs

FIGURE 6-2 *This is an example of a serif font. The little "tails" on the ends of the strokes are called* serifs. *A* sans serif *font, logically enough, lacks these tails.*

However, the combination of screen flicker and poor resolution makes serif fonts hard to read on a computer monitor. This limitation will likely dissipate as soon as high-resolution (300 pixels per inch or higher) displays become commonplace.

The original Web authors planned on hypertext links being unobtrusive, inline items that would not scream for attention. However, since the birth of the Web it has been pretty obvious that users don't grasp the inline-link concept; these kinds of links are frequently overlooked. The popularity of the hyperlink "Click Here" is both frightening and pervasive. Many users I have seen participate in usability studies have been almost oblivious to links that don't say "Click Here."

Therefore, links that stand out from surrounding text seem effective. Burying links inside text may net you lots of errors in navigation on your site.

Additional Heuristic #6: Keep Download and Response Times Low

One of the most pervasive complaints about Web sites has been the same since the beginning of the World Wide Wait: sluggish web site response. Even a well-designed and otherwise usable site can be severely downgraded if the download time is high. Sluggish site behavior can be caused by many things, including client-side bandwidth limitations, server load, and network congestion. Another major culprit is graphic obesity. This heuristic is one that lends itself to automated evaluation (see the "Automated Aids to Heuristic Evaluation").

Is that it?

Not exactly. Again, this list is a nonexhaustive one, but it summarizes some of the most important usability heuristics you are likely to need to do a good evaluation. Do you have suggestions for new heuristics? Pass them along to the community, because they could become widely adopted. I encourage each of you to explore this technique as an addition to your toolbox and to expand and update the heuristic list as technology evolves.

HEURISTIC EVALUATION METHODOLOGY

Now that you have a list of potential heuristics against which you can measure your site, it's important to know how to go about gathering information and making sense of it. One critical thing to note is that heuristic evaluation works best when approximately five experts are involved in the evaluation process. According to Nielsen, the bang-for-the-buck curve begins to flatten out at around five evaluators. If you have too few evaluators, however, you will end up catching only a fraction of the usability problems on the site.

The Environment

Each evaluator should view the site in isolation, as mentioned before. You should plan on the evaluation taking from one to two hours to complete. In the event that the evaluation of the complete site cannot be done in this time frame, plan on breaking the evaluation goals up over two or more sessions in order to keep individual session times to two hours or less.

Some evaluators will have a very methodical manner about examining the site; they might move in a linear fashion from one end of the site to the other. Other evaluators might have a more random approach. The end result, fortunately, is that not everyone will find all the same usability problems, resulting in more problems discovered, so there is much to be said for diversity of technique!

Error Severity Ratings

As each evaluator progresses through the site, they should make a log of usability problems they find, with specific notes about the page on which each problem was located, including the page URL. It is also critical that each problem be assigned a *severity rating*, which is a way of gauging how destructive the error is to the overall functionality of the site. This kind of severity rating allows the usability team to prioritize the components of change that they will recommend as a result of the evaluation. Usually a scale of 1 to 4 is used to rate the problems that are encountered:

1. Cosmetic problem only; need not be fixed unless extra time is available on project
2. Minor usability problem; fixing this should be given low priority
3. Major usability problem; important to fix, so should be given high priority
4. Usability catastrophe; imperative to fix this before product can be released

Debriefing

After all the expert evaluators have rated and scored the site, it is not uncommon for all the evaluators to meet with a moderator to discuss what happened in the test sessions. Individual evaluators can discuss their own subjective experiences with the site; this is also an excellent time for the moderator to ask probing questions about specific areas of usability violations noted on the evaluators' logs. You could even choose to audio- and videotape the debriefing sessions for future analysis.

During the debriefing, it is very likely that the expert evaluators will have suggestions for change, as well as new ideas and new questions that will help the usability team further explore the site's usability. The feedback gathered at the debriefing should be transcribed and presented in the summary report that results from this evaluation.

Assembling Data

Putting your results together and making sense of them is just as important as, if not more important than, gathering the data. Therefore, you need to analyze your data along several lines.

Quantitative Measures

What was the overall number of unique usability problems that were found in this round of heuristic evaluation? If you have a baseline (obtained from previous heuristic evaluations), what is the delta (change) from the last measurement? How many errors did each evaluator find?

Heuristic Violation Proportion Graph

Make a bar graph to show how many violations per heuristic were found. Notice any trends that occur; for example, a huge spike in the "user's natural language" heuristic could mean that there was not enough early interaction with the real user community for the site's designers to develop a user-oriented vocabulary.

Severity Proportion Chart

Make a chart to show how many errors of each class were found. A high proportion of type 4 errors (the severest type) could serve as a catalyst to make the "powers that be" approve major changes for the site. This graphic also gives the team an easy-to-understand snapshot of the overall health of the site's usability (see Figures 6.3 and 6.4).

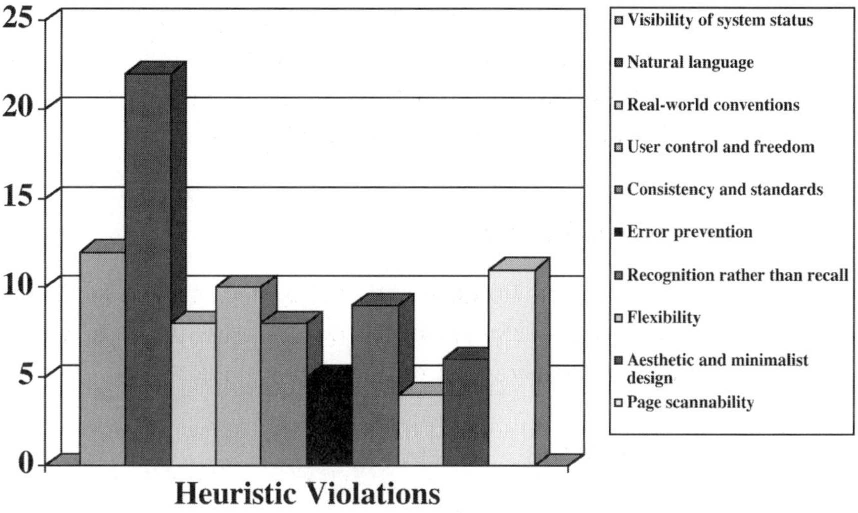
25
20
15
10
5
0
Heuristic Violations
Visibility of system status
Natural language
Real-world conventions
User control and freedom
Consistency and standards
Error prevention
Recognition rather than recall
Flexibility
Aesthetic and minimalist design
Page scannability

FIGURE 6.3 *An example of a chart showing heuristic violation proportions.*

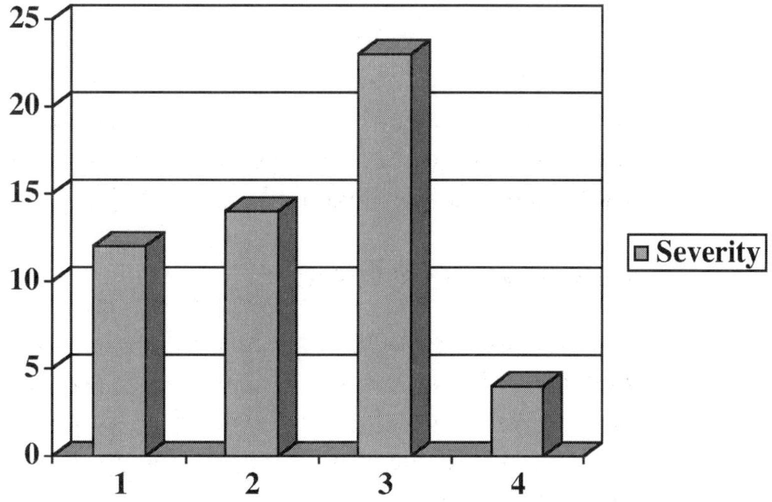
25
20
15
10
5
0
1
2
3
4
Severity

FIGURE 6.4 *An example of a chart of severity types in an heuristic evaluation.*

Thematic Trends

Were there any obvious trends in the located usability problems? For example, if the evaluators found that the terminology used to label various parts of the site was too jargon-filled, falling outside the user population's natural vocabulary, you would again have powerful evidence to support the need to rethink this area and to solicit additional feedback from the user community.

Putting It All Together

Finally, you need to summarize all your suggestions into bullet points so that the team has a clear set of objectives for improved usability. Be sure to cite specific instances and URLs rather than general concepts. Make this list almost impossible to *not* understand. The level of detail that you should include is a stylistic and workflow-dependent decision. The most important idea here, though, is to be specific enough that the "fixes" can be understood and carried out by someone not on your immediate team of evaluators.

Some Criticism of Heuristic Evaluation

Heuristic evaluation is a tool that assuredly has a place in your toolbox. Remember, though, that it should by no means be the only trick up your sleeve! You might hear several criticisms from others in your organization. Take heart from the following excerpt, which comes from Jakob Nielsen's landmark publication, *How to Conduct a Heuristic Evaluation:*[16]

> *Heuristic evaluation does not provide a systematic way to generate fixes to the usability problems or a way to assess the probable quality of any redesigns. However, because heuristic evaluation aims at explaining each observed usability problem with reference to established usability principles, it will often be fairly easy to generate a revised design according to the guidelines*

[16] You can find this article at *www.useit.com/papers/heuristic/heuristic_evaluation.html.*

> *provided by the violated principle for good interactive systems. Also, many usability problems have fairly obvious fixes as soon as they have been identified.*

As you see, this technique was never really intended to be a highly empirical method for obtaining data and systematically transforming it into change; rather, it is a shoot-from-the-hip guerrilla tactic that helps jump-start almost any usability project. And this is not a bad thing at all!

The following sections summarize some criticisms you might hear from naysayers in your organization.

Real Users Aren't "Expert Evaluators"

Obviously, this technique revolves around the idea that expert evaluators "know what's best" for real users. Some people have criticized this technique because it does not attempt to approximate the actual user's frame of reference. My rebuttal has always been that regardless, the expert evaluators do in fact uncover usability errors that would have almost assuredly tripped up a "real" user. This speaks to the concept that I have only recently, and reluctantly, begun to embrace: Some usability is better than none, and it rarely matters how you come to find the problems, as long as you do find them.

Heuristic Evaluation Can't Find All "Show-Stoppers"

This statement is absolutely true. There will almost assuredly be at least one obscure problem with your site that "expert" users won't be able to locate because they don't interact with the site the way a novice user might. It never ceases to amaze me how much trouble some people—even intelligent, relatively computer-literate people—have with their computers. I have seen several users perform the "click of death" on a computer before—that is, they click so rapidly on everything in their visual field that the computer freezes. I have watched at least one very intelligent user trash the contents of her most important directory—irrevocably—because she would not stop to read the warning messages that popped up on her screen.

When I tried to replicate the error just to figure out how it could have been avoided, I found it nearly impossible to duplicate. The novice user had usage habits that were simply alien to me; I would never have stumbled on the chance condition that she had so easily wrought. But remember that you will still have real users test your design, so everything should "come out in the wash."

Automated Aids to Heuristic Evaluation

Although automated techniques should never be used to completely replace real user testing, they can be used quite effectively to augment an existing comprehensive usability plan. In particular, certain types of metrics tend to lend themselves to being evaluated in an automated fashion. Such data, collected automatically, can be a real asset to any usability plan. Remember that automated techniques allow you to acquire large amounts of data that would otherwise be too painful or not feasible to gather by hand.

In particular, automated testing of link integrity (searching for broken links), load times, types of content on a site (HTML, Java, JavaScript, other embedded content such as video or audio data), and the number of ways to traverse to a particular page are easily automated programmatically.

At least one company, WebCriteria,[17] makes a living of implementing just such a technique. For a reasonable fee, you can get the company to do a metrics assessment of your site. The company's current product incarnation uses "Max," an automated browsing agent that is supposed to traverse a site the way a normal human user would. Max is built on a well-known human factors model known as GOMS, which is a type of model human processor.[18] I have not used the service personally. You might opt to outsource such a service to a company like this one, or you

[17] You can visit WebCriteria at *www.webcriteria.com.*

[18] For more information on Max and GOMS, see *www.itl.nist.gov/iaui/vvrg/hfweb/proceedings/lynch/index.html.*

could choose to write your own in-house programs to do site traversal and reporting for you.[19]

CHAPTER SUMMARY

- A heuristic is a rule of thumb.
- Jakob Nielsen developed heuristic evaluation several years before the Web became popular.
- Heuristic evaluation can be done rapidly and with little expense, compared with other testing methods.
- In order to do a heuristic evaluation, you need a list of heuristics to follow and approximately five evaluators.
- The list of heuristics you use might come from the original 10 developed by Nielsen and reviewed in this chapter, or you might choose other heuristics that you or other usability professionals derive from experience.
- Almost every usability problem can be traced to a violation of one or more heuristics.
- To assist in prioritizing change, you should also rate the severity of each usability problem.
- You may hear several types of criticism regarding heuristic evaluation, almost all of which can be dispersed by simply using heuristic evaluation in addition to, rather instead of, other evaluation techniques.
- Parts of heuristic evaluation can be automated using commercial and homegrown software.

HANDS-ON EXERCISES

1. Assemble a team of evaluators. You should shoot for five, but if you can even get one other person to help you with this task, it makes a huge difference.

---

[19]And if you do, may I suggest using Perl?

2. Perform a heuristic evaluation of your site. Decide ahead of time which heuristics you will use, and prepare scoring/comment sheets for your evaluators to use. You can use the sample scoring sheet included on the CD-ROM as a template.
3. After the evaluation, meet with all the members of your group to discuss the findings. What problems did you find that can be immediate action items (problems that obviously need to be fixed without the need for further user testing)? Which might require more input from users?
4. Do a Web search to find out what kinds of automated usability tools exist. Technology is evolving so quickly that the list will have changed by the time you read this book.

DISCUSSION TOPICS

1. What two other heuristics should be included in the heuristics list discussed in this chapter? Why? Note that there might be an unlimited number of heuristics that you could mention; there isn't necessarily a right or wrong way to answer this question.
2. Why even test users at all? If an evaluator is an expert, shouldn't users expect the expert to solve all the problems without their help?
3. If you were forced to use only heuristic evaluation to test your site, what kind of errors would you be most likely to uncover? What types of errors would you be likely to miss? Explain.
4. Do you think that the list of heuristics should vary completely from site to site, should they be completely standardized, or should there be a middle ground? Explain your answer. What are the pros and cons of each stance?

CHAPTER

7

USABILITY LAB SETUP

SETTING UP THE SETUP

Most of the activities described in this book can be done in a plethora of locations; in fact, many of the techniques covered herein are intended to be done "in the field," implying that they can be done anywhere. However, when it comes to usability testing, the tool covered in Chapter 8, it is critical that you have a proper setup in which to work.

In this chapter we look at a variety of potential configurations for your testing lab. You might find that the same area you use for usability testing is the place where you do your other work as well. Many organizations provide an easily reconfigurable room for exactly this purpose.

As mentioned in Chapter 1, you don't need a lot of extravagant equipment to do decent usability testing. We begin our survey of lab configurations with the absolute, bare-bones essentials for a proper lab. As we progress, we introduce increasing levels of sophistication so that as more budgeting becomes available to you, you can grow your facility appropriately. Note also that the more elaborate facilities also require greater staffing to make it all work.

Many companies that profess to do lots of usability testing on their products usually simply have great lab facilities. In fact, often such companies spend the majority of their budgets on state-of-the-art testing labs, with multiple video cameras, high-tech audio-recording equipment, full video-editing facilities, and lots of other bells and whistles. Unfortunately, by the time a company has invested in all this gear (which, admittedly, makes for an impressive tour for people the company wants to impress), sometimes there is little or no budget left over for acquiring the most important resource: participants—oh, and the second most important resource, which is you, of course!

My advice is to start with the simplest configuration you can and plan to upgrade to more and better equipment as your work begins to pay for itself. This means you won't have to spend valuable cycles setting up equipment when what you really need to do is create a great test plan. Keeping it simple pays off here, too!

GENERAL LAB TIPS

No matter where your lab is physically located or which configuration you end up using, you should observe several general tips to make the best possible environment for doing usability testing or conducting other sessions:

- Use modular furniture that can be easily reconfigured, in case you need to lay out the room differently for various types of sessions.
- Make sure that there are no irritating noises in the room (no modem dial-out noises, no noisy racks of file servers humming next door, and so on) and that you have control over any noise that might emanate from adjoining areas.
- Make sure that you can control the climate in the room. Rooms that are too warm tend to make users sleepy.
- It's best to have a reception area nearby so that you can queue participants as they arrive. This is a good place to begin helping them feel at ease. Offering them beverages and a snack (if appropriate for the time of day) is a nice touch.

- Try to avoid using an intercom system to communicate with participants. This can create the "Wizard of Oz" effect; "Pay no attention to the moderator behind the mirror!"
- Be absolutely sure that your pieces of furniture, especially your chairs, are ergonomic and reconfigurable. You don't want your participants to get RSI, nor do you want for a participant in a wheelchair to be unable to use your equipment.
- Just because your lab is being used for experimental testing, it doesn't need to look like an operating room or to look boorish. Try to make the room relatively comfortable but not sterile looking.
- Don't forget a potted plant. It's bad karma to do so.

The most important tip I can give you is to make your lab comfortable. The more sterile and "clean room like" you make your lab, the more uncomfortable your participants will be. Add a little décor, but be careful about things that might be too distracting—lava lamps, although they are a great addition to any room, are probably not things you'd want in your lab! For the same reason, you probably want to turn off screen savers on your test computers.

SIMPLE LAB SETUP

If you are just starting out with usability testing, you probably don't have access to lots of space or technical gizmos. If that's the case, the simple lab setup is for you. The simple lab setup can be in a single room that has no partitions, no control room, no video cameras, and no observation room. You only need the following:

- A PC workstation with the correct operating system and hardware configuration for your target audience
- An Internet connection that best approximates your target audience's connection
- A comfortable chair for the participant
- A chair for the test moderator
- A chair for the timer/data logger (optional)

- Take a look at Figure 7.1, which shows a diagram of a simple lab setup. Note that the test moderator's chair is slightly behind and to the side of the participant's location. The reason for this placement is that the moderator should not sit directly next to the participant; the moderator should be out of the participant's line of sight. Remember that we want to eliminate as many possible distractions from the user's field of sensation as possible, since any such factors might contribute to a participant's performance. Such factors then become what is known as *confounding variables*, which are factors for which the testers did not expressly control, resulting in less reliable data.

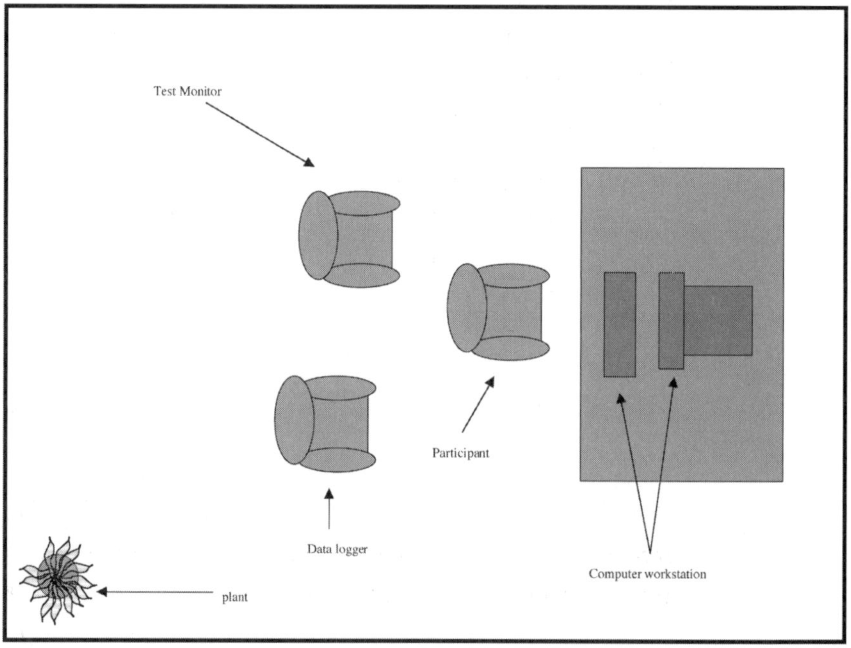
Test Monitor
Participant
Data logger
Computer workstation
plant

FIGURE 7.1 *A simple lab setup.*

As mentioned before, one criticism of such a sterile lab environment is that it does not reflect the highly unpredictable nature of true user environments. Maybe our users really *do* have huge distractions in their environment—for instance, maybe they have large fluctuations in their climate. Nonetheless, we cannot attempt to scientifically and accurately generate such chaos, so we have to take another route: Give every participant the same controlled environment, and that way we get an accurate baseline.

Another reason you might want to avoid sitting directly next to the participant is that psychologically, doing so could make it appear to the participant that you are a peer and that you should share in the frustration of accomplishing the tasks. You have to maintain the "frame" in which you are the moderator and the participant is the participant. Furthermore, I have known several moderators who find it too difficult to resist the temptation of "helping out" when the participant gets into real trouble with a task. After all, it is (arguably) human nature to want to help out when another person is having a difficult time. You must resist this temptation; giving in to it will nullify your data.

Finally, if the participant can see you, he or she might be able to read the subtle nonverbal communication that you, no matter how seasoned a test moderator you are, emit in the way of scowls, hesitation in breathing, subtle motor activity, and a variety of other "signs." These can all signal to a shrewd participant that he or she is off course on a task or that he or she is "warm" or "cold." You want to avoid this type of influence entirely, since once again it can make your data useless.

Nonetheless, it is critical that the test moderator can see and hear everything that is going on with the participant, including facial expressions, screen activity, and verbalized thoughts. All of these can help the moderator understand what is going on in the participant's head as he or she completes tasks. Hence, the moderator sits slightly behind the participant, but not so far behind that the participant's face is no longer visible.

As for the data logger/timer, if you are using an extra crew member, the same is true for that person. The data logger needs to be able to see everything that's going on in the participant's interaction with the screen as well as the participant's reactions to the tasks. Having an extra set of observing eyes and ears in the room can prove very helpful for the moderator. You will not have an easy time doing testing if you are the sole crew member; you really do need someone to handle data logging, unless you are using some sort of automated logging system.

SIMPLE LAB SETUP WITH VIDEO

If you have a single extravagance for your testing lab, let it be video. It can be supremely helpful to have access to video footage after a session is done so that you can review the footage to look for subtle participant feedback that you might have missed during the live session. Additionally, sometimes you simply cannot keep track of what is happening fast enough to do meaningful data logging. If users are making a navigation error in some strange way that escapes you at first sight, you could figure it out after watching the video a time or two.

Note that in Figure 7.2, the location of the single camera setup is such that it is pointed at an angle toward the computer monitor. There are two approaches you can take to positioning the camera. In one approach, you position the camera so that it also picks up at least the side of the participant's face. This placement allows you some, although limited, ability to review what was happening on screen as well as the participant's expressions. Note, however, that this single-camera setup isn't really the best setup for capturing all aspects of what's going on; you sacrifice information all the way around.

The other approach is to choose just one thing to focus on, either the screen or the participant. This means that you will have more video real estate for just the single subject, which normally makes it easier to see what is going on. In the event that you are using a single camera and focusing on the participant, see Figure 7.3 for where the camera should be positioned.

Here's some hopefully sage advice about participants and cameras: Although you are obligated to mention to participants that they are being videotaped, you should never draw attention to this fact during testing. You should never get up in the middle of a session to change a tape. Tape is cheap! Use a fresh tape for each participant if you must, just to avoid this unprofessional action. When you fiddle with the cam-

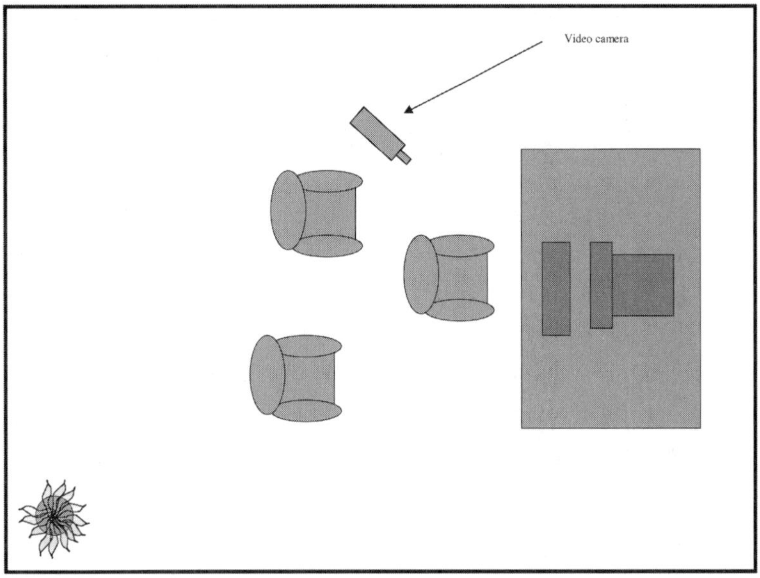
Video camera

FIGURE 7.2 *A simple lab setup with video.*

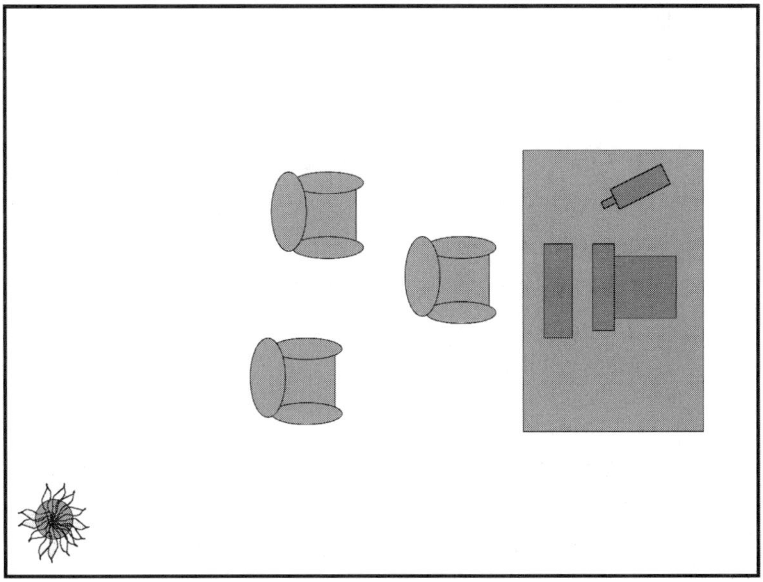

FIGURE 7.3 *Another version of the simple lab with video.*

era, you are reminding the participant that he or she is being taped. That can make a lot of people freeze up and perform poorly, thus negating the point of your test.

In addition, don't leave the camera out in plain sight, especially if the camera has a little blinky light that constantly advertises its presence to the participant. To camouflage your camera, you can use a variety of techniques. I generally use a tall plant or fake potted tree behind which I hide the camera behind. However, any of a variety of hiding techniques will do, and you don't have to make it a totally "hidden" or invisible camera. Just make its placement subtle enough that the participant will forget about it as soon as the tasks begin.

Adding a Direct Video Feed from the Computer

To be honest, using a video camera to record what's happening on screen is a really nasty hack, a real kluge. Video cameras record at a different rate than the rate at which video screens refresh, causing a very noticeable flutter when you view the video. Ever notice this on your local weather forecast? The meteorologist will be talking about some cold front, while in the background you see a bunch of computer monitors that are flickering like mad. For purposes of your test, this effect is annoying and makes it hard to read the screen. Furthermore, the resolution of a typical video camera is too poor to reveal thin lines of hyperlinked text.

The solution to this problem is to purchase a little device that lets you plug your video output of the computer directly into the input of a VCR. Some types of conversion that take place make the screen look great when viewed this way as opposed to the previous method. This method also has the effect of freeing up one video camera, which you can then train squarely on the participant. This is really the best solution because it affords you excellent coverage of both key fields of activity: the screen and the participant.

The previous scenario does present one problem, however: synchronization. How do you link the two videos so that they can be viewed simul-

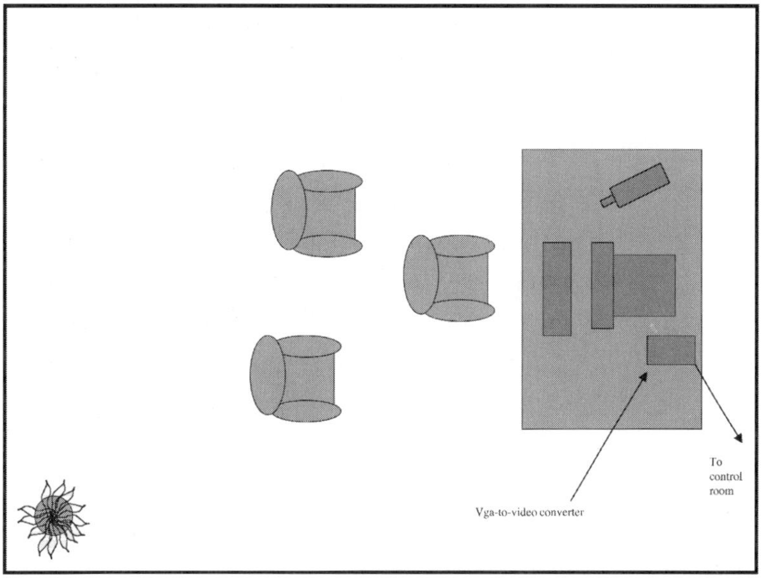
To
control
room
Vga-to-video converter

FIGURE 7.4 *A lab with a direct video feed from the workstation.*

taneously? Otherwise, neither tape makes much sense. There are ways of linking the tapes, but they are outside the scope of this book. If you are able to afford a video operator, the operator should be able to take care of this for you. Additionally, it may be beneficial to make a composite tape that shows a split-screen view of both screen and participant, for illustrating key moments in the sessions. Such footage comes in handy when presenting your findings to the "powers that be" in your organization or to your client.

Modified Lab with Video Control Room

The next extravagance you should want for your lab is a video control room and remotely controllable cameras. There are several "eye-in-the-sky" cameras that can be mounted in a discrete corner of the room and focused on any part of the room via a separate control console that can be located in an adjacent room. Optimally, the video control area would be in a separate room altogether, so that the participant can't see anything in that room or even know that it exists. However, I have seen instances in which the control area was set up behind a partition or in a cubicle, just enough out of sight to work.

Having such a facility greatly enhances how much you can do in the way of recording various angles, since the user needn't know that the camera angle is being changed or that any fancy stuff is happening on his or her behalf. For example, if you do a composite session with a card sort, an interview, and usability tasks, you clearly want to use different parts of the room for different parts of the session. Having a remotely controllable and highly configurable camera allows you to do this and get it all on tape.

The video control room needs to be designed and set up by a video professional, and since I am not one, I won't pretend to know everything that you'll need to set one up. My point is that it is a great asset to your organization to have one of these rooms and the accompanying cameras. See Figure 7.5 for a diagram of this setup.

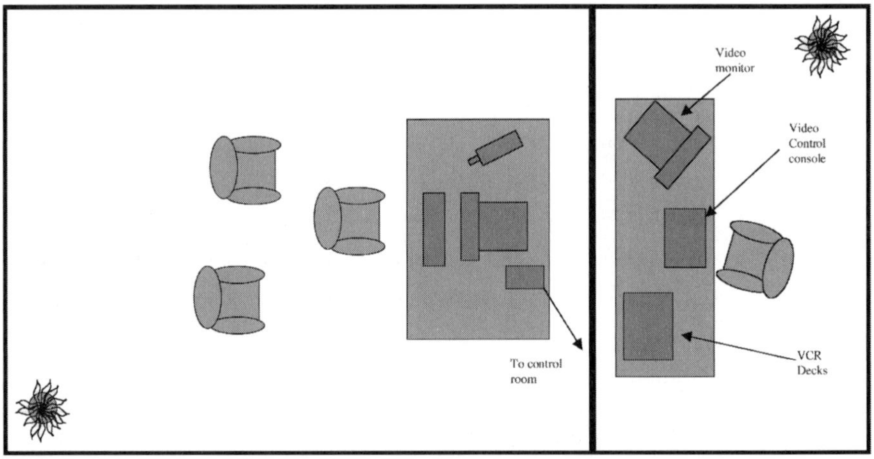
Video monitor
Video Control console
To control room
VCR Decks

FIGURE 7.5 *A high-tech lab with a control room.*

LAB WITH OBSERVATION ROOM

Many classical experimental labs have an observation room—that is, a usually soundproofed room that is joined to the lab area by way of a one-way mirror. An observation room can be quite helpful to the staff conducting the experiment, because it gives them a way to watch the action in progress.

However, I think that these mirrors are often a great way to put your participants on edge. I can't imagine that there is an educated adult in the world who would be fooled by a one-way mirror. Everyone knows what they are and that there are observers behind them. There's something "Big Brotherish" about those mirrors. So you might want to forego this feature. You can achieve much the same effect with a couple of well-placed cameras. However, that's just my opinion (See Figure 7.6).

As mentioned, sometimes letting stubborn designers watch usability trials can be a powerful tool for change. You need to think about the implications of adding such a feature to your lab setup, though. If you have an observation room, who will be allowed to do the observing? How will you maintain ethical boundaries with the people who do get to watch?

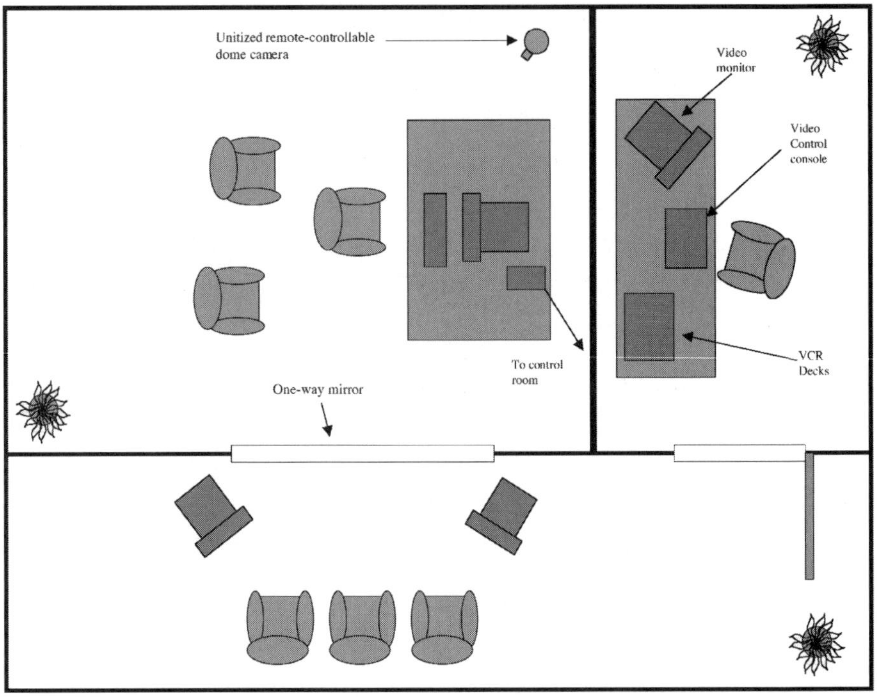
Unitized remote-controllable dome camera
Video monitor
Video Control console
VCR Decks
To control room
One-way mirror

FIGURE 7.6 *An example of a fully equipped lab setup with observation room and video control room.*

potted plant

THE FOCUS GROUP ROOM

Although a focus group room isn't technically a test environment, it is a resource that is great to have. When you're working with focus groups, it's good to have a conference room or the like that can be closed off from interruptions. Depending on how many participants you have for your focus groups, you'll want a round or oval conference table and many comfortable chairs. In addition, since focus group sessions can run for a while, it's a nice touch to have beverages available.

You also need at least one computer workstation with Internet connectivity and some kind of projection system (or, if you have the budget, a large screen plasma display) so that you can project the site being evaluated onto an overhead screen or wall. It is also extremely useful to have one or more whiteboards for drawing ideas and sketches. If you will have a whiteboard, it's well worth having a little device called a *mimio*, and it is a gadget that affixes to your whiteboard via suction cups. It tracks what you write on the whiteboard and captures it to your laptop or desktop computer. You can see more about mimio at *www.mimio.com.* As of this writing, they sell for under $500.

Many vendors make overhead projection units, but the two that I have had the best experience with are from InFocus *(www.infocus.com)* and Sanyo *(www.sanyo.com)*. Sanyo makes an absolutely incredible projector that is the brightest of any I have ever seen, which means that you can see the picture clearly without even needing to dim the room lighting; very impressive! Of course, it costs a mere $25,000, so one would hope it would be at least as bright as the sun.

If you don't quite have the budget for the latest overhead projector, that's okay. You can usually rent one weekly or daily from a nearby A/V supply house. Keep in mind, however, that if you plan to do several focus group sessions, you're much better off buying rather than renting (See Figure 7.7).

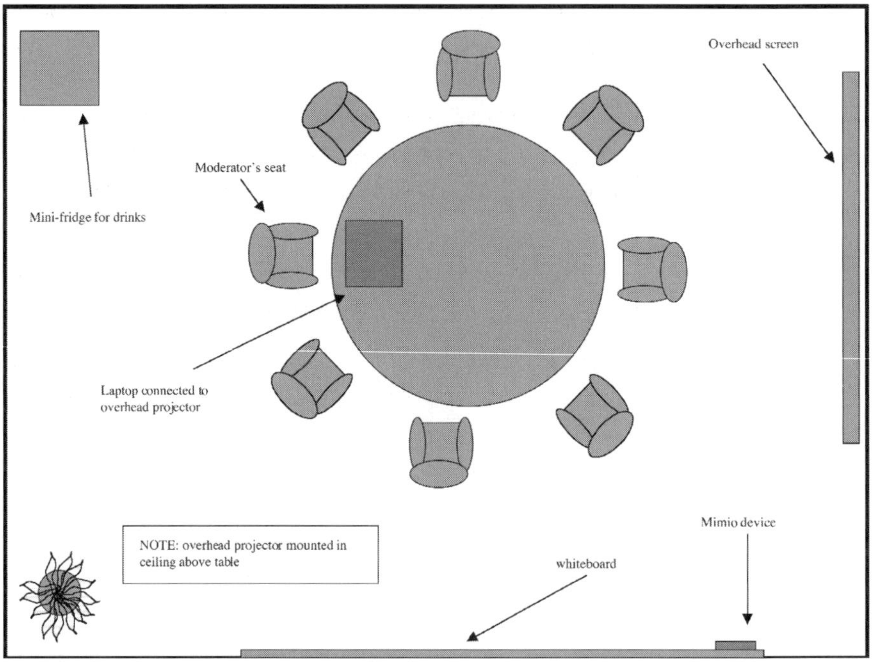
Overhead screen
Moderator's seat
Mini-fridge for drinks
Laptop connected to
overhead projector
NOTE: overhead projector mounted in
ceiling above table
Mimio device
whiteboard

FIGURE 7.7 *A focus room setup.*

SURVEY OF LAB EQUIPMENT

If you do have funding to get fancy equipment—and if you have staff to operate it—it helps to know a little about the different types of equipment that you might need. This section is a topical overview of such types of equipment. My inclusion of a particular brand or model in this book is not in any way an endorsement of that product; I simply chose some representative pieces of equipment for illustrative purposes. Remember too that you don't absolutely have to acquire any of this gear, but if you do have the budget for these devices, you need to educate yourself a little about the best type of equipment to buy for your lab.

Audio

Crystal-clear video should, of course, be accompanied by crystal-clear audio. Although most consumer-grade video cameras come with a type of built-in microphone called a *condenser microphone*, the sound sometimes lacks quality, and if the camera is across the room from the participant or if the room has lots of background noise, the sound quality will suffer.

To combat this problem, you should consider using an external microphone of some sort. There are many varieties and manufacturers of microphones. My favorite type of mic is the pressure-zone microphone (PZM). PZMs work on a different principle than dynamic or condenser microphones, and they tend to reject background noise and pick up sounds such as speech from any location in the room. In my opinion, this makes the PZM mic the best choice of all the varieties. However, you may have your own religious microphone beliefs.

Microphone Characteristics

All microphones can be described along the lines of four essential characteristics:

- Element type
- Polar pattern
- Frequency response
- Impedance

The *element* of a microphone is the part that actually transforms sound energy into electrical energy. The element usually consists of at least a *diaphragm*, which is a thin piece of material that, when moved, induces an electrical current in the mic circuitry. So, essentially, the element *is* the mic. There are several different types of elements; we'll talk about a few of them in a minute.

The *polar pattern* refers to the area around the mic from which sound is "heard." There are essentially four types of polar patterns: omnidirectional, cardioid (also known as *directional*), hypercardioid (another type of directional pattern), and bidirectional. In each case, the microphone is designed to either accept sound from all directions (as does the omnidirectional style) or reject sound from one or more directions (See Figure 7.8).

The *frequency response* refers to the amount of the audible spectrum that the mic can "hear." For reference, a human with perfect hearing can

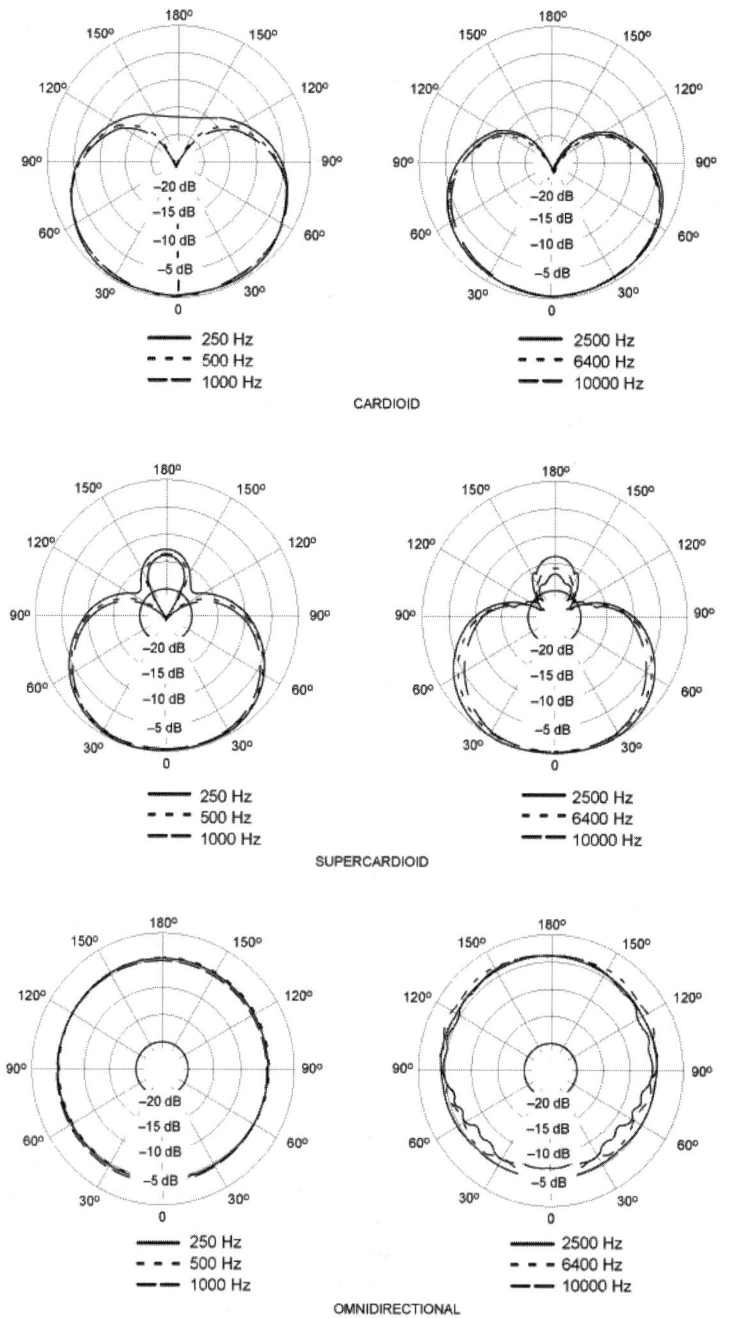
180°
150°
120°
90°
60°
30°
0
-20 dB
-15 dB
-10 dB
-5 dB
250 Hz
500 Hz
1000 Hz
2500 Hz
6400 Hz
10000 Hz
CARDIOID
SUPERCARDIOID
OMNIDIRECTIONAL

FIGURE 7.8 *The four polar response patterns: omnidirectional, cardioid, hypercardioid, and bidirectional.*

hear sounds from 20 hertz (Hz) to 20 kilohertz (kHz). The chunk of this audible range that a mic can "hear" is its *range*. But any given microphone will not have a homogenous response to all frequencies; because of the way they are built and the materials used, some mics "hear" certain frequencies better or worse than others.

Any decent microphone includes a graph of its frequency response when you buy it; you can also ask the salesperson to provide you with the response graph when you are comparison shopping. One tip: Human speech recognition is contingent on a very important frequency range: 1kHz. In the 1kHz range, you'll find many of the sounds that make human speech intelligible. So if you see that a particular mic has an increased amount of response in this region, it's probably because it was designed primarily as a vocal mic.

The *impedance* of a microphone is a measure of the electrical resistance in its circuitry. Generally, low-impedance microphones are of higher quality than high-impedance ones. Sometimes you will hear the term *XLR* (short for "eXtra Low Resistance", so named because of the low impedance of this type of microphone) used to refer to a low-impedance microphone. In a nutshell, you need to make sure that the type of mic that you purchase is the right impedance for whatever you are plugging it into. Most professional devices have XLR connections. Refer to Figure 7.9 for an example frequency response of a very popular dynamic vocal microphone. Note the peak at about 1kHz.

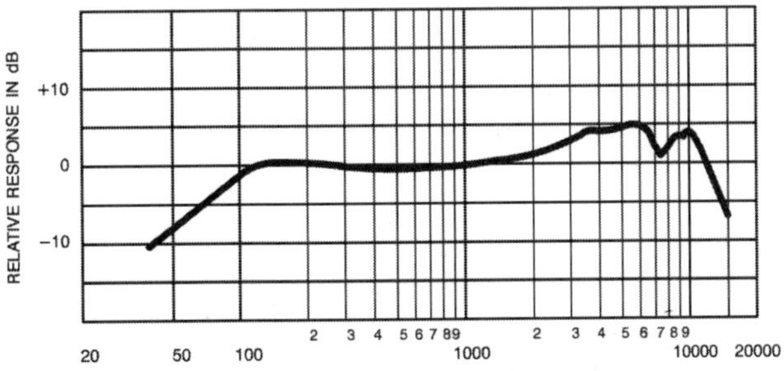
RELATIVE RESPONSE IN dB
+10
0
−10
2 3 4 5 6 7 8 9
2 3 4 5 6 7 8 9
20
50
100
1000
10000
20000

FIGURE 7.9 *A response graph of a Shure SM-58 microphone. Used with permission. ©2000 Shure Brothers.*

Dynamic Microphones

Dynamic mics are the least high-tech form of microphone. They rely on sound waves to move the diaphragm, which in turn induces a weak current in the mic circuitry. The output of a dynamic mic is usually much fainter than the output of a condenser mic. This is absolutely the *wrong* kind of microphone to use for your lab. Don't even think about using one. However, if you abandon your career of usability testing to become a lounge singer, you'll want one of the microphones shown in Figure 7.10.

SM58
SHURE

FIGURE 7.10 *A Shure SM-58 dynamic microphone. Used with permission. ©2000 Shure Brothers.*

Condenser Microphones

The *condenser mic* is an electromagnetic version of the dynamic mic. It uses an active power supply (which can come from either a battery or a "phantom power supply") to amplify the weak inductance caused by the sound waves that strike the diaphragm. The output of condenser mics is strong, and they are very sensitive to sound. Unfortunately, they are also sensitive to background noise, and since they are so "hot" (i.e., sensitive) they can distort easily, making your audio sound like it is coming out of a heavy-metal guitar amplifier.

Condenser mics are really good in the hands of an experienced audio engineer, but in the hands of a novice, they can sound bad. You may find that in certain environments, you need a condenser mic because you have to place the recording gear far away from the source.

Condenser mics can have highly directional characteristics, which means that sound that is "off-axis" is rejected. This can be a good thing if the surrounding area is noisy but you need to "focus" on the subject.

Pressure Zone Microphones

The *pressure zone microphone (PZM)* is a totally different type of microphone. It looks a lot different from the microphones you are probably used to seeing. PZMs are generally flat, often square.

A PZM microphone is mounted on a reflecting surface that causes sound waves to build up a pressure zone within the mic housing before being transferred to the microphone. These mics are often used for group discussions around a table. Their low profile also makes them a favorite when you want to camouflage the recording gear, as is the case in usability sessions.

A variety of manufacturers make PZM-style microphones. Please note that PZM microphones are also frequently called *boundary microphones.*

Video

You may have a regular VHS camcorder lying around that you can use to capture video footage from your sessions. Although such a device is better than nothing, you will run into some pretty severe limitations fairly early on if you use one. For one thing, regular camcorders are bulky, which makes them more noticeable, a trait that you'd rather avoid in a usability lab setup. There are many different types of cameras that you can consider for your lab, but they should all have the following characteristics:

- **Discrete.** Your camera should draw as little attention to itself as possible. Remember that you are not trying to deceive the participants into thinking that they are not being recorded; you have to get their consent to tape them, after all. However, a quiet, small camera will help keep the participant's mind off the fact that he or she is being taped.

- **Remote controllable.** Whether you are controlling the camera from a control room or from within the lab itself, it is very handy to have the ability to remotely start, stop, pause, record, and so on. Better cameras also allow you to zoom remotely. In addition, if you can afford a camera that has motorized pan capability, it will make your life a lot easier.
- **High resolution.** The higher the resolution, the better the quality. This factor is critical if you want to be able to see details in the participant's face or on the screen (assuming that you are not using a VGA-to-video converter to capture screen information; more on that in a moment).
- **Zoom.** Decent cameras should be able to zoom in on the subject. A decent camera has a 10x zoom capability. This feature allows your video operator to zoom on critical events.

One example of my idea of a good camera is the Panasonic WV-CSR654 camera. It can be ceiling or wall mounted for maximizing your angle, is remote controlled, and even has options to be controlled via the Web. In Figure 7.11 we see a "dome" camera that you could hide inside

SUPER DYNAMIC

FIGURE 7.11 *This is the Panasonic WV-CSR654, a "unitized' dome camera, suitable for use in a usability lab. Used with permission. ©2000 Panasonic.*

a plexiglass hemisphere. It's similar to cameras used for surveillance, so it may give off a sort of "Big Brother" feel if you aren't clever about making it discrete!

VGA-to-Video Converters

As mentioned earlier, it can be intimidating to try to capture your participant's moves on the computer screen by pointing a video camera at the monitor. In fact, doing so almost invariably produces lackluster results. Another more suitable approach you can take is to use an off-the-shelf computer video converter that will change your computer video output to National Television Standards Committee (NTSC) or PAL (Phase Alternation Line) video, depending on where you live. NTSC is a video format that is most commonly used in North America. PAL is more common in Europe and other parts of the world.

Several companies make just such a product. One company is AverMedia *(www.avermedia.com).* Another is Focus Enhancements *(www.focus-info.com).* Both companies' products are available from most mail-order PC companies. Note that many of these devices can work only when the computer video is set to a particular resolution (most often, 800 by 600). This setting could have some implications for what you can and cannot do with regard to testing various resolutions for your site.

Of course, many other companies make similar devices, so shop around before you settle on a product. Whatever you choose, you need to configure your device so that the converter "passes through" the computer's video signal to the participant's monitor (if you don't, how are they going to see what's going on?) as well as passing the converted signal through to your video editing and viewing gear.

Note that having several disjointed camera systems that are all attempting to capture assorted angles of the same essential action presents a particular problem: How do you synchronize all this footage later? For example, your video editor might want to transition back and forth between several angles to generate a more powerful video presentation of your results. Although the topic of video synchronization is outside the scope of this book, most companies that sell video equipment will be able to make a suggestion for synchronization. In all likelihood, the solution will involve using Society of Motion Picture and Television Engineers (SMPTE) time code, which is a type of synchronization code that can be "striped" onto videotape. You never actually see the time code, but a SMPTE-aware device will be able to read it.

Overhead Projectors

You should definitely have an overhead video projector on hand for a focus group room (See Figure 7.12). There are many varieties, but the ones I have used and liked are made by InFocus and Sanyo. You can also combine an overhead projector with the mimio device, described earlier in the chapter, to create a large, interactive image on the wall or on a large whiteboard.

FIGURE 7.12 *A typical overhead VGA projector. Image courtesy Sanyo. Used with permission. ©2000 Sanyo.*

PARTICIPANT COMPENSATION

It may sound obvious, but we'll point it out anyhow: any time you use human participants, you should always compensate them somehow. Making sure the participant doesn't walk away empty handed is a critical part of forming a healthy relationship, and it helps keep the participants excited about the work they are helping you do.

The type and amount of compensation varies, from a couple of home-made cookies to a mini-vacation. Cash is always good, but there are plenty of other ways to compensate your participants. Depending on the nature of your organization, your form of compensation could be one or more of any of the following:

- Cash (from $10 to $200 an hour)
- Credit toward your company's goods
- Electronic goods that you don't produce yourself (software, PDAs, CD players, clocks, laser pointers, the list is almost endless); often you can negotiate a co-op with another company to feature its product in a promotional fashion (assuming, obviously, that the company isn't your competitor!)
- Free vacation days or extra flex time if your participants are working on your company's intranet
- Electronic cash
- Gift certificates
- Promotional items with your corporate logo (T-shirts, coffee mugs, and the like)

You can be fairly clever when it comes to compensation, but the bottom line is that participants must feel as though they are getting some value out of the transaction. On some occasions, you are obligated to pay cash (if your participants are from a recruiting agency, for example, you'll need to pay either the participant or the agency).

NO CLOCKS IN THE LAB!

It is quite disadvantageous to have a clock inside the testing lab itself; if your participants are clock watchers, it will affect their performance to be distracted by looking to see how much time they have left. For similar reasons, I discourage showing the participant my stopwatch or announcing how much time is left to accomplish a task. When a participant knows only 15 seconds remain to finish a task, the participant likely to panic and perform differently than he or she might have when oblivious to the time.

CHAPTER SUMMARY

- You don't need several high-tech devices to do real and effective usability testing.
- If you can afford high-tech devices, make sure that you wait to buy them until you have formulated the other components of your usability plan.
- There are several types of lab layouts that you can use, ranging from the very simple to the very complex.
- The first extravagance in which you should indulge yourself is a video system.
- It's also important to have clear audio; most commercial-grade camcorders have microphones that are not appropriate for this sort of work.
- Remote-controlled cameras allow you to capture a much wider range of action and allow you to be unobtrusive at the same time.

HANDS-ON EXERCISES

1. Draft a plan of the lab setup that you think will work best for you. Consider current space allocation, potential for future growth (making sure that all equipment and fixtures are portable), and budget.
2. Call several local audio/video retailers to see what they offer in the way of A/V equipment.
3. Find out where your company gets furniture; price some modest fixtures for the lab. You'll need only basic items: chairs, a table, plants, and possibly some lamps.
4. Inspect the location you'll use for a lab to make sure that it is not in an unusually noisy area and that you can control the climate.

DISCUSSION TOPICS

1. What do you think about one-way mirrors? Have you ever been in front of one? Will you use one in your lab?
2. What are some potential benefits of making your lab setup totally mobile? How can you make a mobile configuration?
3. At how much of a premium is office space in your organization? What are some potential political barriers you will have to cross to get space? How will you cost-justify the space?
4. We didn't look at any lab setup in which the test monitor wasn't in the room, located near the participant. Is this necessarily a good thing? Why should or shouldn't the monitor be in the same room as the participant?

CHAPTER

8

USABILITY TESTING

Research is what I'm doing when I don't know what I'm doing.

—Wernher Von Braun

NOT JUST ANOTHER TOOL IN THE TOOLBOX

Web site usability testing is the most complex tool of our toolbox. It requires the most planning, the most training, and the most resources of all the tools. It is also the most productive of the tools, in that the data that you can gain from testing will be the most detailed and closest to the actual user that you can get.

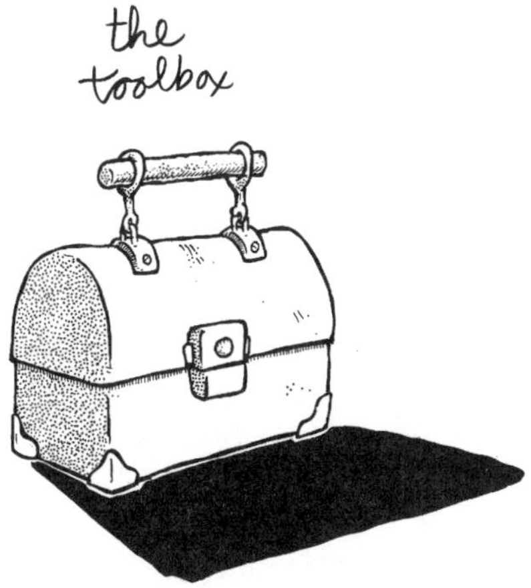
the
toolbox

Remember that the cornerstone of your entire effort at usability is a *comprehensive usability plan*. A usability plan includes details on all aspects of everything that you will do to enhance usability, at every phase of the redesign cycle. This plan is different from the *usability test plan*, which is just one part of your all-encompassing comprehensive plan. The usability test plan is the blueprint and instructions for one particular kind of test – the classical usability test, which is the subject of this chapter.

Every comprehensive usability plan probably includes at least some actual usability testing. The degree to which you use this tool will depend on where your needs fall on the continuum of correctness. Because this tool is by far the most expensive one to implement, the degree to which you can use it is governed partially by your budget. If you are designing a site that runs a nuclear facility, you will do an awful lot of user testing. (We hope!)

CLASSICAL EXPERIMENTAL RESEARCH DESIGN

If you have done any research , perhaps as a student or in your professional life, you will note that the design of our usability tests don't quite follow the rules of traditional experimental research design. This is, in fact, the case, and there are several reasons this is true.

The primary reason is that it is simply not feasible to observe classical experimental conditions in the workaday world, where deadlines overrule science. Most of the projects that you will work on will require such short turnaround that you won't always be able to do "real" experimentation. Normally, you want to maintain perfect control over all factors in your study; you would perform a pretest on the unmodified (original) site, make changes, and then retest, at the very least. Therefore, what we are talking about here isn't real science; it's more like art. Regardless, what we desire are results, and if an unscientific approach will get us there, why not?

Establishing Benchmarks

As your site matures and you perform more and more testing on it, you will certainly want to keep an archive of test results that you can use to compile company standard benchmarks of performance. For example, when you run your first usability test, you'll more or less have to make a best guess at how long each task should take to complete.

However, as you begin your second and subsequent rounds of testing, you will have established a maximum time to complete each task; simply calculate the mean (average) of the successful completion times from your previous rounds of testing. These times will become the milestone by which you can measure future performance. If the figures go up, you know that whatever changes you made were bad, or at least they took you in the opposite direction from where you wanted to be!

Start with a Plan

To get started with user testing, you need the materials mentioned in Chapter 1. Let's refresh your memory—here are the basics you need to get started in Web site usability:

- Digital stopwatch
- Computer workstation (similar to the type your users are using)
- Clipboard
- Web browser that your users are likely to use, plus any other browsers likely to be used to view your site
- Comparable operating system to what your users will be using
- Comparable Internet connection to what your users will be using
- Small, quiet room with minimal distractions
- Two comfortable chairs
- Plastic potted plant

Besides these items, you need to develop a test plan for your site. This test plan will serve as the blueprint for everything that you do as part of your user testing.

Your test plan should be usable as a means of replicating your study. For example, if you develop your test plan for the Chicago branch of your company, a colleague should be able to look at your plan and have no trouble replicating the study at the Sydney branch of the company and get similar results.

Therefore, it is critical that your test plan be written in such a way that you are not the only one who can understand it; it needs to be shared with your colleagues, your clients, and potentially others. Always write your usability plans and reports in a clear and consistent fashion, and never assume that the reader has any *a priori* knowledge of the topic or how to perform usability testing. Particularly, you should make an effort to be clear in the methodology section of your test plan, since this is the section of the plan that communicates the "how-to" to potential colleagues who might try to rerun your study.

The test plan is divided into several logical sections, which are detailed here. It is important to note that initially, you will not have a section for results and discussion of the results; those come later. However, the essential skeleton of the plan will remain the same over various revisions.

For your convenience, this book includes a sample usability test plan in Appendix A that you can reference whenever a topic or point in this discussion is unclear. Feel free to use this sample plan as the basis for your own plan template. The plan is also included on the CD-ROM that came with this book. It is in Microsoft Word format so that you can easily modify it to your liking.

Section 1: Purpose

In this section of the plan, you need to describe the function of the Web site you are testing. What does the site do? Whom does it serve? What is the vision for the site over the long haul? Finally, what is the reason for doing this testing? It is really important to make concrete the site's goals because, without this critical information, how can you tell how to measure the effectiveness of the site?

It is also critical to understand the expectations of the client (or your employer) with regard to this testing. What is expected to result from the testing? Does the client know what usability testing is all about? Is it understood that usability testing is not the same thing as marketing research? You must make sure that you and your client are "on the same sheet of paper," or the potential for chaos and mass miscommunication will be great. (See Figure 8.1.)

The purpose section of the test plan steers the rest of the plan, so if you rush through this part, the rest of your plan will be haphazard, too. Think about this section a great deal before you dive in.

PEPSI WORLD
GO
HOT TOPICS
JOY OF COLA
The JoyofCola
Got an urge to hear that catchy PEPSI SONG? Listen to it here.
Choose between the two formats
real audio
audio
Coming soon: cool stuff from Pepsi, including brand new, toe-tapping commercials!

FIGURE 8.1 *If you had to deduce the purpose of the site shown here from just screen shot alone, what would it be? Is the corporate philosophy clear from page 1, or is the purpose of the site a mystery—perhaps even to the people who designed it? ©2000 Pepsico.*

Section 2: Problem Statements

Your *problem statements* should be short, one-sentence summations of the kinds of questions you are looking to answer by doing this testing. For example, if you are redesigning your site to include a new Web-based storefront, you might be interested in knowing how well customers can use the new features to conduct business. The act of "conducting business" can be broken down into several parts, at least in the case of your site. They might be as follows:

- Can our users easily locate product information they need in order to choose the right products?
- Can our users successfully register for a shopping account?
- Can our users place items in their shopping carts and check out efficiently?

Note the order of things here. The purpose of the site (section 1) is pretty abstract, with only general concepts mentioned. Section 2, problem statements, requires you to be a bit more concrete, to start examining the subtasks that are required to fulfill the purpose of the site. In a bit, you'll need to fully operationalize the problem statements by generating individual usability tasks to answer each problem statement. We'll discuss how to do this shortly.

Section 3: User Profiles

Whenever you do user testing, you test a slice of your entire user population. This slice is called the *sample* (see Chapter 2). One of the things you want to do is test a sample that is representative of your population.

In other words, if you are hoping to generalize to female users aged 18–35, and your sample consists entirely of males over 50, you aren't going to be able to use your results for your originally stated purpose. You can't generalize to your target audience when you have the wrong sample. It's critical that you identify your target audience in this section of the report, explaining the various user profiles in your study.

Once you have acquired your participants and performed the testing, you will be able to show the "actual" sample that you ended up with (data to be taken from the questionnaires sent to the participants). This way, if you have ended up with a less than representative sample, it will be easy to see that fact.

So the user profiles section will undergo two revisions. Initially, you need to say for what group you are aiming in terms of a target audience. Then, after the testing is finished, you can tabulate your participants' demographic and personal information to characterize the group you ended up testing.

Section 4: Methodology

The *methodology* section is critical to the test's ability to be replicated by others. The methodology section is a step-by-step explanation of the things you will do in your test sessions. Note, however, that the methodology section does not include a task-by-task description of each usability activity.

For example, if you are planning a card sort as part of your usability session, you need to indicate this step as part of your methodology. The order of parts of the test and the general flow of things should be summarized in this section. Any unusual conditions that you might require (using only Netscape Navigator 1.1, having loud noises going on in the background, or the like) should also be noted here.

Essentially, the methodology section is your opportunity to explain to a complete stranger how to run the show. Any trained moderator should be able to pick up a copy of your test plan and replicate it without needing to ask you questions.

Section 5: Test Environment and Equipment Requirements

It's always a good idea to include a diagram of your test environment in your plan. This diagram serves as an aid to the people who review your material. You should also mention any equipment or other resources you needed for the sessions (VCR, video camera, computer, overhead projector, index cards, and so on).

Including in your plan a laundry list of required gear serves many purposes. First and foremost, it helps communicate to your team ahead of time what will be needed for your own tests in terms of gear. This means it should be fairly easy and straightforward to extract from your plan a request to give to the A/V department at your company or a rental supplier.

Second, explicitly tabulating the equipment in your plan facilitates drawing up a budget, since equipment costs can be easily calculated from this list. Be sure to figure in magnetic media (tapes and such) because their cost can add up quickly.

Finally, a setup diagram helps people who might seek to replicate your environment. It's a nice touch for your report.

Section 6: Testing Crew

Provide a brief explanation of the team of people who will be involved in the testing process. You will find that it is next to impossible to do a usability session with only one person on crew; two is a bare-bones minimum.

Here's a list of potential members for your team. We talk more about one very special role, that of the test monitor, later in this chapter:

- **Test monitor.** This person interacts with participants, moderates the session, and reads scripts.
- **Data logger.** The logger writes down information and results after participants perform tasks.
- **Timer.** This person uses a stopwatch to measure the time participants required to complete tasks and calls time when time is up.
- **Video operator.** This person operates the camera(s) in the session room; positions tapes for recording, and edits/splices video footage.

- **Site specialist.** This team member knows all the details about the Web site being tested. This person is called on to make judgment calls to determine success or failure on questionable tasks.

Once you've completed your testing, explain briefly who the crew was, what roles they fulfilled, and whether the roles changed at any point. In particularly large usability sessions, you could have more than one test monitor, for example. Note that not just anybody should act as the test monitor; it takes a special person to fill this role, as we shall see in a moment.

Section 7: Evaluation Measures

In this section you need to explain your methods for determining success or failure for tasks as well as explaining any constraints placed on the participant (he or she is not allowed to use search engine, must complete tasks in under three minutes, or the like). Common criteria for task analysis include the following:

- Number of clicks the user needed to complete tasks (you could possibly include the least number of clicks needed, as discovered by site specialists, to give a frame of reference).
- Click path taken; this path can be hard to follow unless you are using automatic link-tracking software.
- Total time elapsed; how long did it take the user to accomplish the tasks? You might need to set an upper limit on how long the user can take to accomplish each task.

It's also not unusual to have two timing milestones: the absolute maximum time you will allow the participant to try a task and the maximum time you'll allow before a task is considered a success. For example, you might set an upper bound of three minutes for a task but not count the task as a success unless it is completed in under one minute. The reason for doing this is that your testing might discover that certain tasks are accomplishable, although not in an acceptable amount of time. This finding can have many implications, depending on the circumstances.

Section 8: Task List

The *task list* is the "meat and potatoes" of the test plan. In this section, present the individual tasks that you have derived to answer the problem statements in section 2. Each task will consist of several parts:

- **The scripted text.** For each task the participants must complete, you must create a short instructive text that you will read out loud. It is critical that the text be short enough for the user to remember while performing the task. If you find that your participants have to stop and ask, "Now what am I doing again?" you have made the task too complex, and it needs to be further broken down. This scripted text is a great thing to beta test on coworkers or friends. If they can't understand your question, your users probably won't be able to, either.
- **Conditions for success.** Each task must have an unambiguous goal, the attainment of which can be easily measured. For example, asking the participant to locate the price of a Wonder Widget 2000 is an easy task to grade. If the participant comes up with the price in the allowed time, he or she succeeds. (See Figure 8.2.)
- **Start state.** This is the state that the computer and Web session are in when the task begins. For example, for a given task, the computer browser might need to be at a totally random spot in the Web site, in which case the moderator would place the browser in this state at the beginning of the task. The start state is important to note; without this information, the test plan is ambiguous.

You can put limits on success beyond simply accomplishing the task itself: You could put a time limit on the task (reflecting the fact that the average user gives up after a short while if progress hasn't been made). You can also put a limit on the number of clicks a participant take to get to the goal state, reflecting the fact that too many clicks dissuade users from continuing with a task.

Make many copies of the task list to facilitate score keeping. Leave blanks where my data logger can enter times, click numbers, and other metrics for each task. Then we have a copy of the task list for each participant.

CONTACT US FOR ADVERTISING INFO
Merriam-Webster
Cool Stuff
Word of the Day
Word Game
Word for the Wise
Products
Licensing/ Network Options
Words from the Lighter Side
Language Info Zone
Inkwell to Internet
Customer Service
Site Map
Merriam-Webster Online
THE LANGUAGE CENTER
Add a Free Dictionary Button to Your Browser
Put a Free Dictionary Search Box on Your Web Site
Click Here for More Downloads
WWWebster Dictionary:
Search
WWWebster Thesaurus:
Search
NEW Web Exclusive! The newest words and meanings! NEW
Search Merriam-Webster's Collegiate® Dictionary © 2000 right here!
Check Out Merriam-Webster's Word Central for Kids!
Cool New Stuff
Dictionary Button / Search Boxes / Newest Titles / Press Releases
Word of the Day
Calendar Archive / Searchable Archive / Word of the Day mailing list
Daily Word Game
Puzzle Archive / Hints and Tips
Word for the Wise
Latest Transcripts / Download Transcripts
Products
Dictionaries / Electronic Products / Word Game References
Network/Licensing
Your Own Intranet Dictionary / Ask about linking to our site
Product Excerpts
Guide to International Business Communications / The Barnhart Dictionary Companion
Company Information
Company FAQ / How a Word Gets in the Dictionary / Brief Look at the History of English
Lighter Side of Language
Flappers 2 Rappers / What's in a Name / Coined by Shakespeare
Customer Service
Technical Support / Product FAQs / Merriam-Webster Retailer List
This site is also available in a text-only version.

FIGURE 8.2 *This site lends itself well to having the participant announce when the goal state has been found; if the participant can define a term found on the site, the goal state has been met! You need to make sure that the participant tells you when the goal state is found, not vice versa. © 2000 Meriam-Webster, Inc.*

Section 9: Results

Note that this section will not exist until you complete the usability testing. Until then, it is customary to include in your plan report an explanation that the data is forthcoming.

When you do have the data, you should provide it in a variety of fashions in this section. First, have a matrix showing all data for each task and each participant. You'll usually want to show success or failure, total time elapsed, and number of clicks per task, and then tabulate the overall success or failure per task. This data can be transformed later into a variety of indexes to gauge the overall health of the site as well as to point out areas that need improvement.

For purposes of our work, use percentage scores to present your results. Note that this practice is actually wrong from a scientific point of view. Percentages are useful only as very, very loose estimates. When I began teaching usability testing I made sure that I included in my syllabus a whole section on research design methods and statistics. I found that most of my students didn't care for the material and would fall back on "folk interpretations" of the data. As mentioned elsewhere, the result was that they still improved the usability of their sites.

My advice is that if you ever expect to do usability testing professionally, take a research design methods course and become familiar with concepts such as standard deviation, z-scores, probability, and confidence.

Section 10: Discussion

This is a freeform section in which you get to talk about your observations, comments that the participants made during debriefing or during the course of testing, and so on. Basically, anything you feel needs to be said can be said in the discussion section. You can usually use this section to build up the case for the recommendations you will make in the next section.

Section 11: Recommendations for Change

The recommendations for change consist of a bulleted list of change items that you believe need to be implemented as a result of your findings. Be careful how much information you give here. Your clients might not be looking for you to write out HTML code to fix the problem; they might be looking for general ideas.

Additionally, depending on how you have billed the job, you could find that if the client is open to your suggestions, implementing the changes will be another totally separate job. You might use a subcontractor to implement the changes, or you could do it yourself.

Appendices: Paperwork and Attachments

You will likely have many different add-ons for your test, such as questionnaires, nondisclosure agreements (NDAs), video and audio release forms, and so on. It is important that you include copies of all this type of paperwork with your final report.

DESIGNING USABILITY TASKS

Arguably, the most important thing you can do with regard to your usability testing plan is develop creative usability tasks that truly measure the things in which you are interested. The method to derive good tasks is simple, but it assumes that you have done a good job of determining the purpose of your site and that you have abstracted the correct problem statements from your purpose. So let's go over this process step by step.

The first step is to determine the purpose of your site. According to its corporate documentation and thought, the purpose of the Mind Hive corporate Web site is as follows:

> *Our Web site is designed to be the technological arm of the company. Its purpose is, first and foremost, to provide technical support to our existing clients. A secondary, but critical, objective of the site is to act as a sales channel for prospective and existing clients alike. Finally, we hope to use the Web site to educate the general public about our services and products.*

That being stated, we can begin to draw out the problem statements. There are three main areas of utility for the site: support, sales, and marketing. Each of these areas can be further refined:

- Can our users find the technical support they need to solve their problems?

- Can customers locate the products they want and purchase them on our Web site?
- Can a potential customer find out about our products and how they compare with our competitor's products?

Each one of these problem statements is pretty general. There isn't a way to directly test them, so we need one more level of refinement. Creating a series of tasks can test each problem statement. That way, the individual, measurable tasks radiate from the problem statements.

From the first problem statement, "Can our users find the technical support they need to solve their problems?" we can generate the following tasks:

- "You are trying to locate a way to repair a damaged Foo format data file under Windows 2000. Please locate this information using the technical support section of the Web site."
- "Someone in your department is wondering if there is a way to import a Frodis word processor document into the Foo processor. Please find out if this is possible."
- "After installing the Foo processor, version 5.5, you notice that your PC crashes a lot when you open older Foo documents. Please find out if this is a known bug."

These statements become the basis for our first three tasks in the testing session. So far, we have the script text for the tasks; now we need to determine the criteria for success for each.

We could determine that our users should be able to find the answer to their questions in less than three minutes, a very aggressive benchmark for technical support. So, one condition for success is that the answer must be located in less than three minutes.

We could also determine that a maximum of six clicks should be needed to find the answer (assuming that it can be done minimally in four clicks, allowing two for errors). This assumption also becomes a condition for success.

Finally, we need to figure out how to determine if the goal state has been reached. We determine that the goal state is to locate the Web page related to each task: *qa12345.html*, *qa23456.html*, and *qa34567.html*, respectively. So our condition for success for the first task looks like this:

- Must locate the page *qa12345.html* in less than three minutes and/or fewer than six clicks

Every remaining task requires us to go through the same process. Once we have determined the script and the conditions for success, we also need to note the start state of each task: From which Web page does the participant start? (See Figure 8.3.)

Spring Travel Tips at Expedia.com
Expedia.com
Welcome - Already a member? sign in
Home Page
My Travel
Deals
Places to Go
Interests & Activities
Maps
Find
Help
Find on Expedia.com
Go
Site guide
msn.com
Flights
Hotels
Cars
Vacations
Cruises
Special Deals
Resorts
Accommodations
Casino Destinations
Family Vacations
Travel Merchandise
Ski & Adventure
Hawaii Vacations
Golf Trips & Gear
Flights at a price you like: Yours!
Specify your price, destination, and travel dates, and let Flight Price Matcher do the rest
Your price:
$ 175 .00
per ticket
Get $100 off a future ticket
Traveler's Alert
US Airways update
Service Notice
Credit cards safe at Expedia.com
Customer Support
Privacy and security
Credit Card Guarantee
Join now. It's free!
Agents on call 24 hrs.
Non-U.S. Residents
Use our sites in Australia, Canada, Germany, UK, Other.
About Expedia, Inc.
Jobs
Press Information
Investor Relations
QUICK ROUNDTRIP FLIGHT SEARCH
Leaving from
Departing (MM/DD/YY)
Time
Travelers
4/15/00
evening
1 adult
Going to
Returning (MM/DD/YY)
4/17/00
evening
Go
This search is limited to adult roundtrip coach fares. More search options...
CURRENT HIGHLIGHTS
To Love and Dye in Myrtle Beach
Chimps and life: Jane Goodall speaks
Score a free handheld computer
More headlines...
FEATURED DESTINATION
Spa Vegas: Relaxing in Sin City is no gamble. Las Vegas has spas in spades. Sponsored by Avis
IN MY TRAVEL
My Itineraries
My Profile
Flight Info: Status on flight arrivals and departures.
Fare Tracker: Weekly fare reports on your favorite cities.
MileageMiner: Track all of your frequent flyer accounts.

FIGURE 8.3 *This site has many potential tasks for testing usability. It contains many goal-oriented tasks, such as reserving a car, booking a flight, and getting a price for a hotel, that can all make for ideal usability testing scenarios. ©2000 Expedia.*

POTENTIAL PROBLEMS WITH TASKS

It is very common to run into many different problems that arise from improperly designed tasks. No matter how hard you try or how well you plan your test, you can encounter the unexpected. For instance, a task that you have designed might be worded poorly, causing the participants to become confused.

You might also design a task that you discover is impossible to complete. This might not be your fault, since sections of the Web site might not be operational when you choose to do your testing. Nonetheless, you must continue. In the event that you discover that a task cannot be completed due to some unforeseen technical problem or a glitch in planning, you can opt to discontinue that particular task for the remainder of the sessions. When you do so, you must drop the task data results from all previous sessions; that data isn't usable anymore. Make sure you document any such last-minute changes.

A way to make your test plan robust against adversity is to always create and plan on using more tasks than you actually need. This way, if you have to omit several questions due to unforeseen problems, you will be able to continue. When you do a test run through the plan with a coworker or friend, you should be able to weed out any potential timing problems, such as having too many or too few tasks.

Another problem that can come up is the result of a phenomenon known as *order effects*, which refers to the fact that the order in which tasks are presented can affect the performance of the tasks.

For example, you notice a gradual increase in a participant's success in navigating the Web site as a test progresses. The scores tend to increase later and later in the session. It could be due to the fact that the user is steadily memorizing the layout of the site and preparing mentally for questions that might pop up down the line. This could happen actively (the participant tries deliberately to memorize the site) or passively (the participant happens to remember the site layout without any special effort).

To counteract this effect, one technique you can use is to randomly shuffle the order in which tasks are presented so that when you average it all out, no single task gets preferential status (that is, no task consistently occurs later in each session) among all participants. Note that if you have a collection of two or more tasks that must be completed in a given sequence, it's okay to keep the group of tasks together and to treat the cluster as one logical unit for the purposes of randomizing. For example, it doesn't make sense to pay for an online order before you select the merchandise you want. In this case, the four steps involved in placing the order can be treated as one logical task and shuffled in with the other more atomic tasks.

EXECUTING THE PLAN

Okay, so once you have the plan together, it's time to implement it. You should plan to have sessions last between one and two hours per participant. I have found that an hour is just about the perfect amount of time. In an hour, you can do a large number of tasks and get input from the participant before he or she gets too tired and cranky. All that testing wears a participant out.

It also will wear you out! Never try to take on too many participants in a single day. Doing so can be quite monotonous and could affect your testing. If you are doing one-hour sessions, about six participants is all you should tackle in a single day. This limit will allow you enough time to get everyone in and out of the lab as well as time to clean up, get the environment back in shape, and finish recording information.

It's a good idea to have a reception area for participants where participants can have a cup of coffee or juice while they wait their turns. If you haven't had the participants fill out a pretest questionnaire, this is a good time to have them do it. If you are lucky enough to have a coworker who can act as the operations coordinator, the coordinator can spend five minutes with the participant while waiting. Just before testing commences, explain the terms of compensation to the participants. If they stay and complete the entire session, they will be compensated in full. If they leave halfway through, they will be compensated half, and so on. In addition, any other bits of administrative trivia can be taken care of at this point. Make sure that you arrange for the participant to arrive a little early if you plan this kind of warm-up activity.

Make a Trial Run

You should actually always do a dry run or two of your test plan on a cohort before you subject your real participants to the test. This practice helps weed out any potential disasters that might happen as a result of tasks that are worded improperly, tasks that are impossible to accomplish, and other unforeseen glitches that might occur along the way.

One of the main things you need to check during your trial run is that you have allocated enough time for all the components of the test. It's not unusual to discover that you have simply included far too many tasks for a one-hour session. Be sure to adjust any timing issues before you test a single real participant.

Just in case it isn't obvious, please note: You shouldn't include the data gathered from the trial run in your final report.

How Many Participants?

According to a recent article by Jakob Nielsen, it is best to have approximately five participants per round of testing.[1] This is in stark contrast to the 700 or more participants a month Microsoft tests! Keep in mind, though, that the number of Microsoft participants is spread out across all the various software programs, operating systems, and so on that the company sells and supports.

Depending on the size of your organization, five participants per session might be just about right. Ultimately, the more participants you have, the more reliable your data becomes and the more usability problems you will find. If this is your first attempt, why not five? It's a good place to start, and if you have created your test plan such that each session takes about an hour, you could conceivably get through all five sessions in a day (not a task for the faint-hearted; this is hard work!).

Keep in mind that if your Web site has many distinct user profiles, you need about five participants from each profile group, not five altogether. One of the biggest mistakes my students have tended to make is to spread the handful of participants they can get over all their user profiles. Remember, it's better to have five participants from a single user profile, so that you get realistic data for at least that profile, than to have a smattering of information from all your user profiles.

Mistakes Will Happen

Inevitably, a mistake will occur. It's just human nature. You might reveal more information to a participant than you meant to, or you might get the wording of a script a little wrong. Keep moving and don't draw attention to your mistake. Most people will never notice the mistake that seems so big to you. They don't know what's going on inside your head; they can't hear your thoughts, so they are oblivious to the mistake.

---

[1]See Nielsen's article at *www.useit.com/alertbox/20000319.html.*

Things You Should Say to the Participant

Being a test participant is nerve wracking for all but the most savvy best-testers (who you probably didn't want coming to your session in the first place!). The test moderator's job is to make the participant feel comfortable. There are several things you need to let the participant know before you begin; however, I can tell you what to say, but I cannot teach you how to say it. I have seen people with little dynamism try to play the role of test moderator, and they are just incapable of handling the position. How you tell a participant something—the genuineness in your voice—can say a lot more than the words you use.

Here are a few helpful statements to tell your participants:

- Be honest with me. I didn't design this site, so you can't hurt my feelings.
- There are no right or wrong answers.
- We aren't testing you; we are trying to find out if there are any design flaws or user-unfriendly parts to this site.
- We aren't going to let anyone outside our research team see these results, and when our team members do see the results, your name will not be associated with the data.
- Try not to act differently than you would at home or at work. We aren't here to rate how you do things, and if you act differently than you normally do, it will affect our ability to make our site better.
- It's okay for you to think out loud; that helps us understand what you are thinking as you go through the tasks.

Get Permission to Tape

If you are planning to video or audiotape your sessions, you need to get the express written consent of each participant to do so. Normally, you inform participants during the orientation script that they will be taped during the session. You should then have them sign release forms.

It's important that you explain to the participants that you will not release the audio or videotape to anyone outside the immediate research group and that the tape will be used only for research purposes. For your convenience, a sample release form has been included as a Microsoft Word document on the CD-ROM.

Role of the Test Monitor

The test monitor is the person in your crew who interfaces with the participants. The test monitor has by far the greatest load of work of all the team members, and it's critical that this person possess a plethora of important qualities.

After reading this section, you might get the impression that the test monitor is almost a sort of therapist! In fact, the qualities of a good therapist and a good test monitor are quite similar.

Here is just a partial list of qualities the test monitor should have:

- **Empathy.** The ability to understand and relate to the feelings of others.
- **Good attention span.** Watching people perform the same tasks over and over again can get really boring. The test monitor needs to pay attention at all times.
- **Warm and comforting.** People can get really stressed out when they are performing usability tasks. A good test monitor must make the participants feel at ease, as though there is no pressure to perform, yet the test monitor must also keep the participant moving through the tasks.
- **Ability to ad lib.** The unexpected will always happen. Being able to roll with the punches and keep things moving smoothly is a must.
- **Good organizational skills.** The test monitor is the hub of the testing process and so must interact with all the other team members and often with the client.

For most of this book, we assume that you, the reader, will act as the test moderator in your usability testing situations.

Watch for Body Language

When your participants are in the middle of a series of tasks, there will be little more revealing about their mental state than the faces they make. Nonverbal expression is one of the defining characteristics of human beings, and facial expressions can be a powerful ally of the observant test moderator.

If I haven't explicitly said it yet, let me do it now: Pay attention to what your participant is going through on every level, cognitive, emotional, and physical. A participant might make it through a task in an acceptable amount of time, and the unobservant moderator will not notice that the participant was completely confused about the task. The participant could very well have happened on the right answer by accident. An observant moderator will notice a grimace on a participant's face and will remember to ask about the task during debriefing.

The Orientation Script

Another important part of your test plan is the *orientation script*, another piece of scripted text that you will read out loud to participants when they arrive for testing. The orientation script is intended to be a general greeting, an explanation of all the activities you have lined up for participants to do, and a chance to explain that participants are free to leave if they begin to feel uncomfortable during the test.

The tone that you take when you read the script should be professional but warm. If you sound like a robot reciting its programmer's instructions, you'll get off to a bad start with the participant.

The script must be the same for each participant; it also needs to be delivered in the same manner to each participant. Do not attempt to paraphrase the script when you get tired of hearing yourself say it over and over. If you do that, you will introduce a potentially confounding variable to your testing. Did participant #6 do poorly because he really would have done poorly, or did your sloppy or inconsistent presentation of the instructions have something to do with it?

The script should be relatively short; it should take no more than a minute or two to read. Don't try to work casual conversational bits into this script; unless you're a trained Laurence Olivier type, it will sound awkward. For example, don't work in a bit of the script where you ask the participant how he or she is doing or what he or she would like to drink. You can do all that before you begin the orientation script. It is normal to provide drinks and a bit of food (especially if it is early morning) for your participants to consume while they are in the waiting area. Keep the beverages in the waiting area, though. Experience has shown that a glass full of fruit juice and a computer tend to mix very poorly!

The normal format of the script should be something like the following:

1. Introduce yourself and other team members.
2. Explain that the participant is here to assist in making your Web site better by taking part in sample tasks that are designed to uncover usability problems in the site.
3. Let the participant know that he or she isn't being tested but rather that the site design is being tested.
4. Give the participant a quick synopsis of what you will do. Describe briefly any types of tests you will do, how long they will take, and so on.

5. Let the participant know that it's okay to ask questions at any time but that you cannot answer questions about how to complete a specific task once the testing has begun.
6. Ask the participant if he or she has any questions before you begin.
7. Have the participant fill out any paperwork (NDAs, video/audio release forms, etc.).

User Tasks

Now, if you have laid out your test plan carefully and you have done a good trial run or two to work out bugs, you're ready to roll through the part you have been waiting for. The user will actually use your site! Be attentive; testing large numbers of users can get tedious.

Remember that you should present all parts of the test in the same way for each participant. The wording you use for tasks should remain constant for all participants. If you change the wording halfway through the day, it will be impossible to rule out the wording as a potential cause of variation in scores. The same is true of the instructions you read during the orientation script. Be consistent.

During the actual user tasks, try to limit your interaction with each participant to a minimum. Save longer issues for the debriefing session at the end of the session.

Keep It Moving

One of the hardest parts about the actual activity section of the test is that you must keep things rolling pretty smoothly without overly frustrating the participant. You will invariably have participants who cannot complete all the tasks; in fact, some participants might not be able to finish any of the tasks. When this happens, your moderator can expect to absorb a lot of natural human frustration. Your moderator must summon up all his or her interpersonal skills to reassure participants and keep them moving right along.

Some of my students have admitted to including some easy tasks throughout the test, just to make sure that no participant feels intimidated. I'm not quite sure how I feel about this; on one hand, it is valuable in keeping up participant morale. On the other hand, you're burning precious time. If you have an ultra-novice participating, this user will almost certainly have trouble anyway and will need some extra assurance and coaxing to continue.

This is the part of the session in which a participant is likely to become too self-conscious and, in some cases, too self-deprecating. It can be very discouraging to try to accomplish tasks set forth by a stranger who the participant probably views as very intelligent and fail at them. After all, all mad scientists are super-geniuses, and your moderator will probably strike the participant as such a person in authority. Humans are proud creatures and want to accomplish tasks.

Therefore, it's critical that your moderator be able to assure the participants that they are doing okay and that other people have made similar mistakes. You don't want to give out information such as "Oh, that's okay, five other people failed at that task."

Resist the Temptation to Lead

If you're the moderator, while the participants are performing the usability tasks you must resist the powerful temptation to help them out when they get into a bind. Remember that you cannot guide them through any part of any task unless you personally plan on being in their presence every time they use the Web.

For some people, it can be very difficult to avoid leading the participant by way of nonverbal cues. You may be unaware that you make a funny little noise when the participant is "cold" or heading for a wrong turn; although the participant might not be consciously aware of the noise, it could still affect his or her performance. Animal trainers have been able to shape the behavior of their animals so that they can read the trainer's subtlest cues; of course, a participant is smarter than a horse! This dilemma reveals yet another benefit of videotaping your sessions:

Although it's painful, you can review your own mannerisms to see if you give away too much with your nonverbal communication.

One other way that you can inadvertently lead a participant is by not allowing the participant to indicate the completion of a task. Normally, the participant is responsible for saying "I think this is it" or "I found it" or indicating success somehow. Once again, if you stop the participant when he or she has "found" the target, you'll also need to accompany that participant through life to provide this helpful service. When the users are on their own, they have to decide on their own whether they have found the information they're looking for. You need to let them do the same thing in your testing.

Don't Push Too Hard

It is an extremely bad idea to attempt to force participants to finish a task if they are absolutely certain that they cannot figure it out. In such cases, let participants opt to fail. In the real world, people give up on Web sites all the time, and if you don't let your participants give up, how will you know if "real" users are going to give up on your site?

The flip side of this coin is that you shouldn't let participants quit every task just because they are angry or "fed up." If you should get a participant in this condition, you might want to consider letting him or her go, since that behavior will waste your time and their own and make for bad feelings overall. Decide on an official policy for such exceptional cases.

Debriefing

This is often the best part of the entire test session, so make sure you allot plenty of time for it. The debriefing session is an informal section of time during which you can allow the participant to ask questions about whatever they want, within reason. For example, quite often participants who were perplexed with a seemingly impossible task will ask me to show them the solution. It's not unusual for such things to happen. Users might also have other questions, such as "Did I do okay?" or "How many other people failed task #4?" Participants also often ask questions about when you're planning on changing the Web site or if you'll call them again, or they could just open up and vent about how bad the site design really is. Be ready to listen.

It is also customary for the test moderator to thank the participant and explain that the data gathered during the session will be a great asset to the future design of the site and that the participant has played a critical role in the effort. In fielding participant questions, you'll obviously need to observe whatever information constraints your situation demands. Although it's probably uncommon, it is still possible that your test participants might be moles from your competitor, using the opportunity to find out critical information about your corporate strategies, insider information on the Web site, or something similar.[2]

Probably the most important thing about the debriefing is that you get to ask questions in an informal fashion. You might have a series of stock questions that you ask everyone (about the site's aesthetics, how interesting or boring the test was, or participants' other preferences), or you might choose to simply leave the talking up to the participant.

While the participant is carrying out the tasks you presented, you should take notes about problem spots, and ask the participant probing questions during the debriefing. It is helpful to bring up the troublesome pages and ask users to repeat out loud the thoughts that they were having as they interacted with the pages. Depending on how receptive and personable you seem to participants, they may tell you lots of things that you can convert into useful design changes.

CHAPTER SUMMARY

- Usability testing is the most complex and most informative tool we have to help us assess a Web site's usability.
- Every comprehensive Web site usability plan should include at least a little usability testing with real users.

[2]Just because I'm paranoid doesn't mean they're *not* out to get me . . .

- Usability testing employs some of the principles of scientific experimental research design but is not strict about adhering to them, primarily due to time constraints.
- Usability testing will yield useful results even if the test design is not completely scientifically sound.
- The blueprint for your testing sessions is called the *usability test plan*, which is not to be confused with the *overall usability plan* for your site.
- You'll need to get your participants to sign and date many pieces of paperwork, including any NDAs, video and audio release forms, and possibly pretest questionnaires if you haven't had them do this previously.
- The test moderator must be a great "people person" so that he or she can effectively communicate with your participants.
- You must observe appropriate ethics when designing and executing a test plan.

HANDS-ON EXERCISES

1. Design your test plan. Be sure to allot an appropriate amount of time for this job; it usually takes two weeks or more to design all the tasks and to do a trial run.
2. Execute the plan. Be prepared for lots of hard work and a very eye-opening experience!
3. Assemble your data and generate your final report. Make suggestions for change.

DISCUSSION TOPICS

1. Why is it important to have at least five participants from each of your user profiles, or is it even important? Explain.
2. What does it mean if all of your participants have a 100 percent success rate on your usability test?

3. Let's say that you are the only person on your usability team (hey! you really *are* somebody!). How will you have to modify your methodology to compensate for this fact? What are some potential problems you will encounter?
4. Which parts, if any, of usability testing can be automated?

CHAPTER 9

WEB ACCESSIBILITY

Then anyone who leaves behind him a written manual, and likewise anyone who receives it, in the belief that such writing will be clear and certain, must be exceedingly simple-minded.

—*Plato,* Phaedrus 275d

USABILITY AND ACCESSIBILITY

Earlier in the book, I mentioned that Web accessibility is not the same thing as Web usability. The difference is more than just a semantic one, but since accessibility can be an important component of usability, I felt it necessary to include accessibility here. So what is the difference between these two concepts ? And why do we need to be concerned with accessibility?

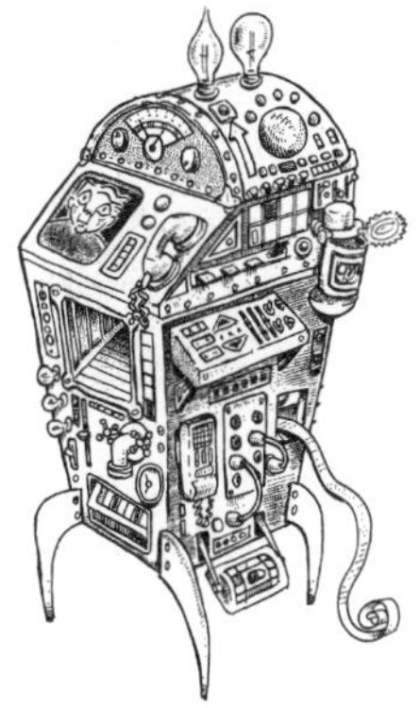

To begin, we need a definition of accessibility. Currently, the World Wide Web Consortium (W3C) heads the Web Accessibility Initiative (WAI), the main goals of which are set forth in a series of guidelines for Web content authors to follow. Here's what the WAI's charter says about the guidelines:

> *The primary goal of these guidelines is to promote accessibility. However, following them will also make Web content more available to all users, whatever user agent they are using (e.g., desktop browser, voice browser, mobile phone, automobile-based personal computer, etc.) or constraints they may be operating under (e.g., noisy surroundings, under- or over-illuminated rooms, in a hands-free environment, etc.). Following these guidelines will also help people find information on the Web more quickly. These guidelines do not discourage content developers from using images, video, etc., but rather explain how to make multimedia content more accessible to a wide audience.*[1]

The thrust of this statement is that people with disabilities need to be able to use the Web as easily as everyone else. However, it is myopic to narrowly assume that only people with disabilities stand to benefit from the implementation of accessibility techniques. Since the initiative's objective is to make content available to users in any context, a side effect of designing for users with disabilities is that users in a variety of other contexts benefit as well. With the rapid popularization of alternative Web browsing devices (WebTV, PalmPilot, and the like), accessibility concepts are critical to making Web content available to users of these newer devices.

In my opinion, accessibility should be taught along with usability as a core part of any course on Internet technology. Some universities have the right idea and are working accessibility modules into their various training programs in computer science and related fields.

For the moment, we focus specifically on how accessibility affects human users in a variety of contexts.

---

[1]From *www.w3.org/TR/WAI-WEBCONTENT/*.

W3C WEB ACCESSIBILITY INITIATIVE DESIGN GUIDELINES

The following material is based on the W3C document *Web Content Accessibility Guidelines 1.0,* available in full at *www.w3.org/TR/1999/WAI-WEBCONTENT-19990505/.* This document is of the Recommendation status, meaning that it is a stable document.

In this section I present the W3C guidelines with my own paraphrasing. It is highly advisable that you read the W3C document in full because it contains many other useful bits of information that are not covered here:[2]

- Never assume anything about how users will try to use your site. They might not be able to see, hear, or move, or they might not be able to process some types of information easily or at all.
- They may have difficulty reading or comprehending text.
- They may not have or be able to use a keyboard or mouse.
- They may have a text-only screen, a small screen, or a slow Internet connection.
- They may not speak or understand fluently the language in which the Web pages are written.
- They may be in a situation in which their eyes, ears, or hands are busy or distracted (e.g., driving to work, working in a loud environment, or the like).
- They may have an early version of a browser, a different browser from the one for which the site was created, a voice browser, or a different operating system than the one used to create the site.

This basic, incomplete list of potential circumstances should give you the general idea that you cannot always know how your user is trying to

[2]The full article is copyright ©2000 World Wide Web Consortium (Massachusetts Institute of Technology, Institut National de Recherche en Informatique et en Automatique, Keio University). All Rights Reserved. See *www.w3.org/Consortium/Legal/.*

access your content. The entire point of accessibility is to ensure that you will reach the largest audience possible by making your content easy to access.

Web site accessibility is essentially broken down into two "themes," or areas of concern:

- Ensuring graceful transformation
- Making content understandable and navigable

Ensuring Graceful Transformation

The first theme, ensuring graceful transformation, is concerned with ensuring that content will remain intact regardless of the presence of any of the previously listed constraints. In other words, you should not design a Web page that works only if the user has Flash installed and JavaScript enabled and 24-bit color and ... you get the idea.

Making Content Understandable and Navigable

The second theme, making content understandable and navigable, concerns itself primarily with ensuring the following:

- Making the language clear and simple (a user's natural language)
- Providing understandable mechanisms for navigating within and between pages

This second area begins to overlap with the domain of usability; providing understandable navigation mechanisms is facilitated by usability studies.

The WAI guidelines have provisions for the concept of priorities, with appropriate wording in the guidelines for three levels of priority. The first level of priority contains items that must exist in a design or else the content will be inaccessible to one or more groups. The second level of priority contains items that should be part of a design or else one or more groups will find it difficult to access information content. The third level of priority contains items that might be included; doing so will improve access in general.

The Guideline List

Now let's examine the guidelines in a little more detail.

Guideline 1: Provide Equivalent Alternatives to Auditory and Visual Content

Always provide text-equivalent content for all parts of your site that would otherwise be inaccessible to text-only applications. For example, use the ALT attribute for image tags. In addition, be sure to end the ALT text with a period (for reasons discussed elsewhere in this book).

For client-side image maps, be sure to provide equivalent text-only links to each hyperlinked region of the image map. One suggestion is to use the LONGDESC attribute that contains a description of an image. This practice allows you to be more verbose than would be stylistically comfortable within an ALT attribute.

Here's an example of a properly constructed client-side image map:

```
<IMG src="welcome.gif"
alt="Image map of areas in the library."
usemap="#map1">

<MAP name="map1">
<AREA shape="rect" coords="0,0,30,30"
href="reference.html" alt="Reference.">

<AREA shape="rect" coords="34,34,100,100"
href="media.html" alt="Audio visual lab.">

</MAP>
```

Another example of providing alternate content is the *D-link*, or the *Description link,* illustrated in Figure 9.1.

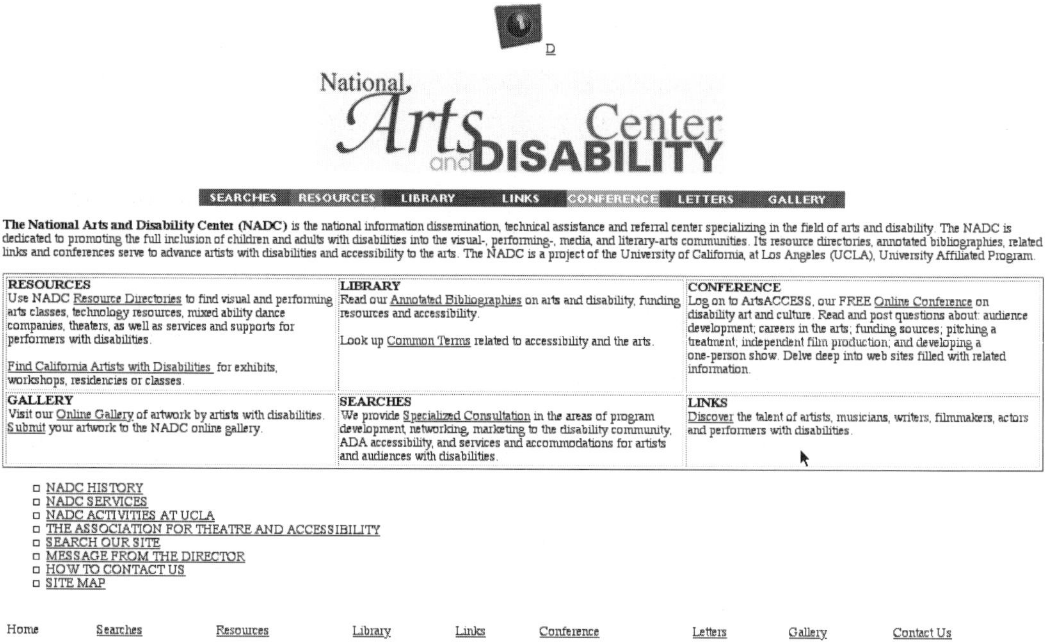
D
National Arts and Disability Center
SEARCHES RESOURCES LIBRARY LINKS CONFERENCE LETTERS GALLERY
The National Arts and Disability Center (NADC) is the national information dissemination, technical assistance and referral center specializing in the field of arts and disability. The NADC is dedicated to promoting the full inclusion of children and adults with disabilities into the visual-, performing-, media, and literary-arts communities. Its resource directories, annotated bibliographies, related links and conferences serve to advance artists with disabilities and accessibility to the arts. The NADC is a project of the University of California, at Los Angeles (UCLA), University Affiliated Program.
RESOURCES
Use NADC Resource Directories to find visual and performing arts classes, technology resources, mixed ability dance companies, theaters, as well as services and supports for performers with disabilities.
Find California Artists with Disabilities for exhibits, workshops, residencies or classes.
LIBRARY
Read our Annotated Bibliographies on arts and disability, funding resources and accessibility.
Look up Common Terms related to accessibility and the arts.
CONFERENCE
Log on to ArtsACCESS, our FREE Online Conference on disability art and culture. Read and post questions about: audience development; careers in the arts; funding sources; pitching a treatment; independent film production; and developing a one-person show. Delve deep into web sites filled with related information.
GALLERY
Visit our Online Gallery of artwork by artists with disabilities. Submit your artwork to the NADC online gallery.
SEARCHES
We provide Specialized Consultation in the areas of program development, networking, marketing to the disability community, ADA accessibility, and services and accommodations for artists and audiences with disabilities.
LINKS
Discover the talent of artists, musicians, writers, filmmakers, actors and performers with disabilities.
NADC HISTORY
NADC SERVICES
NADC ACTIVITIES AT UCLA
THE ASSOCIATION FOR THEATRE AND ACCESSIBILITY
SEARCH OUR SITE
MESSAGE FROM THE DIRECTOR
HOW TO CONTACT US
SITE MAP
Home Searches Resources Library Links Conference Letters Gallery Contact Us

FIGURE 9.1 *An example of a Web page that uses a D-link to describe a lengthy description of otherwise inaccessible media. Note that D-links have been deprecated in favor of the LONGDESC attribute. ©2000 National Arts and Disabilities Center.*

Guideline 2: Don't Rely on Color Alone

As discussed previously in this book, a significant portion of the human race has at least some color deficiency. Make sure that you do not create content that requires the user to differentiate between pieces of information based on color alone.

Instead, you can use a combination of text and shape to provide alternate means of understanding labels on your site. One of the suggestions from the W3C is as follows:

> *To test whether color contrast is sufficient to be read by people with color deficiencies or by those with low-resolution monitors, print pages on a black and white printer (with backgrounds and colors appearing in grayscale). Also try taking the printout and*

copying it for two or three generations to see how it degrades. This will show you where you need to add redundant cues (example: hyperlinks are usually underlined on Web pages), or whether the cues are two small or indistinct to hold up well.

Guideline 3: Use Markup and Style Sheets, and Do So Properly

Don't misuse markup tags to create optical effects. For example, don't use the <address> tag to simply generate an italic effect. Furthermore, avoid using <dt> and <dd> tags to create an indentation effect.

Use style sheets instead to separate content from presentation. Note that your content must still be usable in the absence of a style sheet.

The following example comes from the W3C. It illustrates how to associate the content of table headers with table cells. This practice optimizes the way the data is interpreted by speech synthesizers.

```
<TABLE border="1"
summary="This table charts the number of
cups of coffee consumed by each senator,
the type of coffee (decaf or regular),
and whether taken with sugar.">

<CAPTION>Cups of coffee consumed by each
senator</CAPTION>

<TR>
<TH id="header1">Name</TH>
<TH id="header2">Cups</TH>
<TH id="header3" abbr="Type">Type of
Coffee</TH>
<TH id="header4">Sugar?</TH>
<TR>
<TD headers="header1">T. Sexton</TD>
<TD headers="header2">10</TD>
<TD headers="header3">Espresso</TD>
```

```
<TD headers="header4">No</TD>
<TR>
<TD headers="header1">J. Dinnen</TD>
<TD headers="header2">5</TD>
<TD headers="header3">Decaf</TD>
<TD headers="header4">Yes</TD>
</TABLE>
```

Guideline 4: Clarify Natural-Language Usage

Although the W3C document gives examples for XML, this principle can also be applied to HTML. Be sure to identify the predominant language of a document through metatags or equivalent means (for example, in XML, use xml:lang) so that content is accessible to multilingual users.

Natural-language markup allows search engines to find keywords and identify documents in a desired language. Natural-language markup also improves readability of the Web for all people, including those with learning disabilities, cognitive disabilities, or hearing-disabled people.

When abbreviations and natural-language changes are not identified, they may be indecipherable when machine spoken or in Braille.

Guideline 5: Create Tables That Transform Naturally

The first rule of thumb for this guideline will be a very hard one for most HTML hackers to take. This guideline prohibits the use of HTML tables solely for the purpose of page layout. It's likely that many of the Web pages in the world violate this guideline.

If you do use tables, use them for their intended purpose: for tabular data. Furthermore, if you use tables, the guideline urges you to use the HTML 4.0 table model. The guideline says to use "THEAD, TFOOT, and TBODY to group rows, COL and COLGROUP to group columns, and the 'axis,' 'scope,' and 'headers' attributes to describe more complex relationships among data."

It is worth noting that the guidelines are riddled with disclaimers mentioning that authors should use all these techniques after user agents (browsers) support the advanced features that make them possible.

We all know that you have to use tables to do page layout, since full support for absolute positioning is just a pipe dream (thanks to backward incompatibilities and sketchy support in current browsers). So, unfortunately, a lot of these guidelines are contingent on the browser vendors getting a clue, as well as users getting up-to-date browsers. Alas . . .

Guideline 6: Ensure That Pages Featuring New Technologies Transform Gracefully

Recently, a university redesigned its site to include a plethora of Java applets. These applets make the site look really flashy, but unfortunately, when you try to access the site using Lynx or any other text-only browser, there is no content to see!

This is an example of a site that does not degrade gracefully when all the cutting-edge goodies are taken away. Therefore, the site is verboten to anyone using a speech synthesizer or a wireless PDA.

The best way to test your site for this capability is to view it using many different browsers. Be sure to include the text-only browser Lynx, since it pretty accurately represents the way people who cannot access your images and other multimedia will see your site.

If nothing else, provide a link to an alternative content page.

Figures 9.2–9.4 show what the university's site looked like when viewed through Lynx. Figure 9.5 shows Apple's site, which has been designed with accessibility issues in mind.

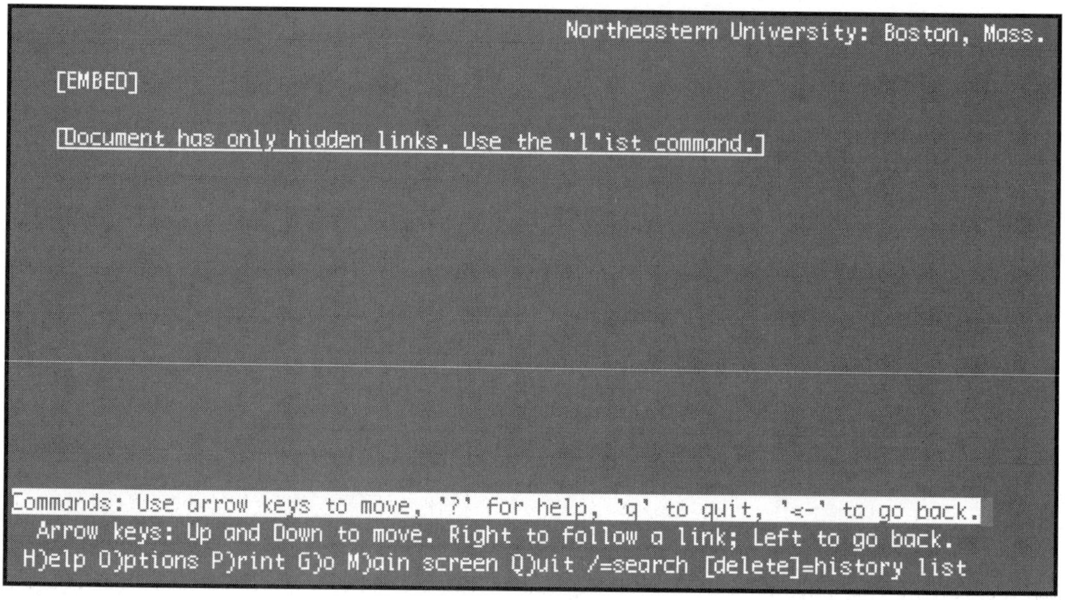
Northeastern University: Boston, Mass.
[EMBED]
[Document has only hidden links. Use the 'l'ist command.]
Commands: Use arrow keys to move, '?' for help, 'q' to quit, '<-' to go back.
Arrow keys: Up and Down to move. Right to follow a link; Left to go back.
H)elp O)ptions P)rint G)o M)ain screen Q)uit /=search [delete]=history list

FIGURE 9.2 *The Northeastern University site as first seen in Lynx.*

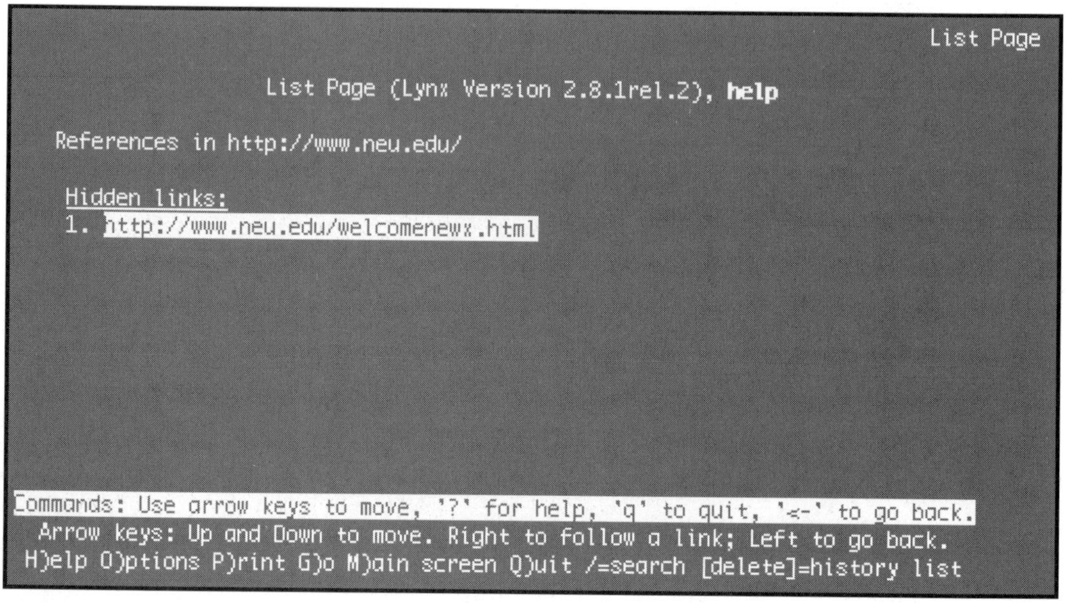
List Page
List Page (Lynx Version 2.8.1rel.2), help
References in http://www.neu.edu/
Hidden links:
1. http://www.neu.edu/welcomenewx.html
Commands: Use arrow keys to move, '?' for help, 'q' to quit, '<-' to go back.
Arrow keys: Up and Down to move. Right to follow a link; Left to go back.
H)elp O)ptions P)rint G)o M)ain screen Q)uit /=search [delete]=history list

FIGURE 9.3 *Screen result when following the "hidden" link.*

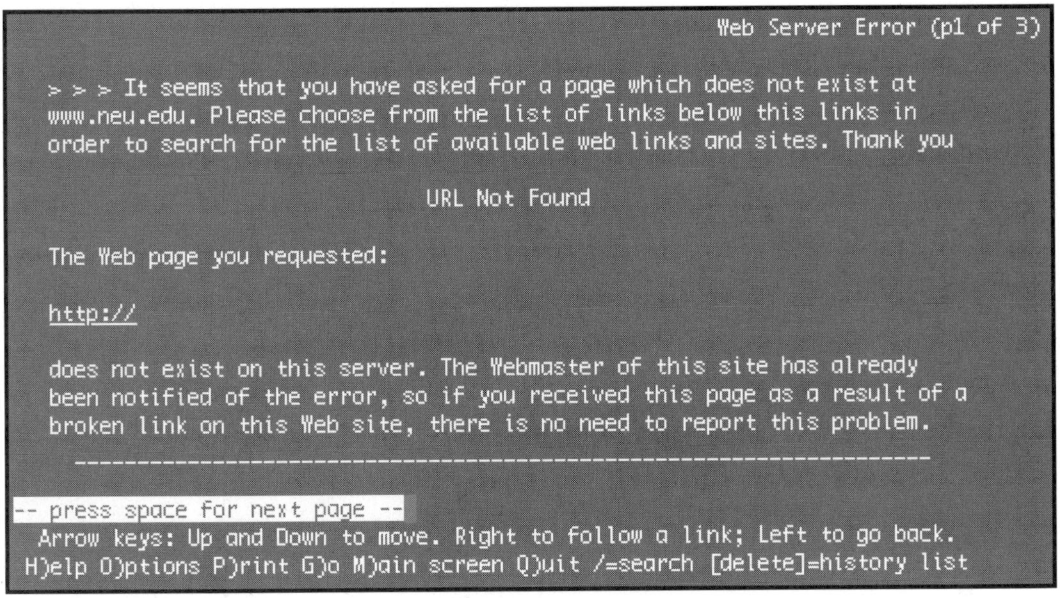
Web Server Error (p1 of 3)
> > > It seems that you have asked for a page which does not exist at www.neu.edu. Please choose from the list of links below this links in order to search for the list of available web links and sites. Thank you
URL Not Found
The Web page you requested:
http://
does not exist on this server. The Webmaster of this site has already been notified of the error, so if you received this page as a result of a broken link on this Web site, there is no need to report this problem.
-- press space for next page --
Arrow keys: Up and Down to move. Right to follow a link; Left to go back.
H)elp O)ptions P)rint G)o M)ain screen Q)uit /=search [delete]=history list

FIGURE 9.4 *Result after following the hidden link shown in Figure 9.3.*

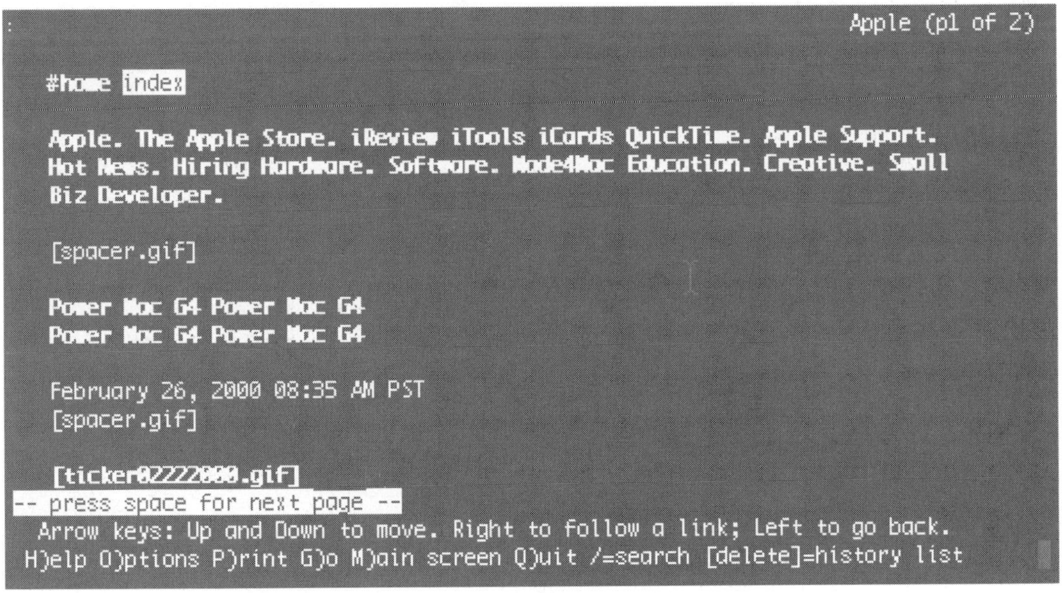
Apple (p1 of 2)
#home index
Apple. The Apple Store. iReview iTools iCards QuickTime. Apple Support. Hot News. Hiring Hardware. Software. Made4Mac Education. Creative. Small Biz Developer.
[spacer.gif]
Power Mac G4 Power Mac G4
Power Mac G4 Power Mac G4
February 26, 2000 08:35 AM PST
[spacer.gif]
[ticker02222000.gif]
-- press space for next page --
Arrow keys: Up and Down to move. Right to follow a link; Left to go back.
H)elp O)ptions P)rint G)o M)ain screen Q)uit /=search [delete]=history list

FIGURE 9.5 *Here's what a cluefully designed Web site looks like in Lynx. ©2000 Apple Computer.*

Guideline 7: Ensure User Control of Time-Sensitive Content Changes

This guideline seems oddly worded to me, but what it is saying is, be careful of allowing your content to change by itself (by using a refresh, push techniques, or animations such as GIFs or Flash). This care is necessary for a number of reasons.

First, if content is scrolling by on the screen, it could go by too fast for the user to be able to read it. Make sure that the scrolling can be stopped or slowed. Perhaps a better idea is to not use scrolling content in the first place.

Another great reason to avoid autochanging content is that people with photosensitive epilepsy can have seizures triggered by the flashing of multimedia images. You might recall that recently a large number of Japanese children experienced seizures after seeing such scenes in a popular cartoon. Do you want your site to have this kind of notoriety? Make this kind of content optional, or consider leaving it out altogether.

Guideline 8: Ensure Direct Accessibility of Embedded User Interfaces

This is basically saying that if you create some kind of a user interface that you embed, such as a Java applet or some other kind of non-HTML format, be sure to make the features accessible via alternate means. You might provide an HTML-only version of your snazzy Java applet.

Guideline 9: Design for Device Independence

This guideline suggests that you make sure that any part of your content that requires user interaction can be accessed through any device. For example, if you design a page that requires a user to perform a mouse rollover in order to access content, you need to either rethink the design or provide alternate content. The user will never be able to actuate a mouse rollover feature with a speech renderer or other alternate input device.

A practical tool that you can get for previewing Web pages to see how they will look when displayed by the WebTV device is the WebTV Viewer, available from *developer.webtv.net/design/tools/viewer/*.

It is important to note that this accessibility tip will gain a lot of steam as more information appliances such as Wireless Application Protocol (WAP) enabled telephones enter the Web arena. Usability and accessibility experts will increasingly need to rely on emulator programs such as the ones downloadable from Nokia at *www.forum.nokia.com/*. (See Figure 9.6 and 9.7.)

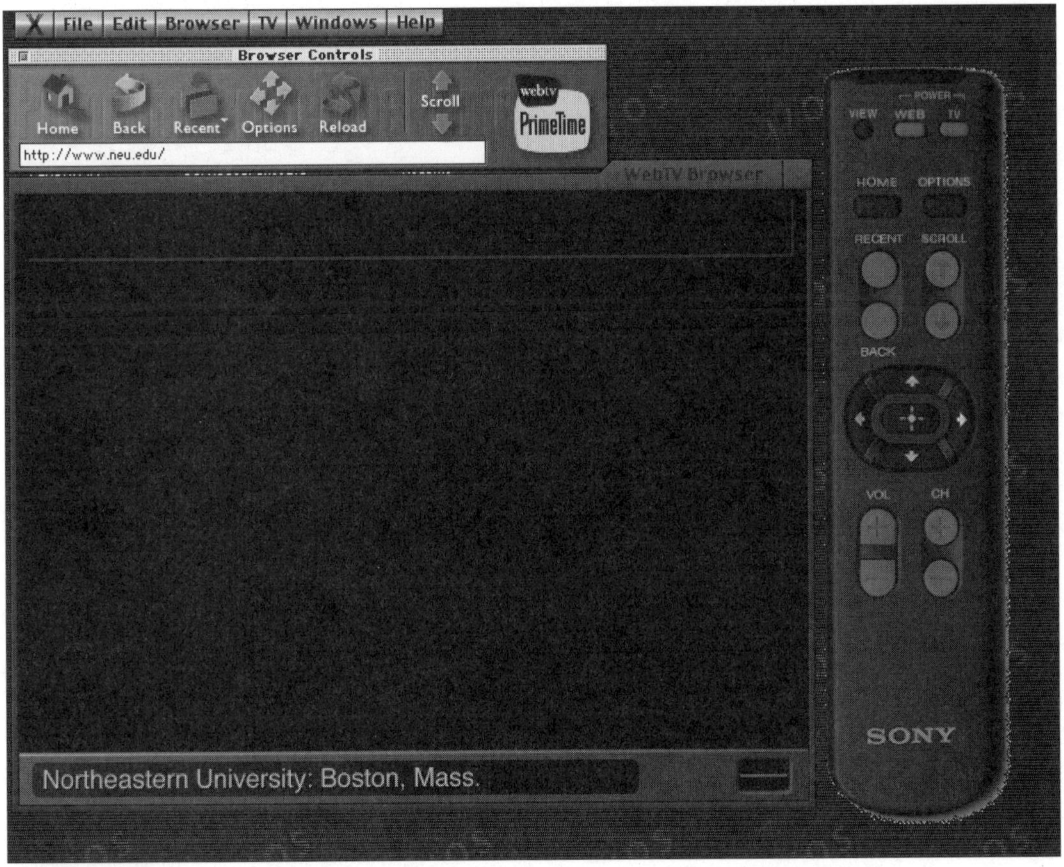
File
Edit
Browser
TV
Windows
Help
Browser Controls
Home
Back
Recent
Options
Reload
Scroll
webtv
PrimeTime
http://www.neu.edu/
Northeastern University: Boston, Mass.
SONY

FIGURE 9.6 *This is how the Northeastern University site looks on WebTV.*

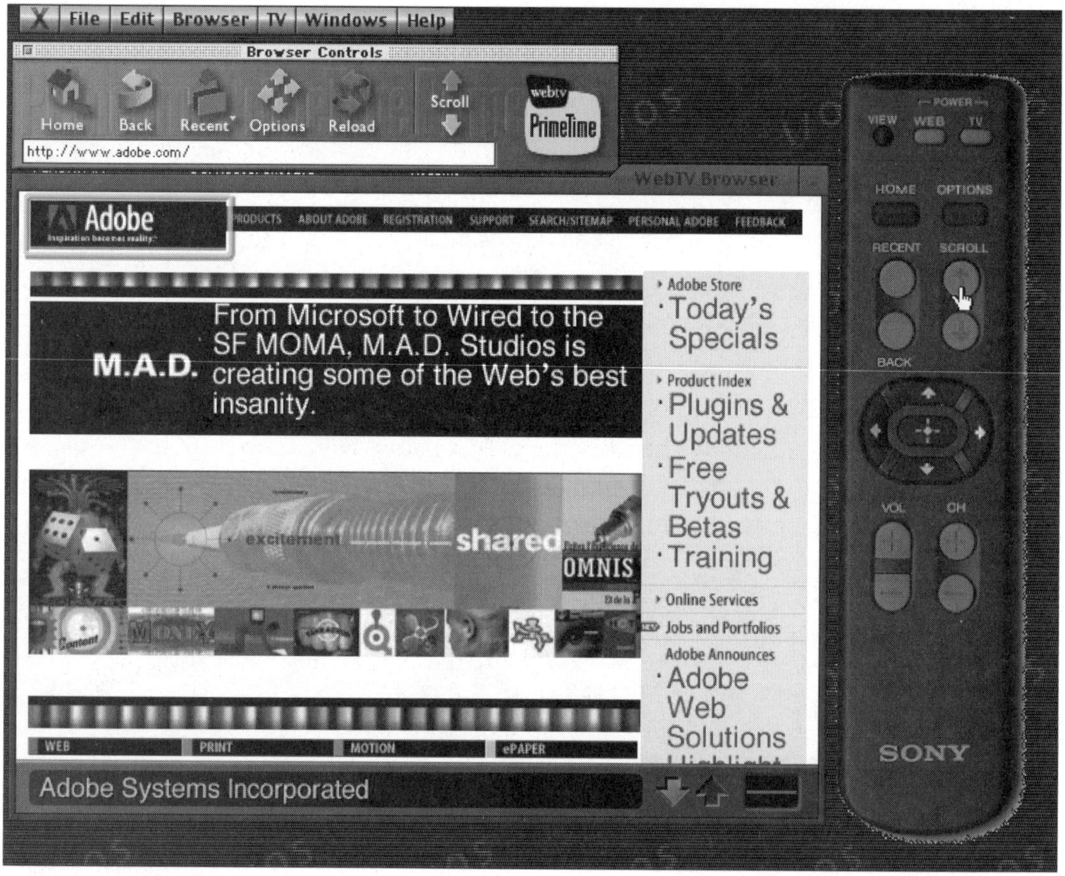
File
Edit
Browser
TV
Windows
Help
Browser Controls
Home
Back
Recent
Options
Reload
Scroll
PrimeTime
http://www.adobe.com/
WebTV Browser
Adobe
From Microsoft to Wired to the SF MOMA, M.A.D. Studios is creating some of the Web's best insanity.
M.A.D.
Adobe Store
·Today's Specials
Product Index
·Plugins & Updates
·Free Tryouts & Betas
·Training
Online Services
Jobs and Portfolios
Adobe Announces
·Adobe Web Solutions
shared
OMNIS
WEB
PRINT
MOTION
ePAPER
Adobe Systems Incorporated
VIEW
WEB
TV
HOME
OPTIONS
RECENT
SCROLL
BACK
VOL
CH
SONY

FIGURE 9.7 *Here's how Adobe's site looks on WebTV.*

Guideline 10: Use Interim Solutions

This guideline is also worded a bit strangely, but it means that you need to provide some backward compatibility only until newer browsers and user agents can support pages designed without backward compatibility.

For example, until user agents allow the user to turn off spawned (pop-up) windows, do not use them. Pop-up windows can be extremely distressful to people who cannot see that a new window has popped up.

This particular guideline would have been well applied to a site that I once had the misfortune to deal with (as a user, not a usability consultant). The designers had included a button on one page that, when clicked, would pop up another window that was smaller than the original and so hidden by it. The company was inundated with calls from frustrated users who complained that the new pop-up window never showed up or that it disappeared suddenly.

I happened to notice what the problem was when watching another user of the site. What had happened is that many users were so used to double-clicking on everything on a computer screen, they were double-clicking on the button, too. When they did this, the first click activated the JavaScript to bring up the new window. The second click, which occurred before the second window had spawned, brought the focus back to the original window, which then hid the smaller window behind it. Subsequent clicks did nothing, since the new window was already open.

The right "interim" solution would have been to simply not use the pop-up window. Instead, the company used a JavaScript function to trap the double-click event and return focus to the new, smaller window.

Guideline 11: Use W3C Technologies and Guidelines

Besides the fact that this guideline is a bit of self-promotion, it suggests the fact that W3C-approved guidelines and technologies are built from the ground up with "built-in" accessibility features. In addition, if you use them, you can add a W3C web badge to your site!

Guideline 12: Provide Context and Orientation Information

This guideline is about making sure that parts of your content use labels and other contextual information to help users find their way around. For example, you should use the TITLE element in each document in a frame set to help the user understand what each page is about. In addition, be sure to associate labels and the controls they represent properly, using the LABEL element.

Guideline 13: Provide Clear Navigation Mechanisms

This guideline contains many basic tips for good navigation. They all have the side effect of making the site more navigable. First, make sure that the text of a hyperlink describes the link destination. Even if you haven't buried your links in the middle of a paragraph, you can still provide better text than "Click here." Next, make sure that you use a site map or a table of contents to help users navigate your site. If you provide a search engine, provide different views of the interface for users with different levels of experience (seems like an odd tip in the context of accessibility, but it's a great tip anyway).

Here's an example that illustrates the use of multiple media types to access information. Note the use of link TITLE attributes to distinguish the various media types.

```
<A href="my-doc.html">My document is available
in HTML</A>,

<A href="my-doc.pdf" title="My document in
PDF">PDF</A>,

<A href="my-doc.txt" title="My document in
text">plain text</A>
```

Guideline 14: Ensure That Documents Are Clear and Simple

This guideline recaps many of the themes that are consistent throughout the other guidelines. Basically, keep it simple, be consistent, and use the simplest language appropriate for the site's content.

Other Accessibility Tips

There has been a rapid rise in the number of older people who are avid Internet users—and the number keeps increasing. This is a great thing, but in order to more effectively reach this audience, you should consider several design tips that will make your content easier for them to use.

After all, when you're getting electronic treasures like these over the Net, you want things to be as easy to use as possible.

Here are a couple of general guidelines to help you design Web pages that are senior-friendly:

- Make your design resize-survivable.
- Make sure that you don't create a page design that will look distorted or become unusable if the default text size is increased or if the resolution is changed from the way you designed it. A good design should be able to scale up or down and still be coherent and usable, even if it isn't quite how you'd like to see it yourself.

Let's look at a few other guidelines that will make Web life easier for all your users, young and old.

Use White Space and Internal Tables of Content

It is true that increasing the amount of white space on a screen can increase its readability. You should do so carefully; it's a pretty good design rule of thumb. Using white space to break up content into logical clusters helps the reader understand the content.

However, using more white space also means that you will cause the user to need to scroll more, so be sure to include "back to top" links at each section break, and use a table of contents at the top of the page.

Avoid Background Patterns

Even if this tip breaks your heart, follow it! Background patterns are pretty unpredictable and usually lead to less readable pages. Therefore, background patterns should be avoided.[3] Also note that what may seem like a faint watermark at one bit depth and resolution combination could become horribly blotchy and distracting at another. (See Figure 9.8.)

---

[3]Despite a study that users were able to read text better on a background that had a subtle grain to it. It seemed that the grain helped the readers track visually as they went from line to line.

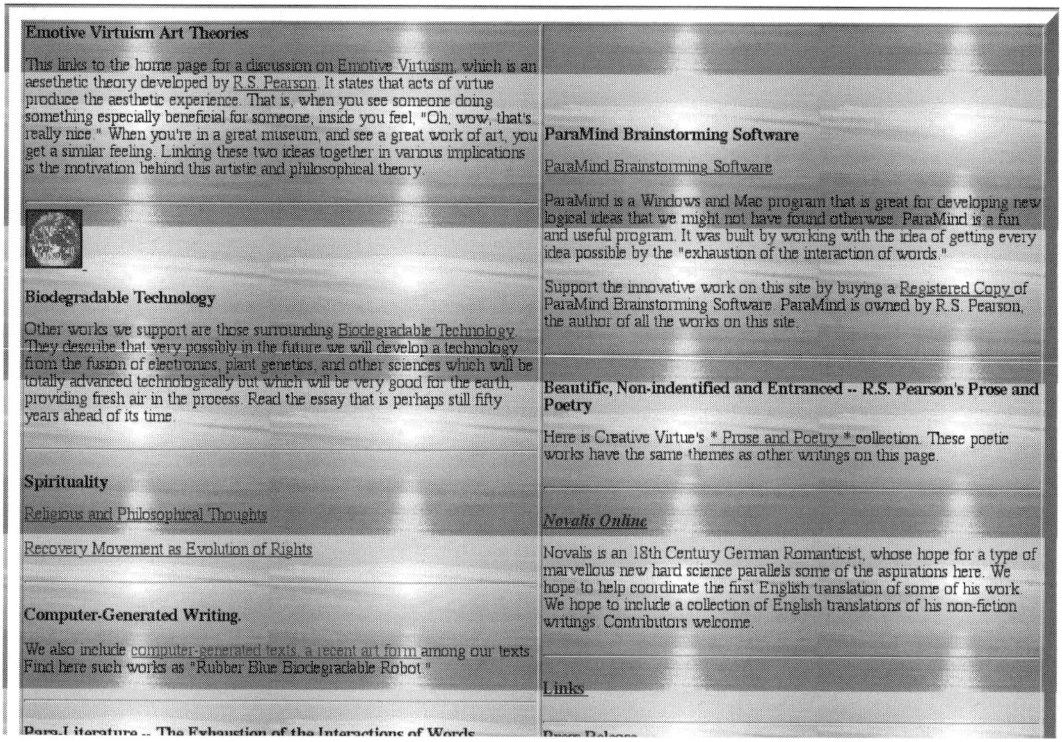
Emotive Virtuism Art Theories
This links to the home page for a discussion on Emotive Virtuism, which is an aesethetic theory developed by R.S. Pearson. It states that acts of virtue produce the aesthetic experience. That is, when you see someone doing something especially beneficial for someone, inside you feel, "Oh, wow, that's really nice." When you're in a great museum, and see a great work of art, you get a similar feeling. Linking these two ideas together in various implications is the motivation behind this artistic and philosophical theory.
Biodegradable Technology
Other works we support are those surrounding Biodegradable Technology. They describe that very possibly in the future we will develop a technology from the fusion of electronics, plant genetics, and other sciences which will be totally advanced technologically but which will be very good for the earth, providing fresh air in the process. Read the essay that is perhaps still fifty years ahead of its time.
Spirituality
Religious and Philosophical Thoughts
Recovery Movement as Evolution of Rights
Computer-Generated Writing.
We also include computer-generated texts, a recent art form among our texts. Find here such works as "Rubber Blue Biodegradable Robot."
ParaMind Brainstorming Software
ParaMind Brainstorming Software
ParaMind is a Windows and Mac program that is great for developing new logical ideas that we might not have found otherwise. ParaMind is a fun and useful program. It was built by working with the idea of getting every idea possible by the "exhaustion of the interaction of words."
Support the innovative work on this site by buying a Registered Copy of ParaMind Brainstorming Software. ParaMind is owned by R.S. Pearson, the author of all the works on this site.
Beautific, Non-indentified and Entranced -- R.S. Pearson's Prose and Poetry
Here is Creative Virtue's * Prose and Poetry * collection. These poetic works have the same themes as other writings on this page.
Novalis Online
Novalis is an 18th Century German Romanticist, whose hope for a type of marvellous new hard science parallels some of the aspirations here. We hope to help coordinate the first English translation of some of his work. We hope to include a collection of English translations of his non-fiction writings. Contributors welcome.
Links

FIGURE 9.8 *An example of a "noisy" background. This page is difficult to read under many conditions. ©2000 R. S. Pearson.*

Don't Use Tiny Text

I'm not sure why, but many, many Web sites have begun using text that is microscopic for important content, especially technical support pages. Don't do this! I'm not too ancient yet, but I can't read text when it fades below the equivalent of nine points or so. Let people with hawk vision reduce the size on their screens rather than putting the burden on the majority of the world.

Make Clickable Icons Obvious

Sure, you want to make your site look interesting, and to do so you might make your clickable images borderless—and you might even make them fade into surrounding, nonclickable areas. Although you might win a design award, though, you certainly won't be doing a favor for anyone who tries to use your site.

Make clickable icons large enough so that people with impaired motor functioning (like me, after typing for 72 straight hours) can easily click them. This can be critical if you have a lot of clickable icons in a small area, such as a navigation bar or other device.

View Your Content with Rose-Colored Glasses

Well, not exactly rose-colored glasses: One good tip is to change your screen properties so that your monitor is only displaying grayscale, then take a look at your site. What you will see is how the site would look to someone with a color deficiency.

You will probably be surprised! Some of your text may fade into obscurity, while other components of the site may become invisible or impossible to recognize.

Don't Try to Beautify Links

Another popular trend is to use style sheets to remove the underlining from hyperlinks. This is similar to removing all of the traffic signals from downtown Boston at rush hour. People have learned that hyperlinks are underlined, so leave them that way.

The converse of this guideline is that you should never underline non-hyperlinked text. Underlining of text for anything other than links may make your site look too amateurish.

Avoid Side Effects of Navigation

Don't use JavaScript or Java code to cause events to occur whenever the user mouses over a certain area. For example, if a user with impaired motor function or impaired vision puts his or her mouse over a part of the page that causes a new page to load or a pop-up window to appear, this will be confusing and detrimental to that user's navigation. At worst, this feature should be a prominently displayed user option; it takes control out of the user's hands (a violation of one of the most important usability heuristics).

If You Use Video, Provide Closed Captions

As of the writing of this book, a promising endeavor is the Media Access Generator (MAGpie) for distribution in SDKs, on the Web, on CD-ROMs, and via other methods. Funding for MAGpie comes from the Trace Research and Development Center at the University of Wisconsin as part of its Information Technology Access Rehabilitation Engineering Research Center, which itself is funded by the U.S. Department of Education's National Institute on Disability and Rehabilitation Research. For more information on MAGpie, visit *www.wgbh.org/wgbh/pages/ncam/webaccess/magindex/html.*

This site has an excellent example of an audio/video clip that has been optimized for ultimate accessibility. The video explains the origin of one of the earth's greatest mysteries: green potato chips. The video clip has been designed with audio captioning for parts of the video that don't have audio (descriptions of scenes) as well as closed captioning for the hearing impaired.

All of this work was done using Apple QuickTime. This is one tool that I can highly recommend, but there are other alternatives as well. The XML language called Synchronized Markup Language (SMIL) also supports the integration of multiple means of content access. Microsoft is also pursuing its own proprietary solution to the problem of closed-captioning for Web content.

XML AND WEB ACCESSIBILITY

One of the problems with the current generation of Web documents is that they implement HTML, which unfortunately mixes presentation of information with the information itself. This means that many of the tags used to mark up information are of a purely visual nature; for example, the bold tag, <b>, contains absolutely no contextual information whatsoever. Its only value is to express that whatever appears inside its start and end tag should be displayed optically bolder.

This fact presents a plethora of problems to people who may not have the benefit of seeing site content, whether the user is visually impaired or retrieving information over the telephone. For example, what does bold text sound like? And how do you distinguish between two pieces of markup such as these:

```
<b>This recipe for Grandma's old fashioned
goulash is yummy!</b>
```

and

```
<b>WARNING! Do not enter the lab without a
respirator—airborne contaminants inside!</b>
```

As far as HTML is concerned, the two pieces of information are equivalent. The tags themselves offer no means of differentiating between the seriousness of the latter sentence and the relative unimportance of the former. This is indeed a problem, and although this is a contrived example, HTML and the current generation of Web documents are absolutely riddled with this kind of inaccessible content.

Take, for example, tables in HTML. Although it is possible to use tables in a fashion that can be accessed by people who lack the benefit of sight, it's a hack at best. What is really needed is the separation of content from presentation. This is exactly what XML allows you to do.

Unless you have been under a rock for the past couple of years, you know that XML, the Extensible Markup Language, is a meta-language that can be used to create an infinite number of application-specific markup languages. XML give the author the flexibility to create tags that are meaningful in whatever context the document exists. For example, the American Medical Association (AMA) could easily contract someone to create an XML language instance (called an *application*, not to be confused with a computer program, which is also called an application) that has only tags that are meaningful to doctors.

Since XML allows the author to use only tags that are not display oriented but are, rather, structure oriented, the notion of how something should be displayed is never an issue with the content. In XML, there are no `<b>` tags, there are no `<font>` tags; there are only tags that represent the logical structure of a document, such as `<chapter>`,

`<heading>`, `<patient>`, and so on. By the way, there are no "pre-existing" tags in XML; the author must create them from scratch by producing a document called a Document Type Definition (DTD).

Now, the problem of making sure that a user-agent (a browser) can understand the format of a table becomes moot, since the XML document isn't concerned with layout but rather with logical representation of data. Take the following HTML table, for example:

```
<!DOCTYPE HTML PUBLIC "-//W3C//DTD HTML 3.2
Final//EN">
<HTML>
<HEAD>
  <TITLE>Example of HTML table</TITLE>
  <STYLE>
  <!—
  TH{font-family:verdana,arial,sans-serif;font-
     style:bold}
  TD{font-family:verdana,arial,sans-serif}
  —>
  </STYLE>
</HEAD>
<BODY bgcolor = "ffffff">

<TABLE border=0 cellpadding =2 cellspacing = 2
       bgcolor = "ccccff">
  <TR>
       <TH>Product</TH>
       <TH>Cost</TH>
       <TH>Rating</TH>
       <TH>Availability</TH>
       <TH>Vendor</TH>
  </TR>
  <TR>
       <TD>Frodis Modulator</TD>
       <TD>$345.00</TD>
```

```
            <TD>***</TD>
            <TD>In Stock</TD>
            <TD>Frodis, Inc.</TD>
      </TR>
      <TR>
            <TD>Gorlox's Space Wrench</TD>
            <TD>$199.99</TD>
            <TD>**</TD>
            <TD>2 - 4 weeks</TD>
            <TD>Hyperspace Warlord Supplies</TD>
      </TR>
      <TR>
            <TD>Electronic Chocolate Bar</TD>
            <TD>$23.95</TD>
            <TD>***</TD>
            <TD>1 Month</TD>
            <TD>Saturn Candies, Inc.</TD>
      </TR>
      <TR>
            <TD>Yak Stampede</TD>
            <TD>$1999.00</TD>
            <TD>****</TD>
            <TD>2 -3 days</TD>
            <TD>Before Creation Tech</TD>
      </TR>
    </TABLE>
    </BODY>
    </HTML>
```

This code gives us a viewable result similar to the one shown in Figure 9.9.

The problem here is that a user-agent (a browser) must have special code that "understands" how a visually laid-out table should be read logically. Although such tools exist, they are again an example of the Procrustean-derived design that we have been trying to avoid. XML allows us to encapsulate the data from the table in such a fashion that no visual for-

Product	Cost	Rating	Availability	Vendor
Frodis Modulator	$345.00	***	In Stock	Frodis, Inc.
Gorlox's Space Wrench	$199.99	**	2 - 4 weeks	Hyperspace Warlord Supplies
Electronic Chocolate Bar	$23.95	***	1 Month	Saturn Candies, Inc.
Yak Stampede	$1999.00	****	2 -3 days	Before Creation Tech

FIGURE 9.9 *An example of a table generated in HTML. This content is harder to access because it is marked up using tags that lay out the content visually rather than tags that bear structural information.*

matting information is included. Instead, that job is left to the Cascading Style Sheet (CSS) engine or the Extensible Style Language (XSL), a much more powerful tool for visual and aural representation of data as well as data transformation. Here's what a comparable data set would look like in XML:

```
<PRODUCT_GUIDE>
  <ITEM id="12345" rating = "3">
        <PRODUCT_NAME> Frodis Modulator
            </PRODUCT_NAME>
        <PRICE currency="USD"> 345.00</PRICE>
        <AVALIABILITY>In Stock</AVAILABILITY>
        <VENDOR>Frodis, Inc.</VENDOR>
  </ITEM>
  <ITEM id="23456" rating = "2">
        <PRODUCT_NAME> Gorlox's Space Wrench
           </PRODUCT_NAME>
        <PRICE currency="USD">199.00</PRICE>
        <AVALIABILITY>2 - 4 Weeks</AVAILABILITY>
        <VENDOR>Hyperspace Warlord Supplies
           </VENDOR>
  </ITEM>
  <ITEM id="34567" rating = "3">
        <PRODUCT_NAME>Electronic Chocolate Bar
           </PRODUCT_NAME>
        <PRICE currency="USD">23.95</PRICE>
        <AVALIABILITY>1 Month</AVAILABILITY>
```

```
        <VENDOR> Saturn Candies, Inc.</VENDOR>
    </ITEM>
    <ITEM id="45678" rating = "4">
        <PRODUCT_NAME>Yak Stampede</PRODUCT_NAME>
        <PRICE currency="USD">1999.00</PRICE>
        <AVALIABILITY>2 - 3 Days</AVAILABILITY>
        <VENDOR> Before Creation Tech.</VENDOR>
    </ITEM>
</PRODUCT_GUIDE>
```

Notice how the information now looks more like data that has been serialized from a database rather than a hacked-together bit of HTML that leaves the user-agent developer looking for clever ways to make sense out of optically formatted—rather than logically formatted—information. Each item has its own explicit members, such as price, vendor, and availability; there is no guesswork involved in figuring out where things should go.

This would normally be only part of the whole picture. For example, to make much use of this data, we'd still need a way to present it on screen, or aurally, or via whatever other presentation device the situation called for. This is the job of style-sheet languages such as CSS and XSL. We could, for example, use the wonderful features found in CSS Level 2 to implement different spoken-word styles for each of the types of information. Or, with the data transformation capability of XSL, we could easily generate HTML output from our original XML input! XSL is very cool; it lets you transform the original XML data into anything else, including a different XML application (good for business-to-business, or B2B, transactions in which the underlying format of data on either side is vastly different).

Okay, so this isn't a book on XML, after all, but let me assure you that the world of accessibility and usability has the potential to be utterly transformed by the capabilities inherent in XML and related technologies. Since XML doesn't paint you into a corner with a particular presentation style, you can use the same data file (an XML document) to output to a Braille machine, a speech reader, a Web browser, and even other media types, such as PDF.

CSS2 AND BEYOND

Cascading Style Sheets, Level 1 (CSS1), provides a minimal set of presentation rules that enable HTML authors to break their content free from presentation. However, CSS Level 2 (CSS2), which is unfortunately not implemented in very many applications at this writing, contains many features that make it highly suitable for use with alternative media presentation devices, such as speech readers.

For example, the following sample CSS2 style sheet comes from the W3C CSS2 Specification, which attained official recommendation status on May 12, 1998. The full text of the section entitled *Aural style sheets* can be found at *www.w3.org/TR/REC-CSS2/aural.html:*

```
H1, H2, H3, H4, H5, H6 {
        voice-family: paul;
        stress: 20;
        richness: 90;
        cue-before: url("ping.au")
    }
    P.heidi { azimuth: center-left }
    P.peter { azimuth: right }
    P.goat  { volume: x-soft }
```

This code directs a speech synthesizer to speak headers in a voice (a kind of "audio font") called "paul" in a flat tone, but in a very rich voice. Before the headers are spoken, a sound sample is played from the given URL. Paragraphs with class "heidi" appear to come from front left (if the sound system is capable of spatial audio), and paragraphs of class "peter" come from the right. Paragraphs with class "goat" are very soft.

The specification allows for many types of control over aspects of speech, including volume, timbre, richness, spatial positioning, and more. This is clearly the beginning of extending the content of the Web to all parties, not just people accessing content via visually accessed browsers. Technologies such as the XSL are another step in the right direction because they allow the transformation of a neutral, structure-rich markup that can control presentation exclusively by external means.

CHAPTER SUMMARY

- Web accessibility is concerned with making sure that the rich content of the Web can be accessed by people—and even machines—in all manner of contexts.
- Accessibility is an essential component of usability, since no one can use your site if the site is inaccessible!
- The W3C's Web Accessibility Initiative (WAI) is a major player in the development of accessibility standards.
- The WAI's Accessibility Guidelines, found at *www.w3.org/TR/WAI-WEBCONTENT/*, is an excellent starting point to learn more about accessibility.
- In addition to users with disabilities, users who will benefit from highly accessible Web sites include users of handheld Web devices, such as PDAs or cell phones.
- Accessibility must become a standard procedure for all Web sites in the same way that wheelchair access, closed captioning, and ergonomic workspace environments have become standardized.

HANDS-ON EXERCISES

1. Perform an accessibility assessment of your Web site. You might model your assessment after the usability task design from Chapter 8, or you might choose to simply follow the W3C Accessibility Guidelines as a design checklist. How many violations are you able to find on your site?
2. Make a report of your findings from your assessment. To which user groups is your site content inaccessible?
3. Make recommendations for change. Estimate how much time it will take to implement changes to improve accessibility on your site.

4. Determine what design habits need to change in your environment to make accessibility a priority from the ground up. Make plans to integrate your findings and recommendations for change into the next round of redesign.
5. Get input from a group of users with disabilities. They will know details of accessibility that you would never think of. Invite them to participate in your accessibility sessions.

DISCUSSION TOPICS

1. What effect will the Baby Boomers have on the need for accessibility for Web sites?
2. Will we always use Web browsers to access Internet content? If not, what are some potential future implications for usability? If so, how will browsers be different?
3. Do you have any real feel for how many of your users have disabilities? How many of your users access your content in a fashion other than a visual Web browser? If you don't know, how can you find out?
4. What is missing from the W3C's guidelines? Are there any groups of users the W3C has potentially overlooked?

CHAPTER

10

PUTTING IT ALL TOGETHER

DEVELOPING THE COMPREHENSIVE PLAN

Now that you have seen all the tools and techniques for guaranteeing Web usability, it's time to see how everything can be implemented together. This chapter shows you the growth and implementation of a comprehensive usability plan conducted by a fictional company called Xolax Software.

I have chosen this method to present the information in this chapter because it lets you see how an almost-real organization executes a comprehensive usability plan for its company Web site and how it deals with adversity. There are two things I want you to "take home" from this chapter: how to develop a comprehensive plan for your site and how another company chose to implement its own.

By reading this fictional account, you will be reading a composite of the experiences of many actual clients and myself. Of course, the names have been changed to protect the "innocent"! You can choose to adopt some or all of this approach for your own sites.

As you read this chapter, be mindful of the tools that are brought into play. Try to determine why a particular tool is used, and imagine how you would be likely to do things differently or the same. In addition, bear in mind that the plan described here is not perfect—deliberately so, for purposes of this example.

THE COMPANY AND ITS SITE

Xolax Software is a software engineering firm located in Austin, Texas. The company's main product is a suite of Java development tools called Xolaxware. According to the corporate vision, the purposes of the company Web site are to provide technical support to its current customers, to act as a sales channel for existing and potential customers, and to act as a vehicle for self-promotion for the company and its products.

The company site is primarily maintained by a small group of in-house programmers and Web designers, although outside consultants are brought in periodically to assist in major design overhauls. Kristen created the original site design in 1995. Since then, the design has undergone two major revisions, and the company is about to completely overhaul the site to better fulfill user expectations. Many new features have been slated for inclusion on the site.

The executives have recently become aware of the need for Web site usability analysis, due in a large part to Kristen's efforts and guerrilla usability studies. The current revision of the site was done primarily by a very expensive Boston agency that is well known for its print media. This new site design is much less content rich than previous incarnations, but it features almost every new cutting-edge Web technology. Xolax's executive committee believed that this display of technology would spread the message that Xolax is a state-of-the-art organization and that it would gain the edge over the competition.

This plan backfired, although the decision makers who initiated the expensive overhaul have been in denial for a while. Nonetheless, Kristen's well-organized data and Hannah's powerful presentation have bowled over the nay-sayers. Consequently, the company has funded a small team of usability specialists to enhance the state of usability of *www.xolax.com.*

THE TEAM

Let's meet the players on the Xolax Web site usability team. The key player in the group is an HTML and CGI guru named Kristen. She was the original designer of the Xolax site and is very familiar with the politics of the company as well as the history of changes the site has undergone.

Kristen was able to acquire the funding to start up a small usability department when she became frustrated with the overwhelming number of negative customer comments about the overall difficulty of using the site. Now she heads a department of four people who specifically focus on the usability of the site.

Kristen was a psychology major in college and had originally intended to open her own practice. However, her fascination for computers got her sidetracked. She possesses fine interpersonal relationship skills, is able to quickly establish rapport with people, and is generally a good listener—a good "people person." In the usability team, she is the test moderator and is the one who interacts with participants.

Jon was previously in accounts payable but wanted a change; since he knew Kristen from college, he was offered the opportunity to come aboard the team. His keen analytical skills and attention for detail afford him the ability to notice subtle trends in data, and almost no event, no matter how subtle, gets past him. He is generally shy with people but feels right at home working with Kristen.

Since Jon is used to working with lots and lots of tabular information and keeping everything in line and organized, he is in charge of data collection and statistical analysis of the data. His latest project has been to assemble a longitudinal study of user demographics as related to Web site features most often used.

Hannah is part of the Web design team but also has a dual role with the usability team. She is a project manager for the Web site and knows most of the intimate details of the site, including upcoming plans. She is the site specialist for the team and is often brought in to consult when the other team members have a question about a feature that hasn't been implemented yet or when they have other questions about the technical makeup of the site.

In addition to this dual relationship, Hannah has clout with the decision makers in the company. She's sharp, makes a very compelling presentation of her ideas, and is well respected by the company executives. She represents the usability team and goes before the "powers that be" to explain the team's rationale for implementing changes based on the studies they perform. It is her duty to keep the company president up to date on the group's activities.

Aaron is a young fellow who is attending the local college of art, where he is studying film. He is also an avid snowboarder; his part-time position with the usability team as a video operator and editor provides him with a little extra money for lift tickets. He works odd hours maintaining the video equipment, setting up the test lab, and, much to his chagrin, coming in early sometimes to film participants.

Scott has worked in various roles for the company since it started. He loves to interact with people and is great at dealing with the red tape of business interaction. He is the operations manager for the group and coordinates participant schedules, equipment use, and virtually all other aspects of the team's day-to-day business. In addition, he fills in as the participant greeter when sessions are running.

IMPLEMENTING THE PLAN

Phase One: User Needs Analysis

Since the whole thrust of the Xolax Web site is changing from a purely superficial model to a rich, content-driven, Web application-based model, the team needs to rethink the site from the ground up. Hannah has been able to provide the team with a database of current Xolaxware customers as well as a rented database of names of people who are likely users of the product. This base forms the the pool of participants the team will use for all its various sessions.

Get Participants

The first logical step is to understand user needs and expectations, so Kristen randomly generates a list of participant names from the supplied database. She begins with a list of 50 potential participants in the hope that at least 20 will be willing to participate in her initial sessions: interviews and a focus group meeting.

After making calls and following up, Kristen has located a total of 23 participants. She sends each participant a questionnaire that she has developed to gather demographic information and other data. The participants are asked to bring their completed questionnaires on the day of their session.

Scott arranges for the participant sessions to take place in a one-week period. The first day, he schedules six of the participants to spend part of the day in a focus group. The remaining participants are broken up over the rest of the week. They will participate in informal interviews that Kristen has designed to accumulate as much information about user likes, dislikes, and expectations as possible.

Assemble and Report Data

The information gathered in the sessions is accumulated, and Hannah presents the data at a meeting. She explains that many of the participants felt that the Xolax site lacks important content and that many of them had tried unsuccessfully to locate technical support information on the site.

Unfortunately, the Xolax FAQs—the sole source of technical support information on the site—are terribly out of date, and many of the links on the page are broken. Every participant mentioned having resorted to tech phone support. This information corroborates her earlier predictions to the company executives. Additionally, information gained at the focus group session revealed a number of features that the participants like on Xolax's competitor's site.

The Web design team is now equipped with a user's-eye view of the new design. Kristen is also concerned with the fact that the current version of the site is completely inaccessible to assistive technologies, due to the heavy use of graphics as navigational items. She proposes that the design team use an approach that includes alternate access to content areas of the site.

Phase Two: Prototype and Test

The design team has come up with two potential concepts for the new site, each of which has its own strengths and weaknesses. The vote is split down the middle, even after hours of conceptual walk-throughs[1] of the potential sites.

Horizontal Prototypes

Kristen decides to get a deciding vote by asking the users what they think. The design team drafts two horizontal prototypes, one for each design. Scott gets on the phone again and arranges for 10 more participants to come take a look at the prototypes. Kristen and Jon decide to take an informal approach to this round of sessions since they simply want to get the users' gut reactions to the two designs. They design a series of questions about the aesthetics of the site and develop a card sort to be given before the two designs are shown to the participants to see if their preconceptions about the site structure match either of the two designs.

Much to everyone's surprise, the users overwhelmingly like one design better than the other; the card sorts back up this preference because the average card sort looks much more like the preferred design. The team forges ahead with the preferred design. Full-scale production begins.

Comparison Tests with Help Interface

Once the foundation for the new site has been created, the design team has come to another wall: how to best implement the technical support interface. There are again two main approaches to the design. This time, Kristen decides to fully implement both interfaces so that they can be used to completion, even though most of the rest of the site isn't ready. This is a vertical prototype that will allow Kristen to perform usability

[1]A conceptual walk-through is yet another tool in the usability toolbox that we haven't discussed. The walk-through is a bit like role playing; you imagine the interface, and imagine using it, predicting what the interface's responses will be. It's very, very inexpensive prototyping.

testing on the two designs. The more usable of the two designs will go on to become the final design.

Scott arranges for 12 participants to take part in a series of usability tasks. Kristen realizes that this part of the design is critical and that time is precious, so she arranges for the sessions to happen in just two days, about one hour per participant. She divides the participants into two groups: one that will use Design A and one that will use Design B. Each group has six members who are randomly chosen from the 12.[2]

The usability test consists of 15 search-and-perform tasks that require the participant to find the answers to many common, and several obscure, bugs. Although the task terminates with the participant finding a predetermined answer, Kristen and Jon both plan to incorporate the next step, to actually implement the solution, as part of a comprehensive joint effort between the software QA team and the Web site team.

One of the two sites has a significantly higher rate of success than the other, but during the debriefing sessions, several of the participants of the less successful site mentioned some features that they really liked. As a result, Kristen and Jon suggest that the features from the less successful design be incorporated into the other design. The hope is that a stronger hybrid will result.

Phase Three: Development and Testing

Heuristic Evaluation

The framework for the site has been completed, and now the design team begins to flesh out the full site content. At this point, Kristen, Jon, Hannah, and Scott all put their heads together to perform a heuristic

[2]The key thing to note here is every participant has an equal chance of being in either group. If Kristen makes the mistake of putting all males in one group and all females in the other group, she will have committed a grave error in research design. Likewise, any subject sorting that is based not on randomness but on an existing condition such as age, gender, experience level, or even alphabetical order of last name can invalidate data.

evaluation of the site. After assessing the site individually, each member of the team presents a summary of observations to the rest of the team. So far, so good, except that Hannah and Scott have noted that in several sections of the site, some of the wording seems jargon laden. The point is taken under advisement, and the design team is provided with alternate vocabulary to use (drawn from the interviews in Phase One).

Accessibility Audit

A series of tests are run in-house to determine if the current site design adheres closely to the W3C's guidelines for accessibility. Although there are some minor problems with the site, it passes the majority of the audit. One major problem is uncovered: The authoring tools that the design team uses do not make proper use of ALT attributes inside client-side MAP definitions. This problem will be corrected before the site goes live.

Usability Testing

Kristen designs a comprehensive test plan that consists of 30 tasks that probe all areas of the site, including membership sign-up, technical support, and product ordering. Scott arranges for 20 users to arrive over the course of four days to participate.

This series of sessions is videotaped from several angles. Aaron pulls an all-nighter to set up, using his brother Matt as a model for the cameras. There will be video coverage of each participant's face, a direct computer output to video (to capture all the action on the screen as clearly as possible), and a third angle that gets the test moderator in the shot as well.

Aaron configures the session recordings so that all three angles can be viewed synchronously, helping the reviewers catch subtle details that they missed during the sessions. He uses plastic potted plants to hide the cameras. Kristen has been amazed at how quickly participants forget that they are on camera as long as no one draws attention to the cameras!

During the sessions, Scott greets participants in the reception area. He offers them a snack and a beverage, but no caffeine—it can make people more nervous and can negatively affect performance. Kristen calls the participants into the testing area when it's time for their sessions.

Kristen explains the nature of the test to each participant and gets each to sign an NDA and a video release form. She explains to each participant that the information gathered in the session will be used only internally by the research team, and that Xolax never rents or otherwise distributes its data.

Once the participant begins the tasks, the session takes about 45 minutes. Jon carefully monitors numbers of clicks, success or failure, and time to complete. Kristen calls time when the maximum time to complete has lapsed. Kristen is also careful to read the scripted instructions for each usability task in the same, consistent tone for each participant, since paraphrasing or revising instructions can affect how a participant interprets the instructions and can lead to problems with the data. Consistency is the key.

During the usability sessions, however, not everything runs smoothly. In fact, there are some major glitches that the team has to deal with quickly and effectively, on the fly. The first snafu is the discovery that one of the usability tasks is impossible to complete because part of the site is not working; an unannounced system maintenance interruption has rendered part of the site's database applications inoperative. After subjecting the first two participants to the task, the team discovers the problem and decides to remove it from the task list. The team notes for their report that this task was dropped due to a site malfunction and that all data from this task should be stricken from the final data.

Fortunately, Kristen designed the test plan to be tolerant of such unforeseen problems; the rest of the tasks are modular enough not to be affected, and the show goes on. This is not the first time that a task has been dropped in mid-session, and it won't be the last.

The next glitch happens when one of the participants shows up a half-hour late for the session, then saunters in and demands to be allowed to complete the session in the remaining time. This participant is quite aggressive, almost belligerent. The team has fortunately made it clear from the first contact with the participants that compensation is prorated based on how much of each participant's session is actually completed. The late participant is reminded of this stipulation and is allowed to participate in a truncated version of the session.

Since Kristen has also planned on this kind of thing happening, she has a backup prioritization for the tasks and is able to present the most important tasks to the late participant. All sorts of people come to participate in these sessions, including people who can be extremely difficult to deal with. Nonetheless, Kristen keeps her cool, collects data, and compensates the participant half the normal amount. Since the team planned on some level of participant no-shows, they are still on track for having enough data. Even if the late participant's data is dropped completely, there will still be enough data for the test.

Unfortunately, the problems do not stop there. On the second day of tasks, a very hostile participant arrives 10 minutes late, and on entering the facility begins loudly complaining about, well, everything! "These directions you gave me to this facility were awful! How did you ever expect that anyone could find their way here?" The participant is red-faced and obviously volatile. Kristen tries to get through the orientation, but the participant keeps interrupting, asking tangential questions and generally getting under Kristen's skin. The last straw comes when the participant responds to every single task with an immediate "I give up!" The participant is clearly here only for the money and expects to be given a free ride for showing up.

The team must decide on a way to handle this irksome person. Jon pulls Kristen aside for a moment, and they decide on a solution. They thank the participant for her time, indicate that they have accumulated enough data for this session, and compensate the participant in full, despite the fact that the session has been a complete waste of time. The participant's name is then removed from the database of potential participants and put on the official blacklist. No future resources will be wasted on this person. If the team had gotten this participant from a recruiting agency, they would have refused to pay for the participant and would have reported the incident to the agency. They would also have requested that the participant be removed from all future potential pools.

After these minor setbacks, the rest of the sessions go smoothly, and the team begins the task of analyzing the data. Jon tabulates the raw data gathered at the sessions and, with the help of Aaron, reviews the footage and pieces together a composite video of key moments throughout the sessions. This video will be presented at an upcoming staff meeting, where the vice president will get to view it. Once the data has been turned into a series of graphs and matrices, the team is ready to present suggestions for change. It seems that only a few minor usability problems have slipped through the cracks, mainly due to the fact that certain parts of the database connectivity are misbehaving. Additionally, several participants had a hard time finding information under certain headings. The team proposes cross-referencing these items to facilitate locating the information.

The team presents the information at a meeting, at which point Hannah takes issue with the fact that the usability team is suggesting cross-referencing items on multiple pages. The design team asserts that cross-referencing will result in unsightly pages that seem cluttered. In the end, the decision is made to implement the cross-references anyway and that further testing on this component should be done to assess the trade-off between aesthetics and functionality.

After the meeting, Hannah instructs the design team to implement the changes suggested in the usability team's report. The Web site is almost ready for launch.

Phase Four: Validate and Launch

The site is now 99.9 percent ready. Kristen designs one small final test and arranges for four participants to take part. The session will be short, designed primarily to address the usability issues found in the last round of testing, to ensure that they were fixed.

Finally, the site launch date is set. Cleverly, Kristen has managed to work a couple quick surveys into the site design to gather user opinions about the new design. This feedback will form the foundation for the next iteration of the whole process, which begins anew as soon as the site goes live.

SOME FINAL POINTS

That's the way the comprehensive test plan for Xolax looks over one iteration of redesign. Your plan might vary from this one, based on your budget and your objectives. Whatever the case, there are some key principles to which I'd like to draw your attention:

Have a Plan

Flying by the seat of your pants is necessary more often that you might like. However, having a plan in place with clear objectives is paramount to making a positive difference in your Web site. Great designs don't just happen; they are the results of good planning and many hours of toil.

But Be Flexible

If Kristen's plan had been inflexible—if she had to totally rewrite it from scratch when she discovered the impossible-to-complete task—many hours and many dollars would have been wasted, not to mention the fact that the competition would be given the opportunity to use the downtime to their advantage. Never "write yourself into a corner"; imposing many contingencies in your plan is a surefire setup for disaster.

Know How to Deal with Problems Ahead of Time

In your usability work, you will deal with some annoying people. I guarantee it. You will also run into other types of unforeseeable problems. Know head of time, as much as possible, how you will deal with late-shows or no-shows who blame their tardiness on you, the weather, sunspots, or any of the host of reasons people have for not keeping up their end of a bargain. Clearly, there will be occasions when your participants have a valid reason for not showing up on time. You should also have a plan for dealing with those situations.

Involve Users at Every Phase

This is one of the core truths of UCD: It is critical that you allow the user to give feedback on the project at every phase. Can you imagine if a book author were to write an entire book without the publisher ever taking a look at it until it was complete? This approach is destined for disaster. So is the approach that many companies take of creating the site in a vacuum, without soliciting user input. Note, again, that this does not mean that you should try to please every user's aesthetic bent. You simply cannot please everyone all the time. But remember that we are not talking about aesthetics here, we're talking about how *usable* the site is.

Record Your Data Carefully

The Xolax usability team was careful to keep good records of all data. When something went wrong, they were sure to note it in their results (for example, when they had to drop the troublesome task from the sessions). Furthermore, by having access to all the video footage, they were able to assemble a compelling video collage of participant trouble spots. Sometimes, watching a real live human struggle with a poor design is the only way to convince a designer to implement your change.

CHAPTER SUMMARY

- In order to succeed at improving your site's usability, you must use many of the tools in the toolbox to form a comprehensive plan.
- In much the same way that the usability test plan acts as a blueprint for a classical usability testing session, the usability plan itself is the overall blueprint for the long-term usable design cycle.
- Expect the unexpected.

- Have contingency plans built into your usability plan. You can never know when things are going to change.
- Be flexible. Rigid test plans don't work.

HANDS-ON EXERCISES

1. Design a comprehensive usability plan for your site. What kind of time frame will you have from the beginning of Phase One to the end of Phase Four?
2. Decide which tools you will need for your plan and operationalize the resources you will need.
3. Build a budget for your plan. How much will it cost in time, money, and other resources, and what do you estimate the return on investment will be over the short and long haul—say, three months? A year?
4. Design a policy for how you will deal with as many types of adversity as you can think of. How will you deal with inclement weather (rescheduling, cancellations, and so on)? Late-shows? Hostile participants?

DISCUSSION TOPICS

1. How would you have dealt with the late participant if you were in Kristen's place? What do you think is just?
2. What tools would you have used in this case study if you had been Kristen? Explain.
3. What improvements to this usability plan would you suggest to Kristen? Did you notice any omissions?
4. How would you handle a participant who wants to talk about anything and everything except the tasks at hand?

CHAPTER

11

TRANSFORMING DATA INTO CHANGE

WHY STUDY STATISTICS?

This chapter is aimed at people who either do not have a formal background in research design or in statistics or who have never taken a course in either topic. It is an introductory chapter, by all means; it does not attempt to summarize the discipline of statistics. Rather, it attempts to give people who have had no prior exposure to the subject a chance to understand the importance statistics plays in any well-designed study.

The most likely criticism of this chapter will be that no one in a Web development team will ever have time to implement the techniques or concepts shown herein. My answer is that if you take even a little time to learn this material and work it into your reporting, it will pay off in large dividends.

If you are proficient in research design methodology or statistics, you can skip this chapter; it's unlikely that it will tell you anything new. If you are new to these topics, reading this chapter will give you a better grasp of the vocabulary used to describe data in a common, scientific tongue.

So far, all the testing you have done has been more an art and less a science. Although I still stick by the notion that it isn't practical to design your Web usability studies around classical experimental methodology, I want to at least equip you with a minimal knowledge of research design methods and statistical measures. In the process, I'll show you how you can transform the data that you have acquired through your sessions into empirically based recommendations for change.

So far, most of your suggestions for change have come from a sort of "common sense" approach; that is, if you see that one usability task has a good deal of failure associated with it, you assume that you need to change something in the interface to make it work better. Part of this guesswork comes from having a solid background in the technologies used to implement your Web site. Another asset in the process is your understanding of human factors. Part of that is just good old common sense, even though common sense isn't really so common!

So here's a disclaimer: I cannot give you a magical formula that says, "If such and such a score is less than *x*, use a text link instead of a graphical link." No amount of mathematical might can replace simple understanding of design and human interaction. Nonetheless, the tools we use to describe many of these things are necessarily mathematical. That's one reason it's helpful to study statistics.

Furthermore, this book hasn't shown you how to do a "real" study in the classical sense. Here's the difference between how we have been proceeding and a "classical" test: Normally, we do a usability test on the original (control) site to establish benchmarks for task completion. Next, we make changes based on our observations that we obtain from the testing. Finally, we run the same test again, this time with a different group of participants (commonly called the *treatment group*). If there is a statistically significant increase in usability from the control group to the experimental group, we can be reasonably sure (assuming that our design for testing is sound) that the changes we made , not some other random act of chance, are responsible for the improvement.

It may sound odd, but many other things can influence an apparent improvement in score, especially if the difference isn't very large. On the path to better research you will find an ally in statistical analysis and research design techniques that combat this randomness.

IT'S ALL ABOUT THE DATA

Statistics would be meaningless without data, so we should focus on the various types of data before we move on. There are four types of data:

- Nominal
- Ordinal
- Interval
- Ratio

Let's take a closer look at each type.

Nominal data is data that cannot be quantified, only named. For example, if you ask 100 people to name their pet peeve about Web sites, you will get responses in the form of words and phrases. There isn't a way to derive an average from this named data per se, so other statistical techniques must be employed. What you can do is count the number of responses that fit a particular nominal descriptor.

For example, the following statistics come from a preference study in 1998. The question was, "Name the five things that you like the most about the Web." The responses were not ranked in any particular order.

There were 10 respondents. The five responses that occurred the most frequently were as follows:

Fast download time: 10 responses

Meaningful content: 9 responses

Well-organized links: 9 responses

No broken links: 8 responses

Good search engine: 7 responses

Ordinal data is data that is rank ordered. For example, if you give people a list of five items and ask them to rate the importance of each item in descending order, you have ordinal data. In the same preference study, I asked respondents to rank order their five favorite things about the Web.

Ordinal data is very popular for communicating information to the lay person, because rank ordering is a common part of our vocabulary. The problem inherent in using ordinal data is that there is no way to display the amount of difference between any two rank orders; for example, 10 people in my study might have responded that they like fast download time, giving this feature a rank order of #1. However, the nearest-ranked feature, relevant content, might have been mentioned by only seven people, giving it a rank order of #2. The difference between rank order #2 and #3 might be yet another amount.

Interval data is the first type of data on which certain powerful types of numerical analysis can be performed. Interval data falls on an interval scale, in which the numbers on the scale have equal distance-value from one another. For example, in an ordinal scale, we have no way of knowing how far apart the difference is between the #1 ranking and the #2 ranking; furthermore, the distance between any two points on the scale might not be the same as the distance from any other two points. In an interval scale, we know the difference between points.

For example, a common household thermometer uses an interval scale. The distance between 10 degrees and 20 degrees is the same distance as between 30 degrees and 40 degrees. But note that in an interval scale, there is no "absolute zero" point that indicates an absence of the measured value. In other words, a thermometer cannot display a total lack of temperature.

Ratio data is the most precise sort of data because it does have an absolute zero point, and like interval data, its units of measurement are all equally sized. An example of ratio data is time. Zero seconds indicates no time, so there is a way of representing an absence of the value entirely. Additionally, the distance between 10 seconds and 20 seconds is the same as the distance between 30 seconds and 40 seconds. Many types of physical measurements—number of clicks, number of errors, and so on—use the ratio scale:.

START WITH A TIMELINE OF PROGRESS

As it stands, we are doing a "before" test, with no "after" test. Although this kind of a pseudoscientific design would never make it into the annals of radiology or particle physics, it can work fine for us most of the time, assuming that we understand the limitations of such metrics. Naturally, over time and over the course of several iterative redesign cycles, you will amass data about the various tasks that you have participants undertake, and after a while you will be able to build a graph to chart the progress your team makes in lowering overall benchmarks. Although this process is different from the design model of conducting a "before" and a more or less immediate "after' test, you will still find such a timeline of progress very handy.

What if your actual tasks change dramatically from one iteration of the test to the next? This is actually pretty likely to happen, given how quickly Web sites must mutate. In this case, your tasks won't be able to directly map to each other across time. Hence, you will be able to report on only a few key pieces of ratio that you can represent in any test:

- Mean time to complete a task
- Mean number of clicks to complete a task
- Total percentage of failures for tasks

For example, the first time I run a usability test on my site, I can figure out the average time for a participant to complete a task (take all of the participant's times and add them, then divide by the number of tasks). I repeat this measure for each participant, then I add up the scores from all participants, then divide by the number of participants. This gives me a watered down, not-very-scientific figure, but it is nonetheless an approximate metric for assessing the state of usability for each task.

Additionally, I can take the mean of all the tasks across all participants to arrive at a single figure that estimates the overall usability of the site. Although this is not a scientifically sound measure, it can at least give you a fuzzy idea of where you are. For example, if your boiled-down average rate of task failure for your site is 98 percent, you don't need an advanced degree to figure out pretty darn quickly that your site is in trouble.

Now, don't tell your statistics professor I said to do that! In reality, the figures resulting from my "formula" can't really tell you very much. Statistics that are based on simple means (averages) aren't terribly useful, since they can be misleading. This is a good first step, however, and if you aren't planning to employ any other statistical means, it will at least give you a longitudinal baseline.

For example, let's say that you are campaigning to be the next governor of your fair state. You know that you have a meeting with only six of the people in a town that is crucial for the election, and you can know only one statistic of the group: you can either choose to know their median income or their mean income. Which should you choose?

Let's say that you choose the *mean* income figure, and you discover that the mean income of the six people is about $91,000. Armed with this information, you prepare your speech in such a way as to emphasize that you will fight for reduced taxes for the wealthy, a better country club, and a decrease in funds to the poor. After your speech, you discover that one of the people had an income of half a million dollars—and that the remaining five were well below the poverty line, with income of $10,000 annually. You lose this round and perhaps the whole race. Had you known to ask for the *median* income, which is the middle value of a set of numbers when they are arranged in ascending order, you might have avoided this debacle.

MEASURES OF CENTRAL TENDENCIES

Which brings us to the next topic. Whenever you need to analyze a large amount of data using statistical tools, you invariably need to employ three types of measurement, one of which you are familiar with from everyday use. The term *central tendencies* refers to the natural phenomenon of data clustering around the "middle" of a set of data. Usability specialists care about central tendencies of data because they tell us much about the general condition of the things they represent. In addition, the measures of central tendencies are used in other types of statistical tools to help us determine whether a change in a participant's performance from a baseline is "statistically significant," meaning that the probability of the change resulting from chance is slim. Depending on how critical accuracy and trustworthiness are for your data, the margin for statistical significance can be quite slim.

The three measures of central tendencies are as follows:

- The mean, which is the arithmetical average of all the data
- The median, or the value that occurs in the middle of the data when it is arranged in order
- The mode, which is the most commonly occurring value in a data set

Each of these measures can be used to describe an arbitrary data set. Let's take, for example, the data from a usability test I did recently. These scores are all the results for task #3 in a series of usability tasks for all participants. First, let's look at the raw data, which is contained in Table 11.1. We use the data set in Table 11.1 for the examples throughout this section.

TABLE 11.1 *Sample Data Results*

Participant ID	Time to Complete Task (in Seconds)
19991114-001	45
19991114-002	23
19991114-003	84
19991114-004	23
19991114-005	31
19991114-006	53
19991115-001	26
19991115-002	35
19991115-003	47

The Mean

First, let's find the mean (average) of this data set. That's easy; we simply add up all the scores and divide by the number of scores we have totaled. Note that converting your times to seconds facilitates this process. So that's:

```
45 + 23 + 84 + 23 + 31 + 53 + 26 +35 + 47 = 367
```

The total, 367, divided by the number of scores (called n) equals 40.78; rounded up, the answer is 41 seconds. Therefore, we know that the mean score on this task was 41 seconds. Remember that *mean* is just a fancy word for *average*.

What good is knowing the mean? First, the mean is the sort of sugary, easy-to-digest statistic that even a child can understand, meaning that it is suitable for presenting data to people who don't think like scientists. Many popular magazines that have surveys and polls describe their results in terms of means. So, the mean is good for summarizing complex data into one easy-to-understand figure.

Additionally, the mean is good for getting a feel for the whole picture, taking all the data into account. Since we average everything together in one big statistical mixing bowl, all the data points are accounted for.

Over a sufficiently large data set, *outliers* (scores that are on the extreme ends) are absorbed by the rest of the scores.

The Median

Remember that in our example above, I said that you really should have used the *median* instead of the mean? Here's why it works out that way. We need to arrange our data values in order first:

```
23    23    26    31    35    45    47    53    84
```

Now we pick the middle value, which is 35. (What if you have an even number of values? Then the median is the average of the middle two values.) Now let's look at our values (the voters' incomes) from the governor's campaign scenario:

```
$10,000    $10,000    $10,000    $10,000
    $10,000    $500,000
```

Obtaining the median income in this case gives us a slightly more realistic assessment of the real income level of the town. Note that in certain circumstances, the median can be misleading. For example, what if we had the following data set:

```
150    175    182    1,350    767,234
    1,000,252    1,000,982
```

Our median is 1,350, which really isn't helpful at all since it is far larger than the bottom-most scores and it is far less than the top-most scores. In reality, this sort of thing doesn't happen regularly. If the items that you are measuring are truly comparable, the scores should fall within a fairly normal distribution; that is, the gathered values will actually tend to clump neatly around our measures of central tendencies. Have ever seen a bell curve before? That is the kind of distribution I am talking about. Data that does not fit the normal distribution should be a cause for alarm, because something could be wrong with your measurement techniques; you need to retrace your steps to see where your measurements went awry.

The Mode

Our final measure of central tendencies is the *mode*, which is the value that occurs the most in a data set. Many people think that the mode is a useless measure, but it's really quite helpful in the right circumstances.

If you look at our data set from Table 11.1, you see that the mode is 23, which is nowhere near our median or our mean. This kind of distortion can be caused by many different factors, but most commonly, it occurs because our sample is so small. Typically, over a sufficiently large sample, these kinds of disparities "come out in the wash," and you see a tighter clustering of the three measures of central tendencies. So, in our sample set, the mode isn't particularly telling; it's probably just random chance that the mode was 23.

One place that the mode is particularly effective is with nominal data. For example, if you have a survey question such as "What is your favorite Web site overall?" the response is not going to be something that you can plug into an equation and for which you can figure out a mean. (What's the result of adding *cnet.com, slashdot.org,* and *palmpilot.org* and dividing by 3?) However, it is easy to pick the mode out of such a data set, in which case it is quite useful. In fact, the mode is the only measure of central tendency that can be used with any type of data—ordinal, nominal, ratio, or interval.

It bears mentioning that sometimes you can have data in which more items than one have the same high frequency of occurrence. In this case, the data set is called a *multimodal* set.

Population and Sample

We're already seen that in a study, the *population* is the entire set of potential candidates, and the *sample* is the much smaller, randomly selected group that you pick from the population to participate in the study. However, we have not discussed the fact that it is important to determine how many sample members it takes to constitute a useful study.

For example, if you suffer from asthma and have heard about a new drug that helps alleviate the symptoms of asthma, would you be willing to try the drug if only two other people had ever tested it? I sure wouldn't! There are millions of asthma sufferers in the world, and having only two test participants doesn't make for significant results. The drug might prove lethal in 98 percent of people who take it, and the drug trial might have chosen the 2 people in 100 who are impervious to this side effect.

As Jakob Nielsen said in a recent article,[1] you need to test only about five users to get a relatively accurate reading of usability problems on your site. I agree that efficacy can be obtained with this small sample. Dr. Nielsen is a big advocate of low-cost usability testing, and clearly, limiting the number of users who participate in your study is a key to reducing cost. Making people aware of low-cost techniques for usability is critical; far too few companies do any kind of testing, and at least initially, the usability specialist community must push for acceptance, so canceling out cost as a potential barrier is smart.

However, I tend to think that if you can afford it, you're better off having about twice that many participants per round. It's not significantly better, as Nielsen shows in the previously cited article, with his formula for computing the percentage of errors found compared with the number of participants. It remains a fact that the larger your sample, the more confident you can be in your data.

On Randomness

I have mentioned several times throughout the book that when you select your sample to enroll as participants in your sessions, you need to make sure that they are randomly chosen. Let me drive that point home: *It is imperative that your selection of participants be random,* or else you will run into serious problems. Why? Because random selection weeds out any factors that might confound your study.

---

[1] To see the article, visit *www.useit.com/alertbox/20000319.html.*

For example, let's say that you have a Web site that is geared toward professional software developers. You design a series of usability sessions, including preference questionnaires, usability tasks, and extensive debriefing questions. To enlist participants, you send a team member to the annual Perl conference to gather potential participant information. You call back the respondents, they arrive, they participate, and you employ their input to shape your site.

The result? Your site fails to penetrate the target audience because the people you selected for your sample all shared a very nonrandom trait. They were all very likely to be major Perl fanatics, and that type of person naturally has a certain nonrandom set of preferences that will not be representative of your larger target population. For example, in your preference questionnaire, Visual Basic might have not even made it onto the list of commonly used programming languages. In reality, many people use VB. Focusing on a specific subset of your overall population led you down the wrong path; although you probably generated some good data that you could generalize to the Perl community, you cannot use the data to represent the entire population.

Any time you use nonrandom sampling techniques, you create problems for yourself in the way of *subject variables*, which are tendencies, habits, experiences, and other traits that a participant may bring to the study that could affect results. Of course, every human has personal traits; there's no avoiding that, thankfully! But having a random pool of participants makes it harder for many participants to share confounding traits that might throw your data off course or pigeonhole it erroneously.

How do you get a random sample? There are many techniques. One way that is easy to do if you have a large database of potential participants is to assign each participant a number. Most database systems do this anyway. You can then pick participants randomly by number using a random-number generation program (do a Web search for *random number generator* and you'll uncover a load of C source code as well as precompiled binaries that will spit out however many numbers you ask for).

If you don't have access to a database with this kind of feature, you can resort to a more low-tech approach. Print the participants' information, cut up the paper into strips that have a single participant on each strip, put the strips in a hat, and draw until you have enough participants. There are, of course, many other variations of random selection, but these two should get you started. Sometimes recruiting agencies allege that they use random-sampling techniques for choosing participants. Be sure to ask them for a description of their methodology, because they may not actually be very random at all.

RESEARCH DESIGN CONCEPTS

Although you aren't expected to don a white lab coat and carry around a beaker full of some iridescent, bubbling liquid, you can certainly benefit from knowing a little about principles of research design methodology. To begin, let's touch briefly on the *experimental method.*

The entire goal of the experimental method is to reduce ambiguity in the way you interpret results of change that you make. If you decide to make a change to your Web site, and there is a subsequent change in the way your users interact with it (better usability, poorer usability), how do you know for certain that what you changed was the cause of the new behavior? Plenty of other factors that might contribute to the new behavior; for example, a new Web browser might have come on the market with bugs in it, or your users might have become so used to your site over the past few months that their ability to use it has improved in spite of its shabby design. The point is, without experimental methodology, your assumptions are mere guesswork that is unfounded in anything reliable.

Experimental Control

One of the keys to the experimental method is *experimental control,* which is the act of making sure that the experimenter has the capability to control any factors, called *variables,* that might influence the outcome of the study. The other side of control is that there should normally be two groups of participants in a study: a *control group* (participants who receive the "untreated" experience—for instance, the original Web site before the redesign) and an *experimental group* (sometimes called the *treatment*, or *Tx, group*) that experiences the "treated" site (i.e., after you've made changes). The only difference between the two groups should be the Web site changes you have made.

In real experimental work, you would make only a single change at a time and then test for each change, since simultaneously making hundreds of tiny design changes introduces far too many variables to track. How could you tell which of the hundreds had the positive impact on your participants? In the real world of Web usability, it is highly unlikely that you will ever move with such precision. Nonetheless, you can employ the principles, even if only in a pseudoscientific fashion, to attain better usability.

If the experimenter can be certain that the only things that are different between the two participant groups is the design change, the experimenter can be reasonably sure that any observed difference in behavior can be attributed to the design change. On the other hand, in a poorly designed study, you could have confounding variables, such as having all men in the control group and all women in the experimental group (a problem called *non-equivalent groups*). In a case such as that, the data is more or less useless, since the difference in performance could be due to the innate difference between the two groups. Experimental control seeks to eliminate this sort of dilemma.

Randomization

As mentioned earlier, having a random sample derived from your entire population is key to getting meaningful results. The bottom line with randomness is that there should never be a way that any one member of the population has a better chance of being selected as a participant than any other. For example, choosing all the graduates of a particular college to represent a much more comprehensive population would be nonrandom selection, and therefore data gathered would be invalid.

Randomization is so important because it is impossible to control for personal traits of participants. Therefore, having a random sample helps cancel out the idiosyncrasies of individuals.

Independent and Dependent Variables

In all experimental designs, there is at least one independent variable and one dependent variable. An *independent variable* is one that the researcher controls entirely. For example, the Web site researcher has the ability to control whether a given hyperlink is a graphical or a textual link. The *independent variable* that the researcher might want to measure is the time it takes a participant to recognize the link and follow it. When the researcher manipulates the independent variable, the dependent variable changes as a result. The way to think of these variables is that the dependent variable depends on the researcher's actions to change.

Bad Research Designs

I'd like to show you some examples of classical "bad" study designs to help illustrate how *not* to set up your own studies. There are several well-known pitfalls that you can hopefully avoid!

The Lemon Pledge Design

The *Lemon Pledge design*, also know as the *missing control group design* or the *one-shot design*, is flawed because it has no control group against which to compare anything. The name *Lemon Pledge design* comes from the old TV commercials of happy people spraying furniture polish on a table before showing the audience the table, and then showing the result and glowing over it. What did it look like before? How do we know if the treatment really did anything to change the table's appearance?

Imagine if you upgraded your old Web site—without testing it at all—and then performed a usability test on the new design. What would you hope to accomplish with the data you gathered? You can't make any inferences about anything because you didn't measure the previous state of the site. At best, you now have a "before" snapshot of the site that you can use to compare to future usability session results.

One Group Pre-Test/Post-Test Design

The *pre-test/post-test pseudo-design* is also called the *snake oil design*. The idea is that you use the same set of participants for your "before" test and your "after" test. The name *snake oil test* comes from the Old West frontier days in the United States, when crooked peddlers would sell "magic snake oil" miracle cures for all manner of ailments. The proof that the medicine worked would come when a test participant, who had a cold at the time, would consume a dose of the snake oil. A week later, the cold had miraculously been cured!

Clearly, other factors were actually responsible for the "miracle" cure; for example, the illness would normally have gone away on its own in sufficient time. This effect is usually called *maturation*, which simply refers to any change that naturally happens over time. Another potential problem can result from the actual act of testing itself. If you retest the same group of participants for your second test, they will be armed with memory of the old site—and practice makes perfect! The change in performance from pre- to post- sessions could result from simple practice. I hope that I have convinced you to never cut costs by reusing participants in this fashion; it is a very bad idea!

Nonequivalent Groups Design

I spoke briefly about this bad design earlier in the chapter. The basic idea here is that you make the extra effort to actually have a control group and an experimental group, but you fail to make sure that the participants are equivalent; in other words, you should randomly assign participants into the two groups. As I mentioned above, having a control group of all people who have never used a Web browser before and an experimental group that consists of all veteran surfers is a shortcut to uselessness.

CONCLUSION

I have deliberately siphoned off the vast majority of detail with regard to statistics; there isn't a single formula in this chapter. I haven't given you an exhaustive coverage of research design, because I don't want you do be exhausted or turned off to the process. But my sincere hope is that if you have found any of this chapter helpful, you will be encouraged to pursue more education in the area of statistics and research design methodology.

There is a vast wealth of information that you can integrate into your overall usability strategy; with this book, I have tried to give you a taste of the possibilities. I wish you all the luck in the world, and I strongly encourage you to spread the word about usability. Remember to publish any findings, insights, anecdotes, or other wisdom you can, because many more pioneers like you are looking for answers and might have something to teach you (and me), too.

WEB SERVER LOG ANALYSIS

The following paragraphs are not meant as a tutorial in server log analysis; this topic is outside the scope of this book. However, included with the CD-Rom in this book you will find a free copy of the Webalizer, an open source suite designed to do professional web server log analysis. Note that this software must be installed by your system adminstrator on your web server; *it is not intended to be used on a personal desktop computer.*

Although many web developers use server log analysis to track variables like length of user visit, hot pages, and so on, primarily for marketing purposes, a web usablity specialist can certainly benefit from this practice as well. How you implement log anaysis can vary from the very simple (using UNIX utilities like grep to wade through the logs) to the very expensive and sophisticated. There are several commercial log analysis packages available "off the shelf." You may also find that making your own custom tools in Perl or another scripting language works better for you, if you are so inclined.

The basic ideas are simple. Server logs tell you who has been looking at your site, what pages they have been requesting, and in the case of search engines, they can tell you what people are searching for. If an item comes up repeatedly in web searches, it's usually a sign that you haven't located that item in a user-friendly place. Looking at the logs, you can prioritize the content of your site based on your user's needs. Remember the example of the FedEX web site in Chapter 5? How many times do you think their logs would show searches for "tracking" if they hadn't located it on the home page?

Another use for web logs can be to give yourself baseline times for the completion of multipage forms and similar interface elements on your web site. For example, if your web site currently has a registration form for a conference that spans several pages, you might want to know how long it takes the average user to go from start to finish. By examining your server logs, you can get a handle on this pretty easily. Most of the better commercial applications will allow you to do this. (Once you take all the completion times from unique visitors implemented through a session ID or through IP address, though the latter isn't always helpful.) Having this baseline is valuable for use in future usability trials on revisions of the same form, or similar forms.

In Figure 11.1, you can see that the Webalizer can produce a report of the most frequently requested URLs. This can give you a good feel for what the hot content on your site is, possibly enabling you to rethink your site design to make the hottest items more accessible. Most commercial search engines will also allow you to see the most commonly requested search strings; this can also be very helpful in determining what people are having a hard time finding. A hidden benefit of this sort of tracking is that it allows you to build a user-centered vocabulary. Have you used jargon or a fancy term for an important concept on the site, while users are searching for a different—more user-friendly—term?

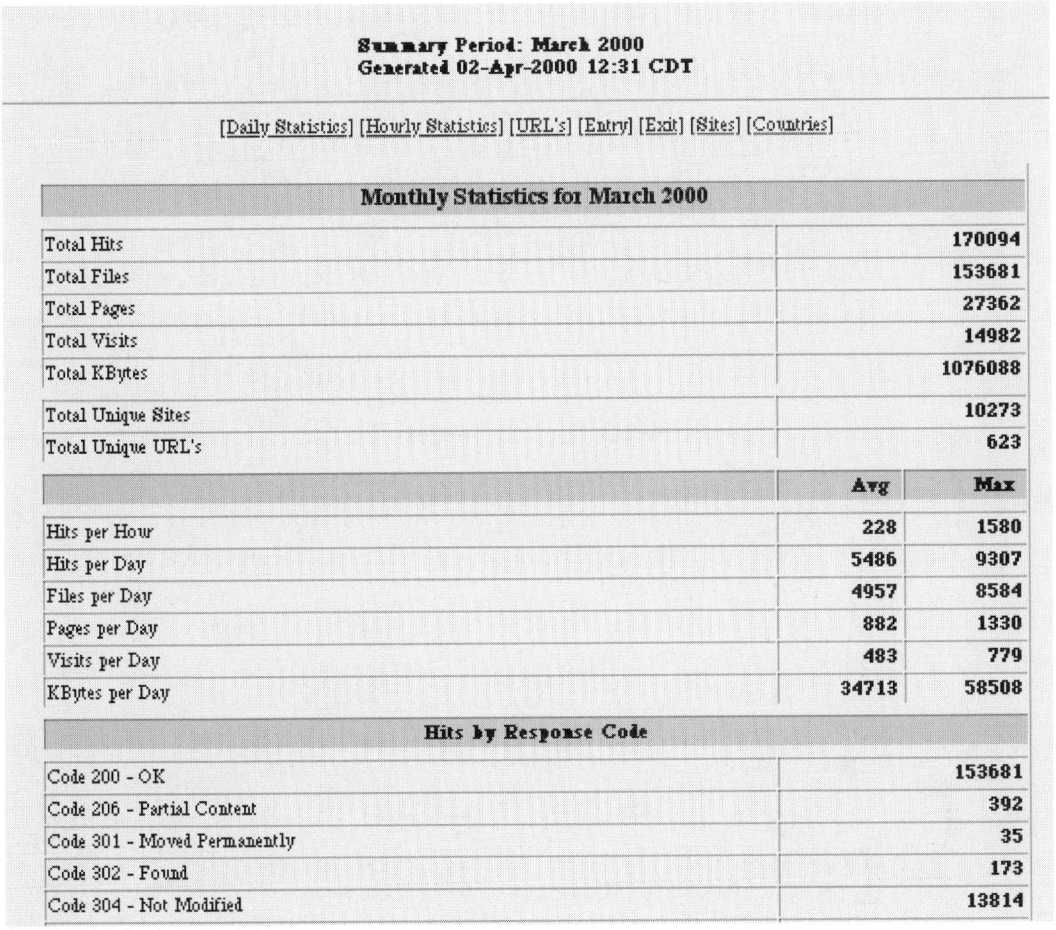

Summary Period: March 2000
Generated 02-Apr-2000 12:31 CDT

[Daily Statistics] [Hourly Statistics] [URL's] [Entry] [Exit] [Sites] [Countries]

Monthly Statistics for March 2000		
Total Hits		170094
Total Files		153681
Total Pages		27362
Total Visits		14982
Total KBytes		1076088
Total Unique Sites		10273
Total Unique URL's		623
	Avg	**Max**
Hits per Hour	228	1580
Hits per Day	5486	9307
Files per Day	4957	8584
Pages per Day	882	1330
Visits per Day	483	779
KBytes per Day	34713	58508
Hits by Response Code		
Code 200 - OK		153681
Code 206 - Partial Content		392
Code 301 - Moved Permanently		35
Code 302 - Found		173
Code 304 - Not Modified		13814

FIGURE 11.1 *Log analysis reports provide important marketing and evaluation information.*

In Figure 11.2, we have a listing of the most common entry pages for people coming to your site. As you can see, not everyone comes in through the front door! You can never know where users are coming from; so it is important to make sure that your site doesn't rely on the user entering and exiting in a controlled fashion.

Top 10 of 623 Total URL's By KBytes					
#	Hits		KBytes		URL
1	4224	2.48%	92764	8.62%	/
2	1314	0.77%	75509	7.02%	/demos/htmltm/MACFILES/clipart.html
3	381	0.22%	23344	2.17%	/distr.html
4	289	0.17%	16087	1.49%	/books/bryce.html
5	154	0.09%	15140	1.41%	/books/bhchap6.html
6	586	0.34%	8609	0.80%	/mult-grph.html
7	693	0.41%	7986	0.74%	/titles/truefx.html
8	18	0.01%	6478	0.60%	/movies/hawk2.mov
9	160	0.09%	6275	0.58%	/books/intrsecchap.html
10	441	0.26%	5844	0.54%	/titles/bryce.html

Top 10 of 266 Total Entry Pages					
#	Hits		Visits		URL
1	4224	2.48%	3627	26.05%	/
2	1314	0.77%	1251	8.98%	/demos/htmltm/MACFILES/clipart.html
3	729	0.43%	610	4.38%	/titles/wdogEnt.html
4	693	0.41%	580	4.17%	/titles/truefx.html
5	441	0.26%	350	2.51%	/titles/bryce.html
6	586	0.34%	305	2.19%	/mult-grph.html
7	353	0.21%	252	1.81%	/titles/poser4.html
8	305	0.18%	220	1.58%	/titles/poser.html
9	584	0.34%	193	1.39%	/titles/advbrycecre.html
10	289	0.17%	179	1.29%	/books/bryce.html

FIGURE 11.2 *Visitors to your site may enter from a variety of locations.*

CHAPTER SUMMARY

- You will greatly benefit from an understanding of statistical methods and research design principles, even if you never get the chance to conduct a full-on, whole-hog experimental design study.
- Statistical methods are used to translate raw data into a meaningful picture of the state of your Web site.
- There are four types of data. They are, in increasing order of descriptiveness, nominal, ordinal, interval, and ratio.

- There are three measures of central tendencies: the mean, the median, and the mode.
- The population is the group of people that represent all of your potential users in the world.
- The sample is a much smaller, randomly selected pool of participants who will actually take part in your studies. The data gathered from them will be generalized to the entire population.
- Randomness is a critical component to good design methodology.
- Experimental control is also a key component of the experimental method.
- There are several well-known "bad" study designs that you should avoid.
- Web Server log analysis can be a useful evaluation tool.

HANDS-ON EXERCISES

1. Take a course on research design methods and statistics at your local college or university, if you haven't already.
2. Plan how you will generate the next version of your usability test plan to be used as an experimental (post-test) group against your existing control group (pre-test) from the relevant exercise in Chapter 8.
3. Get your hands on as many case studies of experimental designs as you can and look for weaknesses in the design. Specifically, look for places where there were no equivalent groups, where there was no control group (a "Lemon Pledge" study), and where experimental control was not exercised. Do a Web search for *Web site usability findings* to get started.

DISCUSSION TOPICS

1. What other research designs have you heard of that are as flawed as the three examples given in this chapter? How about ones that you hear on radio and television ads?

2. How can statistics be used to deceive?
3. What are steps you can take to avoid ambiguity in reporting changes in performance of your participants following a change in your Web site?
4. Which concepts from this chapter did you find the most helpful? The least helpful?

APPENDIX

A

USABILITY TEST FOR XOLAX CORPORATION'S CORPORATE WEB SITE

INTRODUCTION

Following is the test plan for conducting usability tests of the corporate web site for Xolax Corporation. The plan covers the following sections:

- Purpose
- Problem statements
- User Profiles
- Methodology
- Task list
- Test environment and equipment requirements
- Evaluation measures
- Test report contents and presentation

PURPOSE

The XOLAX Company is a software engineering firm located in Austin, Texas. The company's main product is a suite of Java development tools called XOLAXware. As per the corporate vision, the purpose of the web site is to provide technical support to its current customers, to act as a sales channel for existing and potential customers, and to act as a vehicle for self-promotion for the company and its products.

The XOLAX web site has recently undergone a major facelift: both content and look-and-feel have been recreated from scratch to produce a more modern, professional look. Additionally, vast amounts of new informational content (primarily in the way of online documentation and technical support) have been added to enhance the value of the site to our users.

The purpose of this battery of tests is to determine if the changes that have been made have produced an overall improvement in site usability, as compared to our previously established baselines (1998). We hope to implement changes suggested by this study before the GOOGOLPLEX trade show in Las Vegas in July.

TEST OBJECTIVE/PROBLEM STATEMENTS

After analyzing the purpose of this web site, we have determined that there are several broad categories of questions that need to be answered about its usability.

1. Can our current users find the technical support information they need on the XOLAX web site?
2. Can potential customers locate product information and ordering instructions?
3. Can existing customers locate upgrade information and place an order for an upgrade?
4. Can press personnel locate news releases and other related information?

5. Can potential employees find job information and apply for a job?

USER PROFILES

Through research performed by the XOLAX marketing department, we have been able to identify several target audiences for the XOLAX web site. They are classified as two groups, a main target group and a secondary target group. Both of these groups may be further subclassed into more groups.

Main Target Groups

Purchasing authorities for large, multinational hi-tech companies are the main target group for this website. This main target group can be separated into two distinct subgroups.

- **Potential Customers** - People that already make decisions regarding equipment purchases. They are most likely to be highly educated with advanced degrees in engineering and/or business. They may currently do business with one of our competitors via the web or traditional purchasing channels.
- **Current Customers**– Also have a high degree of education. Our research shows that this group has a high loyalty rate but that it also expects a high degree of quality and service. One of our focuses is on heightening our level of service to them.

Secondary Target Groups

Members of this category are likely to use the XOLAX web site, but are not considered primary users.

- Investors
- Press/ Media
- Future Employees

User Profile		
Characteristic	Range	% Frequency Distribution
Age	18-30	12,5
	31-40	50
	41-50	25
	51-60	12.5
Sex	Female	62.5
	Male	37.5
Education	College	75
	Some College	25
Major Area of Study	Electronics Technology	12.5
	Electrical/Biochemical	
	Engineering	25
	Computer Science	25
	Education	12.5
	English	25
	N/A	
Learning Style	Trial and Error	62.5
	Consult with Others	75
	Documentation	37.5
	Other	12.5
PC Experience in Years	0-3 Years	25
	4-7 Years	25
	8-11 Years	25
	12-16 Years	25
PC Daily Usage	0-2 Hours	12.5
	3-5 Hours	12.5
	5-8 Hours	75
Computer Application Experience		
Database	0	50
	1-3 Years	37.5
	4-7 Years	12.5
	8-11 Years	0
	12-16 Years	0

User Profile *(Continued)*		
Characteristic	Range	% Frequency Distribution
Spreadsheet	0	0
	1-3 Years	87.5
	4-7 Years	12.5
	8-11 Years	0
	12-16 Years	0
Word Processing	0	12.5
	1-3 Years	37.5
	4-7 Years	25
	8-11 Years	12.5
	12-16 Years	12.5
Desk Top Publishing	0	87.5
	1-3 Years	0
	4-7 Years	0
	8-11 Years	12.5
	12-16 Years	0
Design CAD/CAM	0	87.5
	1-3 Years	12.5
	4-7 Years	0
	8-11 Years	0
	12-16 Years	0
Operating System Experience		
DOS	0	12.5
	1-3 Years	12.5
	4-7 Years	25
	8-11 Years	25
	12-16 Years	25
UNIX	0	62.5
	1-3 Years	37.5
	4-7 Years	0
	8-11 Years	0
	12-16 Years	0

(continues)

User Profile *(Continued)*		
Characteristic	Range	% Frequency Distribution
MSIE	0	0
	1-3 Years	87.5
	4-7 Years	12.5
Netscape	0	37.5
	1-3 Years	50
	4-7 Years	12.5
Familiarity XOLAX Corporate Web Site	YES	37.5
	Slightly	50
	I Know it Exists	12.5
	Not at all	0

METHODOLOGY

The usability test will consist of the main performance test designed to gather extensive usability data via direct observation.

The main performance test is composed of the following four sections:

1. Participant greeting and background questionnaire

Each participant will be greeted by the area receptionist and offered a seat and a complimentary drink. The participants will be given a very short questionnaire that gathers basic background information. Participants will be notified that they will be anonymous throughout the session, and that they will be assigned a unique ID number, which will be used in place of their name.

2. Orientation

The participant will listen to a short, verbal script that will explain the agenda for the day. All parts of the test will be explained. The participants will be notified of their right to leave the session should they become uncomfortable. They will also be notified that we wish to videotape the session. If they agree, they will then be asked to sign a video consent form. Finally, the participant will be asked to sign a non-disclosure agreement (NDA) that states that they will not discuss this session to anyone outside the research team.

3. Performance test

During this section of the test, the participants will be asked to perform a series of usability tasks on the XOALR corporate web site. Each task will be introduced by way of a short, scripted instruction from the test moderator.

For each task, the test moderator and the data logger will record the participants' actions, including time elapsed, number of clicks, and success/failure.

The individual tasks are enumerated below.

4. Participant debriefing

After all tasks are complete or the time expires, the test monitor will debrief each participant and the debriefing will be videotaped. The debriefing will include the following:

- Participant's perceptions about usability and aesthetics of the site
- Participant's overall comments about his or her performance
- Participant's responses to the test monitor asking about errors or problems during the test

The debriefing session serves several functions. It allows the participants to say whatever they like, which is important if tasks are frustrating. It provides important information about each participant's rationale for performing specific actions, and it allows the collection of subjective preference data about the site.

After the debriefing session, the participants will be thanked for their effort, and the compensation will be given to them.

TEST ENVIRONMENT AND EQUIPMENT REQUIREMENTS

Our testing lab will be a simple lab setup, including a video camera, a computer workstation, and three seats: one for the participant, one for the test monitor, and one for the data logger.

EVALUATION MEASURES

The following evaluation measures will be collected and calculated:

1. The average time to complete each task, and average number of clicks, across all participants.
2. The percentage of participants who finished each task successfully versus those who had errors from which they could not recover.
3. Error classification: to the degree possible, each error will be classified and a source of error indicated. Error classes are as follows:

- **Observation and Comments** — The test monitor notes when participants have difficulty, when an unusual behavior, or when a cause of error becomes obvious.
- **Non-critical Errors** — An individual makes a mistake but is able to recover in the allotted time.
- **Critical Errors** — An individual participant make a mistake and is unable to recover and complete the task on time. The participant may or may not realize a mistake has been made.

4. Participants ranking of usability and aesthetics of the site. (Some questions may be essay-type, rather than rankings.)

TASK LIST

Task List for XOLAX Web Site Usability Test

TASK LIST LEGEND:

MTC = Maximum time to complete
P = Participant
SCC = Successful completion criteria
TM = Test monitor
ATC = Actual Time to Complete

TASK NO.	TASK DESCRIPTION	TASK DETAIL
1.	Locate the recent press release about XOLAX's involvement with a local University	**SCC**: Navigate to the URL shown below. http://www.xolax.com/press/university.html **MTC**: 1 Minute
2.	You would like to apply for a software engineer position. What are the job requirements for this position?	**SCC**: Locate requirements on page listed below. http://www.xolax.com/jobs/main.html **MTC**: 1 Minute
3.	What is the availability of the FOO++ software module?	**SCC**: Availability is: shipping in mid-may. Locate information in one of the two following pages: http://www.xolax.com/products/foo/index.html or http://www.xolax.com/store/products.html **MTC**: 1 Minute
4.	You have a damaged FOO format file. You need to use the recover utility. Find out how to use it.	**SCC**: Locate technical article #4982734 via Tech Support Search page **MTC**: 1 Minute
5.	After you installed Service Release 8 for the XOLAXware compiler, your computer has begun crashing. Find out if this is a known bug.	**SCC**: Use Tech Support Search page to locate article # 94875334 **MTC**: 2 Minutes
6.	What is the cost of the QUUX-12 filter plug-in module?	**SCC**: Price is $350 – find this via one of the following pages: http://www.xolax.com/products/quux.html http://www.xolax.com/pricing/index.html **MTC**: 2 Minutes

(Continues)

Task List for XOLAX Web Site Usability Test (Continued)

TASK NO.	TASK DESCRIPTION	TASK DETAIL
7.	Is there a competitive upgrade path from SPORKTECH's SNOO++ package?	**SCC**: Yes, for $399 USD. Find at following page: http://www.xolax.com/upgrade/spork.html **MTC**: 2 Minutes
8.	You want to purchase the XOLAXware Professional package. Please use this (fake) credit card to place the order.	**SCC**: Navigate to the URL below, fill out form, and complete transaction http://www.xolax.com/store/index.html **MTC**: 4 Minutes
9.	Are there any know XOLAX Y2K or other related date problems?	**SCC**: Yes, certain products are not year 2038 compliant. Locate article on page shown below. http://www.xolax.com/y2k/index.html **MTC**: 1 Minute
10.	What are the system requirements for the XOLAX Vaporware suite?	**SCC**: Windows 98 or NT 4.0 SP6 +, 128 MB RAM, 333 MHz Pentium II or better. Find on page shown below http://www.xolax.com/vapor/index.html **MTC**: 1 Minute
11.	What is the maximum size for a FOO bytecode file?	**SCC**: 128 GB. See page listed below. http://www.xolax.com/kb/limits.html **MTC**: 1 Minute
12.	Please sign up for a free XOLAX developer account.	**SCC**: Locate form at URL below, fill out form and submit. http://www.xolax.com/accounts/go.html **MTC**: 3 Minutes

RESULTS

Performance Data Summary

TASKS	% of participants performing Correctly (within benchmark)	% of participants performing Incorrectly (within benchmark)	Mean Time (minutes)	Mean clicks
1. Locate the recent press release about XOLAX's involvement with a local University.	0	100	1.01	3.57
2. You would like to apply for a software engineer position. What are the job requirements for this position?	43	57	.67	4.00
3. What is the availability of the FOO++ software module?	86	14	.30	.86
4. You have a damaged FOO format file. You need to use the recover utility. Find out how to use it.	100	0	.16	2.43
5. After you installed Service Release 8 for the XOLAXware compiler, your computer has begun crashing. Find out if this is a known bug.	100	0	.30	3.43
6. What is the cost of the QUUX-12 filter plug-in module?	57	43	1.45	7.43
7. Is there a competitive upgrade path from SPORKTECH's SNOO++ package?	43	57	1.39	5.86
8. You want to purchase the XOLAXware Professional package. Please use this (fake) credit card to place the order.	57	43	1.56	9.29
9. Are there any know XOLAX Y2K or other related date problems?	**29**	**71**	**.80**	3.86
10. What are the system requirements for the XOLAX Vaporware suite?	86	14	.24	**2.57**
11. What is the maximum size for a FOO bytecode file?	100	0	.18	2
Please sign up for a free XOLAX developer account.	29	71	1.68	*

Preference Data Summary

Questions	%SA	%A	%N	%D	%SD
1. Was the language on the Task List you were given, easily understood?	71	29	0	0	0
2. Was the amount of information on the home page adequate?	0	43	29	29	0
3. Was the use of color appropriate?	0	57	43	0	0
4. Was information grouped consistently?	0	29	14	57	0
5. Was the navigation inherently intuitive?	0	14	14	57	14
6. Were colors and navigation consistent through out the site?	14	43	43	0	0
7. Were you able to move around the site without getting lost?	0	29	43	29	0
8. Was there too much information on individual pages?	14	29	29	29	0
9. Was there too little information on individual pages?	14	43	14	29	0
10. Was there adequate cross-referencing of topics and information?	0	29	29	29	14
11. Was more important information highlighted in some way?	29	14	14	43	0
12. Were topic and page headings self-explanatory?	14	43	14	29	0
13. Was it necessary to scroll often to reach desired information?	86	14	0	0	0
14. Was the "Table of Contents" (commonly called a Sitemap) helpful?	29	29	14	14	14
15. Was the site "Search" helpful and reliable?	14	14	43	29	0
16. Did you receive adequate information from the "Search" feature?	14	14	43	29	0
17. Was the terminology understandable throughout the site?	0	71	29	0	0
18. Was there an adequate use of graphics?	29	14	14	43	0
19. Were the graphics clear and sharp?	29	29	29	14	0
20. Were text and graphics presented in a visually aesthetic manner?	29	43	29	0	0
21. Was there an adequate use of white space?	29	43	14	0	14
22. Overall, were the pages quick to load?	43	56	0	0	0

PART A

BACKGROUND QUESTIONNAIRE

Name: ______________________ **Company:** ______________

Job Title: ______________________

Please answer the questions below in order to help us understand your background and experience.

Age:

(Circle One) **18-30** **31-40** **41-50** **51-60** **Over 60**

Sex:

(Circle One) **Male** **Female**

EDUCATION: (Please check the highest grade level achieved below)

☐ Grade School

☐ High School

☐ Some College

☐ College Graduate

☐ Post Graduate

If you graduated from college, please list your major area of study.

____

(Continues)

BACKGROUND QUESTIONNAIRE *(Continued)*

LEARNING STYLE:

1. Which way do you prefer to learn?

   ☐ Trial and Error

   ☐ Consult with others

   ☐ Documentation

   ☐ Other:____________________

COMPUTER EXPERIENCE:

1. How long have you been using a personal computer?

______________yrs ______________ mths

2. How often do you use a personal computer to complete your daily job tasks?

____

3. Please circle the types of computer applications you have used before, followed by the approximate months of experience with each one used. (Excluding Internet Browser experience.)

<u>Application</u>	<u>Months of Experience</u>
Database	____________
Spreadsheet	____________
Word Processing	____________
Desk Top Publishing	____________
Design (CAD/CAM)	____________
Manufacturing	____________
Engineering	____________
Other:	____________
____________	____________

BACKGROUND QUESTIONNAIRE *(Continued)*

4. Which Operating System do you have experience with?

DOS ______________yrs ______________ mths

UNIX ______________yrs ______________ mths

INTERNET EXPERIENCE:

1. Are you familiar with Internet browsers? If so, which ones? What versions?

a. Netscape Navigator : How long have used it? _______yrs_______mths

b. Microsoft Internet Explorer: How long have used it? _______yrs_______mths

c. America Online: How long have used it? _______yrs_______mths

d. WebTV: How long have used it? _______yrs_______mths

2. Which browser do you prefer using when accessing the Internet?

____

3. Are you at all familiar with the XOLAX corporate web site?

(Check One)

☐ **Yes** ☐ **Moderately** ☐ **A little** ☐ **Not at all**

4. If so, how often do you access the site?

____

PART B

ORIENTATION SCRIPT

Hi, my name is ______________. I'll be working with you in today's testing session. Let me explain why we've asked you to come in today.

We're here to test how easy it is to use the XOLAX corporate web site, and we'd like your help.

You will be performing some typical tasks with this web site, and I'd like you to perform as you normally would. For example, try to work at the same speed and with the same attention to detail that you normally do. Do your best, but don't be all that concerned with the results. This is a test of the web site, and it may not work as you expect. You may ask questions at any time, but I may not answer them, since this is a study of the usability of the web site and we need to see how it works with a person such as yourself working independently.

During today's session, I'll also be asking you to complete some forms and answer some questions. It's important that you answer truthfully. My only role here today is to discover both the flaws and advantages of this web site from your perspective. So don't answer the questions based on what you think I may want to hear. I need to know exactly what you think.

While you are working, I'll be sitting here nearby taking some notes and timings. In addition, you and I will be in a room with others observing. The session will also be videotaped for the benefit of those who could not be here today. For confidentiality, your name will not be used, instead a unique testing identification number is assigned to each test participant.

Do you have any questions?

PART C

TAPE CONSENT FORM

XOLAX Web Site Usability Testing

Thank you for participating in our usability testing for the XOLAX corporate web site. This is to inform you that we will be videotaping your session for the benefit of our group members who can not be present and to enable us to review information at a later date. We will greatly benefit from your feedback and appreciate your time. Please read the statement below and sign where indicated. These tapes will not be released outside of our team of researchers, and will only be used for reference in our research.

I understand that video and audiotape recordings will be made of my session. I grant the usability test group permission to use these recordings for the purposes mentioned above, and waive my right to review or inspect the tapes prior to their dissemination and distribution.

Please print name: ______________________________

Signature: ____________________________________

Date: ______________

PART D

POST TEST QUESTIONNAIRE

Please answer the following questions based on your experience using the XOLAX corporate web site.

Legend

SA = Strongly Agree

A = Agree

N = Neither

D = Disagree

SD = Strongly Disagree

Task Questions/Issues:

1. Was the language on the Task List you were given, easily understood?
   SA A N D SD

General On-Screen Issues:

2. Was the amount of information on the home page adequate?
   SA A N D SD

3. Was the use of color appropriate?
   SA A N D SD

4. Was information grouped consistently?
   SA A N D SD

5. Was the navigation inherently intuitive?
   SA A N D SD

6. Were colors and navigation consistent through out the site?
   SA A N D SD

7. Were you able to move around the site without getting lost?
SA A N D SD

8. Was there too much information on individual pages?
SA A N D SD

9. Was there too little information on individual pages?
SA A N D SD

10. Was there adequate cross-referencing of topics and information?
SA A N D SD

11. Was more important information highlighted in some way?
SA A N D SD

12. Were topic and page headings self-explanatory?
SA A N D SD

13. Was it necessary to scroll often to reach desired information?
SA A N D SD

14. Was the "Table of Contents" (commonly called a Sitemap) helpful?
SA A N D SD

15. Was the site "Search" helpful and reliable?
SA A N D SD

16. Did you receive adequate information from the "Search" feature?
SA A N D SD

17. Was the terminology understandable throughout the site?
SA A N D SD

18. Was there an adequate use of graphics?
SA A N D SD

19. Were the graphics clear and sharp?
SA A N D SD

20. Were test and graphics presented in a visually aesthetic manner?
SA A N D SD

21. Was there an adequate use of white space?

SA A N D SD

22. Overall, were the pages quick to load?

SA A N D SD

Overall impression of the site

On a scale of 1 to 10, 1 being the worst, and 10 being the best, how would you rate this site based on what you have seen today? (Circle 1)

1 2 3 4 5 6 7 8 9 10

Please add any comments or suggestions in the space provided that you feel will help us evaluate the usability of the XOLAX web site. Positive and negative comments will all be appreciated and addressed accordingly

APPENDIX

B

ABOUT THE CD-ROM

This CD is packed with useful tools to use in your Usability testing and Web site design.

- Includes two complete packages for Web Site design from Charles River Media: *THE JAVASCRIPT CD COOKBOOK,* Third Edition and *THE HTML/CSS DEVELOPER'S RESOURCE GUIDE.* Both of these programs run on Windows 95 or later and Macintosh System 8.0 higher. See below for detailed system requirements.
- *Web Metrics Suite of Tools* from NIST. This free testing package is for Solaris machines only. The suite includes the following:

  -*The Web Static Analyzer Tool* (WebSAT) checks the html of a web page against numerous usability guidelines. The output from WebSAT consists of identification of potential usability problems which should be investigated further through user testing. WebSAT can be executed from any web browser for non-intranet users.

  -*WebCAT* is a variation upon traditional card sorting techniques. It allows a web designer/usability engineer to test a proposed or existing categorization scheme of a web site to determine how well the categories and items are understood by users. The WebCAT process of categorizing and analyzing information is interactive.

- *MAGpie Accessibility Software* for Windows 95/98 Using MAGpie, authors can add captions to three multimedia formats: Apple's QuickTime, the World Wide Web Consortium's Synchronized Multimedia Integration Language (SMIL) and Microsoft's Synchronized Accessible Media Interchange (SAMI) format. MAGpie can also integrate audio descriptions into SMIL presentations.
- Webalizer Web site log analysis tool. Webalizer is a free, open-source tool that is widely used on many web sites. It produces highly detailed, easily configurable usage reports in HTML format, for viewing with a standard web browser. Sample reports are featured in the book.
- Sample files included for your own customization (Macintosh and Windows formats – Microsoft Word and Microsoft PowerPoint format)
- All of the images from the book in full color for your reference

SYSTEM INSTRUCTIONS:

The files included are broken into directories by respective platforms. The two-top level directories, Solaris , PC ,or Mac, contain files for those platforms respectively. The WebMetrics suite from NIST only runs on Solaris 2.6. The complete installation instructions are included in the Solaris directory. To obtain the latest version of this free software suite, please see http://zing.ncs1.nist.gov/webmet/. This software will be installed by your system administrator. All documents regarding installation can be located at the url listed above.

Inside the directory either Macintosh, Windows, or Solaris you will find many of the sample files mentioned in the book, as well as video clips, the MAGpie software, The JavaScript CD Cookbook, and The HTML/CSS Developers' Resource Guide.

System requirements for these programs include the following:

PC: Windows 95 or higher or NT, 8MB of RAM, CD-ROM drive, mouse or other pointing device, QuickTime 4.0 or higher, and a web browser such as Microsoft Internet Explorer or Netscape Navigator.

Macintosh: System 8.0 or higher, 8MB of RAM, CD-ROM drive, mouse or other pointing device, QuickTime 4.0 or higher, and a web browser such as Microsoft Internet Explorer or Netscape Navigator.

You can find updates for the book and CD-ROM at http://www.usablesites.com/handbook/

BIBLIOGRAPHY

Anderson, J.A. (1995). Learning and Memory; An Integrated Approach. New York: John Wiley and Sons. ISBN 0-471-58685-4

Baron, J. (1994). Thinking and Deciding. Cambridge, UK: Cambridge University Press. ISBN 0-521-43732-6

Coe, M. (1996). Human Factors for Technical Communicators. New York: John Wiley and Sons. ISBN 0-471-03530-0

Cozby, P. C. (1981). Methods in Behavioral research, Sixth Edition. Mountain View, California; Mayfield Press. ISBN 1-55934-659-0

Eysenck, M.W., & Keane, M.T. (1995). Cognitive Psychology: A student's handbook. Hove, UK: Lawrence Erlbaum Associates.

Faulkner, C. (1998). The essence of Human-Computer Interaction. Hertfordshire, UK: Prentice Hall Europe. ISBN 0-13-751975

Fiske, S.T., & Taylor, S.E. (1991). Social Cognition (2nd ed.). New York: McGraw-Hill.

Fortner, B. & Meyer, T.E. (1997) Number by Colors. New York: Springer-Verlag. ISBN 0-387-94685-3.

Hubel, D.H. (1988). Eye, Brain and Vision. New York: Scientific American Library. ISBN 0-7167-5020-1

Miller, G.A. (1956). The Magical Number Seven, Plus or Minus Two: Some Limits on Our Capacity for Processing Information. The Psychological Review, 1956, vol. 63, pp. 81-97

Nielsen, J. (1993). Usability Engineering. San Diego, California; Academic Press. ISBN 0-12-518406-9

Norman, D.A. (1990). The Design of Everyday Things (published previously as The Psychology of Everyday Things). New York: Doubleday Books. ISBN 0-385-26774-6

Norman, D.A. (1998). The Invisible Computer. Cambridge, Massachusetts; MIT Press. ISBN 0-262-14065-9

Raymond, E. S. (1996). The New Hacker's Dictionary. Cambridge, Massachusetts: MIT Press. ISBN 0-262-18178-9

Rubin, J. (1994). Handbook of Usability Testing: How to Plan, Design, and Conduct Effective Tests. New York: John Wiley and Sons. ISBN 0-471-59403-2

Shneiderman, B. (1998). Designing the User Interface. Reading, Massachusetts; Addison-Wesley. ISBN 0-201-69497-2.

Solso, R.L., Johnson, H.H., & Beal, M.K. (1998). Experimental Psychology, Sixth Edition. Reading, Massachusetts: Longman Press (an imprint of Addison-Wesley). ISBN 0-321-01146-5

Strothotte, C. & Strothotte, T. (1997). Seeing Between the Pixels: Pictures in Interactive Systems. New York: Springer-Verlag. ISBN 3-540-59417-5

Spool, J. et. al. (1997). Web Site Usability: A Designer's Guide. New York: Morgan Kaufmann Press. ISBN 1-558-60569-X

Tufte, E.R. (1997). Visual Explanations. Cheshire, Connecticut: Graphics Press. ISBN 0-961-3921-2-6

Wixted, J.T. & Ebbensen, E.B. (1991). On the Form of Forgetting. *Psychological Science*, 2, 409–415.

INDEX